Get Out of the Ring:

An Equestrian's Guide to Riding the Trails in and around Rocky Mountain National Park

Kim Starling

PublishingWorks
Exeter, NH
2008

Maps copyright © 2008 by Deanna Estes.

Published by:
PublishingWorks, Inc.
60 Winter Street
Exeter, New Hampshire 03833
603-778-9883
www.publishingworks.com

Designed by K. Mack

Sales:
Kim Starling
P. O. Box 1022
Loveland, CO 80539-1022
970-203-9995
970-203-9994
E-mail: kimstarling@mesanetworks.net
Fax: 303-225-5460

ISBN: 978-1-933002-51-4

LCCN: 2007936208

Get Out of the Ring:

An Equestrian's Guide to Riding the Trails in and around Rocky Mountain National Park

This book is dedicated to my husband David, who encouraged me to start riding again after many horseless years. He has hauled our horses to every trailhead and has been with me on every trail as I gathered information for this book. Without him, this book would never have become a reality.

PREFACE

This book is intended for all trail riders: those who are just beginning to ride, those who have experience in other riding disciplines, and those who already have trail riding experience. Anyone who wants to take a horse trail riding can benefit from this guidebook. Trail descriptions range from **Easy**, for horses or riders who are new to trail riding, to **Demanding**, for experienced riders with well-conditioned mounts. This book covers trails in the foothills for cooler weather and shorter drives, in the mountains for hot summer days, and on the eastern side of the Continental divide, near Grand Lake, for multi-day summer trips.

Whenever I go riding near Fort Collins, Loveland, or Boulder, I see quite a few horses in the areas where horse trailers can easily park. These areas are included in this guidebook. However, my favorite riding trails are in the mountains, and when I go to these places I see few horse trailers. Taking a horse to the mountains can be a little more challenging than the more popular trails because it is further to drive, the places to park are not as obvious, and the weather can be changeable. However, in July and August when temperatures at the lower elevations are soaring, or in September when the aspen trees turn gold, I cannot think of anything as gratifying as going for a ride in the mountains.

Each trailhead description in this trail guide has detailed driving directions, including instructions on where to park a horse trailer, and a list of amenities available to trail users. The trail descriptions are comprehensive and include headings with ratings for the difficulty of the trail and obstacles horses may encounter along the way. A map is provided for each trail showing mileages and difficulty ratings. Each individual section of the book is self-contained, so the description of the desired trail can be photocopied and carried along on the ride.

Information on trail riding basics is also included. As long as you are comfortable that you can control your mount in an arena, you can go trail riding. Most horses enjoy trail riding as much as their owners. I love to go trail riding, and I hope others will use this book to share my passion. If I am lucky, I will see you on the trails. If you recognize our horses or our rig, please say hello. Happy trails to you!

TABLE OF CONTENTS

PART I. TRAIL RIDING INFORMATION

General Information

Trail Riding Basics

PART II. TRAIL DESCRIPTIONS

Legend to Maps and Trail overview

Trails South and East of Rocky Mountain National Park

Trails accessed from Colorado State Highway 7 and U.S. Highway 36

Trails in Rocky Mountain National Park, East of the Continental Divide

Trails accessed from Colorado State Highway 7

Trails accessed from U.S. Highway 34 and U.S. Highway 36

Trails in Rocky Mountain National Park, West of the Continental Divide
Trails accessed from U.S. Highway 34 near Grand Lake

Trails North and East of Rocky Mountain National Park
Trails accessed from Larimer County Road 43, near the town of Drake

PART III. REFERENCES

PART I

TRAIL RIDING INFORMATION

Introduction

We began as two greenhorns with two green horses. We made mistakes, and so did our horses, but we all became seasoned trail riders and mounts. The information in this book is designed to help you avoid mistakes, and to make all your trail riding experiences great ones.

It may take awhile for you and your horse to become comfortable trail companions who take all obstacles in stride. Caution should be always be exercised when encountering anything your mount has not seen before. Read Part I of the book before planning your first trail ride, particularly if you are new to trail riding. Reading books and magazines with articles about trail riding, horse training, and trailering horses can also help you have successful rides. See Appendix A for information on some useful books.

Start by riding trails described as **Easy**, and then work up to more challenging ones. Ride some trails at lower elevations before going to the mountains. Horses feel the difference in the altitude too, so they may need to travel more slowly, rest more, or turn around sooner than at lower altitudes.

Arrive at trailheads early in the morning to secure a parking space, and to have plenty of time to complete your ride. Plan another ride as a second choice, in the event the trailhead you have chosen is full, being repaired, or otherwise unavailable. The trailheads that are grouped together under the same heading are the closest ones to drive to. Keep this book in your vehicle to get directions to other trailheads.

Let someone know where you are going, when to expect you back, and when to call for help if they don't hear from you, especially when you are riding alone. Then remember to let them know you arrived home safely!

Colorado has developed a search and rescue insurance fund. Colorado Outdoor Recreation Search and Rescue cards cover the cost of rescuing people who become lost or injured on public lands. These cards are valid for five years, regardless what activity a person is engaged in when they become injured or lost while visiting a Colorado recreation area. The cards cost $12 each and can be purchased at many outdoor recreation stores. This is a small price to pay to avoid having to foot the bill for a search and/or rescue effort done on your behalf. See Appendix B for specific locations.

In Colorado, brand inspections are required to transport livestock, including horses, whenever you are more than 75 miles from home or crossing a state line. A brand inspector will come to inspect your horse and provide a permanent brand inspection that you can keep in your trailer for around $25 per horse. This gives law enforcement a way to ensure ownership of horses, and is intended to deter livestock theft. See Appendix B for more information.

Trail Descriptions and Ratings

Detailed directions are invaluable when pulling a horse trailer. Because changing lanes, stopping, turning around, and parking are not as simple as in a car, precise driving instructions are provided for each trailhead. Directions are given from Colorado State Highway 66 and U.S. Highway 36 in Boulder County, U.S. Highway 34 in Larimer County, and from U.S. Interstate Highway 25, whenever it is reasonable. Directions to the trails on the western side of Rocky Mountain National Park are given from U.S. Highway 34 in Grand County.

The trailheads are described from southeast, to west, to northeast. Parking is rated as good, acceptable, and poor. Parking rated poor is acceptable for a two-horse trailer, but not for a four-horse living quarters trailer or a convoy of trailers. Ratings are based on the size of the

Drive Ratings:

Simple

Moderate

Difficult

parking lot and number of designated trailer parking spots, the ease of the drive due to road surfaces or conditions, and the level of safety, such as being adjacent to a highway or requiring crossing a road.

Each trailhead and trail description is complete, giving you the option to photocopy the description of the trail you plan to ride, rather than having to carry the book along on the ride. This results in some directions being repeated from section to section. Trails that are accessible from one trailhead are grouped together under that

Parking Ratings:

Good

Acceptable

Poor

trailhead description. In order to be able to vary your route and still have a trail description available, carry all the trail descriptions from that trailhead on the ride. When a trail description suggests that it could be combined with another trail for a longer ride, the trail number of that description is given.

Use the trail information section to choose a trail with a length and difficulty level suitable for you and your mount, and to determine the best time of year to ride each trail. Check the maximum elevation of the trail to avoid areas above snow line. In the springtime, snowdrifts often block the trail below the actual snow line. In July and August snow is not an issue, but it may be every other month of the year, including June. You can call Rocky Mountain National Park to obtain information on the current snowline in the park. See Appendix B for contact information.

National Forest areas allow hunting in the fall. Some riders put orange material on their horses to keep hunters from mistaking them for game animals. To determine the dates for deer and elk hunting seasons, call the Department of Wildlife. See Appendix B for contact information. National Parks, Colorado State Parks, and County Open Spaces areas are safe options during hunting season, as they generally do not allow hunting.

The trails are rated as **Easy**, **Moderate**, **Advanced**, **Demanding**, and **Closed** or **Dangerous** for horses. This book rates every trail from the trailheads listed in it. Trails that are **Closed** or **Dangerous** for horses are not described, but they are noted when a trail description passes one, and are marked by an **X** on the maps. The map legend and the headings for each trail

Trail Ratings:	
Easy	- - - - - - - -
Moderate	··········
Advanced	·—·—·—·—·—
Demanding	♦ ♦ ♦ ♦ ♦ ♦ ♦
Closed or Dangerous	x x x x x x x x

give more information about trail designations.

Compare similarly rated trails for relative difficulty by using the round-trip mileage and elevation gain measurements. These numbers are determined from the preferred trailer parking, rather than from the trailhead, and therefore vary somewhat from other trail guides. Horses generally travel about 2.0 miles per hour uphill. The return trip is usually quicker than

6

the outbound ride, since most horses like going home, and it is usually downhill. An overall speed of 2.0 miles per hour for a leisurely ride, including rest stops or lunch, is reasonable. You will soon learn whether you and your mount travel at a faster or slower pace.

The Difficulty heading for each trail has two subsections. Terrain is the rating for a trail's footing; a trail surface that is too difficult may be dangerous, especially on the way home when horses are tired. More symbols signify greater difficulty. These ratings are: mostly smooth, rocky or steep areas, steep stairs or loose or large rocks in some areas, and extensive challenging footing. Training Ability reflects the amount of trail experience recommended to complete the trail. The specific obstacles encountered on the trail are listed so you can judge whether this trail is appropriate for your mount. More than one or two new obstacles may take the fun out of the ride. The overall trail rating reflects these ratings, as well as the length of the trail and elevation gained.

Last, but not least, whenever the weather or trail conditions are challenging, remember that arriving home healthy and happy is more important than making it to your planned destination.

Terrain Ratings:

Mostly Smooth	♘
Rocky or Steep	♘♘
Steep Stairs or Loose Large Rocks	♘♘♘
Extensive Challenging Footing	♘♘♘♘

Training Ability:

No Obstacles	+
Some Obstacles	+ +
Lots of Obstacles	+ + +

Maps

When trail riding, always take a map and a reliable trail description. This information is invaluable to determine where a side trail goes, how much further it is, and where you are, especially if you make a wrong turn. I carry at least one map with me when trail riding, and whenever I reach a trail junction I check the map to confirm that I am choosing the correct trail. I also enjoy being able to identify mountain peaks, lakes, and other highlights along the way. Even if you do not share my enthusiasm for maps, it is vital to learn to read a map well enough to know where you are. I have made a wrong turn more than once when I thought I knew which way to turn, and didn't check the map. When I realized I was lost, being able to use the map to determine my location was critical.

Read the trail and trailhead descriptions, and find the route on the map before the ride. Marking the route with a felt pen makes it simple to see the trail when you are in the saddle. Refold the map so that the trail you will be riding is facing out, put it in a zip-lock bag, and take it along on the ride.

Each trailhead description lists the most appropriate maps for that area. For most areas I prefer the National Geographic Trails Illustrated maps, because they cover a large area, and they are waterproof and long lasting. I often take USGS maps with me as well because they show more detail. The Colorado Atlas and Gazetteer by De Lorme consists of topographic maps of the entire state. It is a great, inexpensive reference book for finding trailheads.

Maps can be purchased at many hiking and camping stores. REI generally has the most complete selection of maps for sale. See Appendix A for more information about purchasing and learning to read maps. The trails at most city and county open space areas are not yet shown on commercially available maps, but trail maps of the area are available at the trailhead or entrance to each of these areas.

Entrance Fees

Some of the trailheads listed in this book charge an entrance fee. Areas administered by the following governments and agencies do not charge user fees: City of Fort Collins, some of Larimer County's Open Space, Boulder County, the National Forest Service, Comanche Peak Wilderness and Indian Peaks Wilderness. In addition, many of the trails leading into Rocky Mountain National Park originate at trailheads that do not collect fees. The trailhead descriptions list which fees, if any, apply. Where fees are collected, the money is used to maintain trails and other amenities in these wonderful places, and to preserve them for the future. The yearly pass for Rocky Mountain National Park is quite reasonable compared to the daily fee. At Lory State Park and Horsetooth Mountain Park, it may be a better value to pay the daily fee. Below is a summary of the fees charged as of 2008. I store my park passes in our tow vehicle to ensure they are available when needed.

Rocky Mountain National Park

Purchase at any of the three entrance stations.
- The one time fee is $20.00. This fee grants access to the park for seven consecutive days.
- The yearly pass is $35.00. This pass grants access to the park for twelve consecutive months.
- The Golden Eagle pass is $65.00. This pass grants access to all the National Parks for twelve consecutive months.

Larimer County Lands and Open Space

As of 2008, the two Horsetooth Mountain Park trailheads are the only Larimer County trailheads described in this guide where fees are collected.

- The daily fee is $6.00. Purchase this at the trailhead by putting the correct amount in a lock box, and putting the parking stub on your windshield. A ranger is sometimes available to collect fees.
- The yearly pass is $65.00 ($75.00 for out-of-state). This pass expires at the end of December regardless of when it is purchased. It is best to purchase passes in advance from County Offices near Carter Lake, the County Courthouse, or from the entrance station at the Horsetooth Reservoir marina when it is open. They can also be purchased on the Internet at larimer.org/parks. Click on the green buffalo.

Lory State Park

This pass is good at all State Parks, such as Eldorado Canyon, Golden Gate Canyon, Barr Lake, and Boyd Lake. Pay the daily fee or buy the yearly pass by driving through the fee station near the entrance to Lory State Park.

- The daily fee is $5.00.
- The yearly pass is $55.00. This pass expires at the end of December.

Options for Lodging and Horse Boarding near Rocky Mountain National Park

In Estes Park, the options for daily horse boarding are extremely limited. Horses can be boarded at the fairgrounds if you are participating in a horse show. Elkhorn Lodge and Stables is the only facility that boards horses short-term. Guests staying at the Lodge are allowed to board their horses at the stables, which is a typical dude stable operation.

It is in a nice location within walking distance to town, and has trails leading into Rocky Mountain National Park as described in trails #20 and #21. Elkhorn Lodge can be contacted at (970) 586–4416, or www.elkhornlodge.org. Otherwise, contact the Estes Park Equestrian Club who will attempt to find a club member who can accommodate your horses. See Appendix B for contact information.

Camping is not a particularly viable option near Estes Park. The National Forest Service does not allow horses in developed areas (i.e. campgrounds), and the undeveloped camping areas in the national forest near there are difficult to access. The trail descriptions mention areas where camping with horses is allowed and accessible to horses and vehicles, although not all of them can be reached with a trailer. See trail #2, #3, and #5. The National Forest Service requires all hay and hay cubes to be certified weed-free. Hay pellets are exempted from this requirement, due to the high heat used to process them. Do not tie horses to trees; a high line or portable corral is acceptable. Call the forest service ahead of time to find out the current fire restrictions for campfires and portable stoves. See Appendix B for contact information.

Rocky Mountain National Park does not have campground facilities for horses. However, some backcountry campsites are approved for livestock, and many of these are mentioned in the trail descriptions. Animals are not allowed to graze in national parks, so horse feed must be packed in and must be certified weed-free. Hitching posts are provided at all stock campsites, but corrals are not provided for public use. Backcountry camping requires a reservation made in advance and a $20 permit from the National Park Service. Refer to their "Backcountry Camping Guide" for more information. See Appendix B for contact information.

Grand Lake is less than two hours from Estes Park via U.S. Highway 34, otherwise known as Trail Ridge Road. Two stables near Grand Lake will let you and your horses stay for one or more nights. Neither is luxurious and both have trail horses available for guided rides. They are each described below.

The Winding River Resort is a huge campground with pancake breakfasts, chuck wagon dinners, and ice cream socials. It is located just south of the park entrance and has a trail to the Green Mountain Trailhead, so you can leave your trailer parked when you use that trailhead. The horse facilities consist of small round pens made of pipe panels set up near a few of the campsites. Hookups are available for living quarters trailers. In addition, a few old cabins are available to rent by the night. Horses belonging to guests staying in the cabins are kept in a run (no stall) by the barn. Rain is more common in Grand Lake than on the east side of the divide, and the rain runs off the barn into these runs, so they tend to be muddy. Horse owners are expected to feed and water their horses with their own feed, feed tubs and buckets, and to clean up the corral daily. Shovels, water and hoses are provided. They can be contacted at P.O. Box 629, Grand Lake, CO 80447, (970) 627–3215, 1–800–282–5121, or on the Internet at www.windingriverresort.com

The Winding River Ranch is just south of the campground above; the names are similar because at one time it was all one ranch. They have a few cabins and pens for short-term horse boarding. The pens don't have any shelter, but the ranch has a fabulous barn with enclosed box stalls where they allowed us to keep our horses, even though we were staying elsewhere. They provided bedding and fed our hay, kept our water buckets full, and the stalls clean. We rode every other day, so the horses got plenty of exercise, and they were happy to have dry, bedded stalls to rest in on their days off. If you want to take your horse on a nice **Easy** ride without hooking up your trailer, ask if you can ride through the fields, following the river that runs through their property. They can be contacted at P.O. Box 359, Grand Lake, CO, 80447, by phone at (970) 627–3251, or on the Internet at wrranch@rkymtnhi.com.

Proof of a negative Coggins test done within the last year may be required to board a horse in Colorado, even for a few days or at a horse show. This rule ensures that horses are not carrying Equine Infectious Anemia (EIA) and protects our healthy horses. It is simple to have your veterinarian draw blood for this test at the same time spring shots are done. Have the horse's teeth floated at this yearly appointment as well. A horse with sharp points on his teeth is not going to be happy with a bit in his mouth all day.

Trail Riding Etiquette

In general, horses have the right-of-way on trails, and most other trail users willingly make room for horses to pass. Many hikers do this even when they don't know the proper etiquette. Areas that allow bicycles usually point out this guideline, and bicyclists are typically very cooperative. However, when a bicycle is following you, your mount will be happier if you find a place alongside the trail where you can pull over to let the cyclist pass.

Hikers are often surprised to see horses, and don't know what to do. Say hello, and ask them to stand on the side of the trail if they seem confused. Before riding past, make sure they are holding any loose dogs, as even nice dogs can be aggressive toward horses. The only negative incidents I have had with other trail users, besides vicious dogs, have been with trail runners who continued to run by my mount, causing the horse to spook. So now I initiate voice contact with runners before they get too close, and I ask them to walk past the horse. I also advise my riding partners when other trail users are approaching, so they are aware of the person's location and mode of travel. All trail users, including horses, should slow to a walk when approaching other trail users.

While I cannot do much when my horses leave a little manure on a steep spot along the trail, I do have the option of cleaning up after them at trailheads and lunch stops. I carry a small trash can and a shovel in my trailer. When my horses relieve themselves in the trailer or the parking area, I place the manure in the trash can and dispose of it at home. Do not clean out your trailer and leave the offending material in the parking lot because it is unsightly and it attracts flies. At popular lunch spots, I try to kick manure off to the side, except at hitching posts. Trail riders should be courteous and follow the rules of the jurisdiction they ride in, so they continue to be welcome trail users.

All areas require staying on the trail, even when the trail is muddy. It doesn't hurt horses to get muddy feet, but widening the trail degrades the environment. After a heavy rain or spring snowmelt, wait a few days for the ground to dry before trail riding to avoid doing damage to the wet trails. After opening gates on the trail, make sure they are secured properly. Use a hitching post, hobbles, or a person to hold horses at lunch breaks; tying horses to trees is not good for the trees. Take your litter with you. Whatever you brought with you, even things that may seem organic like orange peels and peanut shells, should be taken home.

Dogs are not allowed on most of these trails; where they are allowed, it is mentioned in the special notes section and on the maps. The national forests allow dogs to be off-leash. Wilderness areas, state parks, and county open space areas that allow dogs, require them to be on a six-foot leash. It is impossible to abide by this regulation while riding a horse.

Dogs need places to get out too, and many areas have denied access to them, due to negative incidents that have occurred when their owners failed to control them or otherwise follow the rules. I encourage all dog owners to adhere to the posted rules, so that their pets will continue to have the privilege of enjoying these areas. I leave my dog at home, because I have more fun riding when I am not concerned about the dog.

I recommend riding with at least one other person. All horses should stand still while other riders mount and dismount. Before starting to walk or increase the pace, check with the other riders. Discuss a schedule for rest breaks before starting the ride. A ten-minute break for each hour ridden, and a half hour break for lunch is reasonable. If your horse is hot, you may want to remove his or her saddle during long breaks. Horses should not kick at, bite, nip, or get too close to other horses. Any horse that

may kick at people or other horses should have a red ribbon tied on his or her tail. A horse that behaves badly around other horses should not be taken on group rides, until he or she is better socialized.

When riding with other horses, or behind another party, keep your horse at least one or two horse lengths behind the horse ahead of you. If your horse is traveling faster than another party, and the trail is wide enough to pass, call out "on your left" or "on your right" before passing at a walk. When crossing a stream, each horse should be given adequate time to drink without other horses entering the water. Horses should not be allowed to paw at the water; it muddies the water, making it less useful as drinking water. Splashing water can also get other riders and their tack wet and dirty.

Finally, consider joining a horseman's association that supports trail riding. These groups are the ones who ensure that so many trails are open to horses and that parking at the trailheads is appropriate for trailers. They need your support to keep doing their job. Trails that have numerous horses on them require ongoing maintenance, and some of these organizations provide this service as well. Maybe you'll find that you enjoy making repairs to your favorite trail in the company of other horse owners, or you may choose to participate in competitive trail rides, which have levels for new competitors as well as more experienced ones. A list of local horse organizations and how to contact them is in Appendix B. Numerous local groups restricted to specific breeds exist as well, and many of them support trail riding in addition to horse showing.

Rocky Mountain National Park Information and Regulations

The U.S. Congress established Rocky Mountain National Park in 1915 so that this area would be preserved forever. All trail users are reminded to tread lightly upon the land, so that generations of users after us will have the same opportunity we have to experience this remarkable area. Hikers and backpackers use many of these trails and campsites heavily. Maintaining the park in good condition for all users is a huge task, and the park service does an amazing job in this respect.

The park service prints a pamphlet entitled Horses and Other Pack Animals that can be obtained at visitor centers located near the entrance stations. Pick one up and be familiar with the current rules specific to horses; it is your responsibility to know and follow park regulations. Some of the rules are highlighted here. Horses should be gentle, well broken, properly

shod, and in good physical condition. Horses must stay on the trail; grazing is not permitted anywhere in the park. Walking, trotting, and cantering are allowed as long as they are safe and appropriate to the trail; galloping is not permitted. Slow to a walk when approaching other users, and let them know you are approaching. Hunting is not allowed at any time, and firearms cannot be carried. Horses are not permitted in campgrounds; they are permitted in designated backcountry sites with a permit obtained in advance. Carry any food your horse may need and do not leave litter anywhere. In other words, leave no trace; take nothing and leave nothing, so the person who comes behind you will be able to have the same experience that you have had.

The further we get from the trailhead, the fewer people we see. Our horses help us leave the crowds behind. The park has approximately 260 miles of trails open to horses, representing about 80% of their trail network. Trails that are not open to horses are listed on the horse regulation pamphlet. Please respect the signs that read, "No horses beyond this point." These signs are posted for good reasons; perhaps because the trail is too difficult for horses or to prevent contamination of the lake, or even to reduce interaction with hikers on extremely popular trails. Some popular trails have been paved with asphalt, and none of these trails are open to horses. These trails are mentioned in the trail descriptions in this book, and they are identified on the maps. Trails Illustrated maps also indicate which trails are not open to horses.

Most trails have hitching posts for horses at the furthest point they are allowed, usually near a lake or mountain the trail is named for. Please do not continue with your horse past this point. On some trails the hitching posts are a short distance from the lake. If the horses are happy being left tied to the hitching post, you can walk to the lake and enjoy your lunch there. Otherwise, someone should stay with them while the others take a hike to see the views.

In order to reduce damage to the environment and to offer privacy to trail users and campers, Rocky Mountain National Park provides toilets at most of their trailheads and at over 70 backcountry campsites. The trail descriptions mention these facilities when they can be seen from the trail. Please do not put anything into the toilets that is not human waste or toilet paper. Feminine hygiene items should be packed out along with all other trash.

I love riding in Rocky Mountain National Park; it is beautiful, and the trails are both well designed and well maintained. Many of these trails have existed for over a hundred years and need continual maintenance, especially to mitigate the damage that horses cause. Please respect the environment and other park users, so this valuable resource will continue to be available to horses and riders. Rocky Mountain National Park accepts volunteers for everything from fence and trail work to crowd control during elk bugling season. See Appendix B for contact information if you would like to volunteer some of your time at this fabulous national park.

Larimer County Parks and Open Lands Information and Regulations

Larimer County Parks and Open Lands trails are growing by leaps and bounds. In 2006 they opened the Blue Sky Trail, an 8-mile trail connecting several open space areas. A developer previously owned part of the large valley the Blue Sky Trail follows. He had planned to sell it as individual home sites. Due to various circumstances he was forced to sell this parcel in 2003. With the exception of the few lots that had already been purchased by individuals, it was sold as one parcel to Larimer County Parks and Open Lands. They have recently made other large purchases as well. Today some of these areas are fee areas, some are free, and some are not yet open to the public. The ones that are open to the public are all open to horses.

The opening of the Blue Sky Trail created a network of trails that starts at the Devil's Backbone Trailhead on U.S. Highway 34 in the south, and extends to Lory State Park near La Porte; 15 miles from end-to-end. It can be accessed from several different trailheads, all offering parking that can accommodate horse trailers, thanks in part to the Larimer County Horseman's Association that advocates for horse friendly trails and trailheads.

The Coyote Ridge Trailhead, the Horsetooth Trailhead, the Soderburg Trailhead at Horsetooth Park, the Devil's Backbone Trailhead and Lory State Park all provide access to this area. It encompasses over 50 miles of trails, and also includes the Rimrock Open Space, which does not have a trailhead. All of these trails are open to horses and bicycles as well as hikers and runners, with the exception of a few short trails that are reserved for hiking only. This unbelievable asset near an urban area has been made possible through the combined efforts and/or funding of the Citizens of Larimer County, the Help Preserve Open Spaces sales tax, the City of Fort Collins, the Colorado State Parks Trails Program, the Colorado State Department of Transportation, the Larimer County Parks and Open Lands Department, the Northern Front Range Metropolitan Planning Organization, Volunteers for Outdoor Colorado, and Great Outdoors Colorado, which is funded by the Colorado Lottery. These organizations have teamed-up to provide an amazing network of public, multiuse trails that, hopefully, will provide an opportunity for urban dwellers to easily enjoy the outdoors for generations to come.

The main rules in these areas are that dogs are on a six-foot leash, hunting is prohibited, and horses must stay within 10 feet of the trail. These trails and parking lots open at dawn and close at dusk.

With time, open space rules may be adjusted; the most current information regarding open space regulations can be found in brochures available at the trailheads. These brochures are chock-full of interesting information about the flora, fauna, and geology of these areas, and have the only maps available for these new trails.

How Do I Get My Horse Ready for Trail Riding?

You should do two things with your horse before he or she is ready for the mountains: The first is to expose your horse to items that might be seen on the trail, so he or she is comfortable with them. Horses are very perceptive, and seemingly normal things may scare them. Backpacks are one example. Have someone put on a large backpack, and have your horse approach this person in an arena or other safe area. When the horse is comfortable with the look of the pack, have him or her stand still while the person approaches the horse and walks on by. Next, they could pass each other while they are both walking, then have your horse walk somewhere with the backpack following. This exercise can be done while leading the horse and then mounted. Do only as much in one session as your horse is comfortable with, and end with the horse feeling satisfied about conquering his or her fears.

Other things you will encounter are hikers with hiking sticks. Hiking sticks and fishing poles can be scary to horses. Try the above exercise using ski poles or hiking sticks instead of the backpack. Use the same exercise with someone jogging. If your horse is not comfortable with dogs, the same exercise could be done with various dogs.

Bicycles are not allowed in Rocky Mountain National Park, but you will encounter them almost everywhere else. Have someone ride a bicycle in your arena following the example in the above exercises before riding your mount at any areas that allow bicycles.

When the horse is comfortable with the bicycle, have the rider go fast, apply the brakes to create noise, and shift noisily. Have the rider speak while riding.

Being able to put on additional clothing in a hurry without spooking your mount is important when it starts to rain or hail. Start this invaluable exercise with your rain gear in its usual storage place on the saddle, and then put it on while mounted; let it flap a little bit to simulate wind blowing. Horses that are not used to the higher pitch and loud voices of children can be fearful when encountering them, especially when they can hear them, but cannot see them. If your horse is not used to children, have someone bring one or more children around. Without being close to the horse, have the children play loudly. If they happen to cry, the exercise will be even better.

The second thing to do to prepare for trail riding is to get your mount in condition so that he or she has the ability to carry you on the rides you would like to do. Start by increasing the length of time you ride your horse at one time. Add hills and short trailer rides, progressing to rides at higher elevation and further from home, and then trails with elevation gain. An underweight horse should not be expected to carry you on trail rides, so make sure your horse is healthy and able to add muscle.

When you are ready to take your horse out on the trail, the best thing you can do is to take a seasoned trail horse and rider along with you. After seeing another horse calmly splashing across a stream, clomping across a bridge, or grazing by the side of the trail while a legion of bicycles zoom by, your horse will realize that he or she can negotiate that obstacle. Your mount is probably a good judge of the footing and of his or her abilities. When my seasoned trail horse refuses to do something, it is usually because whatever I am asking him to do is not safe, and his refusal gives me a chance to reconsider whether the task is appropriate or not.

When trail riding, periodically give your mount a chance to rest until his or her pulse and respiration are normal. A normal pulse rate for horses is below fifty beats per minute and normal respiration is twenty-five breaths per minute or less. To familiarize yourself with what is normal for your horse, learn how to take his or her vital signs at home (ask a veterinarian or other horsey person to help). At the end of a few months, a healthy horse conditioned in this way, should be able to do a four-hour ride, or about 8.0 miles, in addition to an hour or more ride each way in the trailer. I usually try to do a long ride, like Thunder Lake or Lost Lake, at the end of August when the horses and their riders are in their best condition.

What Should I Wear?

When you are planning to spend a day in the saddle, the answer to this question will be less about fashion and more about comfort. Dressing in layers helps you stay comfortable throughout the day, and anything that opens in the front is more versatile and easier to remove while riding than pullover type apparel. It may take some time to figure out what works best for you.

In the heat of summer at lower elevations this may simply be a short-sleeved top, paired with a long sleeved shirt for the early morning chill and afternoon thunderstorms. In the mountains, in addition to this combination, warm clothing and rain gear should always be packed on your mount. Synthetic fabrics can keep you warm even when they are wet and they dry more quickly than natural materials like cotton and wool.

Jeans can rub and they stay wet and cold after being rained on. Synthetic riding pants are a better choice if you like them. Some horse catalogs carry underpants designed for riding, with padding added in the right places, and no seams in the wrong places. Using baby powder to dry the area, or an ointment such as Vaseline™ to moisten it can alleviate chafing. I always wear sunscreen and carry a lip balm with sunscreen that I can reapply as needed.

Most riders wear boots, although endurance riders often opt for athletic type shoes. Difficult areas of the trail may require dismounting and leading your horse up or down steep or slippery areas, making a sole with good tread advantageous. Many trails don't allow horses to go quite to the end of the trail, so to be able to reach mountain tops that are too rocky for horses, or to have a view of the lake you came to see, your footwear should be safe and comfortable for hiking as well as riding. My favorite boots are designed as a riding boot but they look like a hiking boot; they are comfortable for hiking and have good traction on rocks. My boots are from Mountain Horse, but other companies make similar boots as well. I recommend wearing socks that are specially designed to keep your feet dry and provide cushioning, as well as thin sock liners, which reduce chafing. These can be purchased at outdoor recreation stores and western wear stores.

In the wintertime, I wear a lined leather glove. Summer gloves come in various styles, or you may prefer not to wear them at all. Keep a pair of gloves made of polypropylene or other fast drying material with your rain gear. Your hands can become quite cold while holding the reins in the rain or a hailstorm, and, even when wet, these gloves help keep your hands warmer. Leather work gloves are handy when encountering trees that have fallen across the trail or are clogging a river ford, but that can be moved off the trail by hand, allowing you to continue your ride.

Last but not least, is the most important piece of clothing: your head wear. I wear a hat to keep my hair and the sun off of my face, and to protect my scalp from sunburn. I want my head cool in the summer and warm in the winter, so why not have a riding hat that can do all these things? It just happens that my hat is also designed to protect my brain and skull if something causes me to end up on the ground unexpectedly, or when encountering low-hanging branches. It weighs ten ounces, has lots of airflow in the summertime, a fleece cover for the wintertime, costs about as much as two baseball caps, and will last indefinitely. This hat is referred to as a helmet in riding stores and catalogs, and the best ones are ASTM approved.

What Should My Horse Wear?

You may ask what is wrong with what you use now. The answer may be nothing, however if your gear isn't working for you, or if you are planning to buy some new tack, you may find an idea that you want to try.

Starting at the bottom, secure shoes are the basis for a relaxing ride. Colorado's mountain range is not called the Rockies for no reason! Nine trails in this book may be appropriate for a horse without shoes. These are trail #16 Moraine Park, and trail #33, the North Fork Trail as far as the Deserted Village, or somewhat further. The Bobcat Ridge Natural Area has trail #35, the Valley Loop Trail. Both trail #40 the Nomad Trail, and trail #42 the Blue Sky Trail, leave from the Soderberg Trailhead at Horsetooth Park, and trail #43 the Valley Trail, starts at Lory State Park. Trail #1 the Nighthawk Trail and Nelson Trail at Hall Ranch can be ridden up to and including the prairie dog village. Do not attempt to ride the entire Bitterbursh Trail barefoot, as the end of it is very steep and rocky; return the way you came. Two of these trails, #26 the East Shore Trail and #31 Little Yellowstone, are on the east side of the Continental Divide.

Trail horses deserve to have hooves that are trimmed and shod properly. You can do some simple things to check your horse's feet. Measure the length of each hoof from the coronary band to the ground on the inside and outside of the hoof, to ensure they are the same length from side to side. Measure the length of each toe from the coronary band to the ground. You can purchase a simple device that measures the angle of the hoof, if desired. Front and back hoof angles and hoof length should not match, left and right hooves should match. More information about

hoof angles can be found in various publications. Because it takes nine to twelve months to completely grow a new hoof, but just a few minutes for an inept farrier to damage one, we believe that a good farrier is worth his weight in gold. We happily spend twice as much for the farrier as we do for feed. Proper shoes should last six weeks. If a horse continually loses shoes in less than six weeks, having clips put on the shoes may help. Have your farrier show you how to use a nail clencher if you want to carry one in your trailer. I did this after driving an hour to a trailhead on a beautiful day only to find that one of the horses had a loose shoe. Since we cleaned his feet at home, we knew the shoe was fine when he got in the trailer. Although disappointed, there was nothing we could do but drive back home and make an appointment with the farrier, but a quick nail clinching would have lasted through the ride.

If your horse is being ridden in the wintertime, the farrier can add snow pads between the shoe and the hoof. These pads eliminate the need to pick snow out of the hooves to avoid slipping. Shoers can also put borium on his or her shoes to make them less slippery. If your horse might kick another horse when turned out, this is not an option.

What about boots? You know best whether your horse is athletic or if he or she occasionally clips a foot. If your horse is coming home with nicks or cuts, putting boots on can protect the problem areas. I always put bell boots on my gaited horse before leaving home, to protect his heels and coronary band area during the drive as well as on the ride. When my horse was young, he wore more leg protection.

Headgear is strictly a personal issue. Leather bridles are traditional, but nylon, biothane and beta are easier to maintain. I avoid Chicago screws because there is no good time for a bridle to come apart, and they occasionally come unscrewed. When using a bridle with these screws, use Loctite Threadlocker™ or similar products available in hardware stores when putting them together, and carry extra screws on the ride. Check Chicago screws for tightness when putting the bridle on. Any bridle should have a throatlatch, so the horse cannot remove it while scratching his or her head.

A halter and lead rope are required equipment for the trailer ride and trailhead, as well as lunch breaks or emergencies. I prefer to use a halter/bridle combination so I can just add the bit to the halter at the trailhead and my horse is never without his halter. I keep a lead rope in my cantle bag for use during lunch breaks. My husband prefers a rope halter, which he removes at the trailhead and puts in his saddlebags. Some riders and most dude ranches simply put the horse's bridle on over the halter. As long as it is comfortable for the horse, keeps him or her from becoming loose on a busy highway, and can be taken along on the ride for tying the horse to a hitching post or while he or she is eating lunch, it should work fine. When using a bit, make sure that it is comfortable for your horse; a large smooth bit is the most comfortable to carry all day. I use a bit with a mild three piece mouthpiece made out of sweet iron or copper, with or without a roller depending on the horse, and a short shank for control in stressful situations.

Reins also offer many options. I prefer a one-piece rein so I cannot accidentally drop a rein, and I can loop it over the saddle horn when changing a jacket or taking a photograph. Unfortunately, the reins are then too short for the horse to lower his head to drink water or scratch his face, so I use a custom made rommel rein which gives me something to hold onto when he lowers his head. I use a swivel, snap-hook for attaching the reins to the bit. When I need to lead the horse I can snap the reins off the bit and onto the halter, or for a longer lead I just attach one end of the rein to the halter. I have read that this metal attachment to the metal bit may bother the horse, but mine seems happy with this arrangement.

Entire books are written on how to choose a saddle, and I am not an expert in this area. Make sure, however that the saddle is comfortable for the horse. A saddle that seems fine for half hour training sessions may become a torture device on a five-hour ride. The same may be true for the rider. I have tried every type of seat saver carried in equine catalogs to keep me comfortable on long rides. The ones I like the best are sheepskin with the wool still on it, and the full sized tush cushion made by Cashel™. These can be used together.

Horses deserve a thick absorbent saddle pad on a long ride. Make sure that the saddle and pad stay in place. If they slide around, try other combinations until you find one that stays where it belongs, regardless of the terrain. Wash dirty saddle pads in mild soap rather than detergent so that neither dirt nor chemicals irritate the horse's back.

Some riders are happy riding trails in an English saddle. I prefer a western saddle as I use the horn for horn bags, and I can hang lots of stuff on it, as well as using it as a handle to mount my large horse. Endurance saddles are designed primarily for the rider to be comfortable when standing in the stirrups at a trot. Australian and treeless saddles seem interesting, and although they don't seem to fit my round horse, they may fit yours. As long as you and your horse are comfortable and balanced, the design doesn't matter. Make sure that you can sit with your shoulders, hips, and heels in a straight line perpendicular to the ground, to make it easier for your horse to negotiate obstacles and carry you on long rides. Some western saddles are designed to put your feet forward of the rest of your body, causing the rider to lean back in the saddle, and the horse to be off balance.

If your saddle is designed with a flank or aft cinch option, make sure to use one and adjust it so it is snug, because it helps the saddle stay in place. When using a western cinch, consider using a latigo on both the off and near side of your cinch as horses seem to get smaller around during the ride. My young gelding's cinch became detached from the off-billet when he started to sprint up a hill. The cinch hanging around his legs terrified him and he ran as fast as he could to escape it. Luckily, he ran out of breath before taking any sharp turns, and I realized the problem before I attempted to dismount. I now make sure my cinch is foolproof by using a latigo tied to the saddle on both ends of the cinch.

The other accessory the horse needs is a breast collar. Many styles are available, so choose one that keeps your saddle from slipping back and is comfortable for the horse. Some people insist on cruppers, but my horses have never needed them. If the saddle slides forward and bumps your horse's withers when riding down hills, learn to use a crupper properly. Artificial aids, such as tie-downs and martingales, should not be used when trail riding. They restrict your horse's range of motion making awkward spots in the trail more difficult, and they may be dangerous in the event he or she trips or falls.

What Should I Take with Me?

Take food and water for yourself. For a long ride, take something for your horse to eat as well. Hay pellets in a nosebag or a sack of carrots work well. Feed grain only after the ride, in the same amount as you usually feed grain. A small first aid kit for people and horses is recommended, and a bandana has many uses.

A hoof pick, a whistle, which can be used to signal for help in an emergency, and a multi-tool such as a Leatherman™, are small and invaluable items to take. If you take a cell phone for emergency use, program phone numbers into it for your regular veterinarian, another veterinarian who is available when your regular vet is not, your farrier, and someone who can take care of your children and your other animals in case you cannot get home, or need to drive directly to the veterinarian.

Some riders take an Easy Boot™ to use in case of a thrown shoe, but they are cumbersome to carry and the older type can be difficult to keep on the horse. I have not tried the newer, more expensive alternatives on the market. A small roll of duct tape can protect a hoof that has a loose shoe, or can be used as a substitute for a thrown shoe for a short distance.

A camera and small binoculars can be carried on your belt, or in saddle horn bags so they are easily accessible. A gallon-sized zip-lock bag takes up little space, and can be used as a bucket to water your horses at lakes they are not allowed to approach. Always take a halter, lead rope, and a map.

When heading into the mountains, rain gear and extra clothing, like a sweater or a fleece to keep you warm, should always be available, even when the weather looks terrific. Afternoon thundershowers can come in quickly at higher elevations and can be severe, with lightning and hail. These storms can lower the temperature considerably. Be prepared to wait out a storm, or if it lasts more than half an hour, to ride to your trailer in the storm. Various types of rain gear can be used while riding. Nylon ponchos are lighter and more comfortable than plastic ones, and are simple to pack. Guided trail horses always have a yellow slicker tied to the back of the saddle; Australian waxed canvas jackets can be tied to the saddle and used as a lightweight coat as well as rain gear. A large trash bag can protect your saddle and keep the seat dry while you are waiting out a storm under a tree. In the event you are caught above tree line in a lightning storm, dismount and lead your horse to an area downhill from the closest trees.

How Can I Carry Everything?

Many options are available for carrying items while riding. Miniature saddle bags that fit over the saddle horn, called horn bags, are great for things you want to be able to reach. For larger items use a cantle bag, or saddle bags. Saddlebags are roomier than a cantle bag, but tend to become lopsided on the horse if they are not balanced for weight. Spare clothing can be tied behind the cantle with saddle strings. Just remember, anything that is on your mount may not be available if he or she takes off without you, so carry essentials in a backpack or fanny pack, on your belt, or around your neck.

A great way to carry water for yourself is to use one of the many water delivery systems that consist of a small backpack with a plastic bladder to fill with water or other liquid. On a hot day, ice cubes can be added to the water. Water is sipped through a tube so your hands are virtually free while riding. Some of these can hold up to one hundred ounces of liquid and have enough extra room for a lunch, a first aid kit, and a cell phone.

Trailer Talk

Take water in your truck or trailer and a bucket for your horse to drink from, especially when going to trails where water is scarce, and in the wintertime when sources of water on the trail are likely to be frozen. In the summertime, you can also use the water and a sponge to rinse your horses off after the ride. You may want a cooler or sheet to put on them for the drive home if they are sweaty or wet from rain or sponging. Bring hay for the drive home when they will be hungry.

Keep a good first aid kit in your trailer. The things I use most often are Ace bandages and cold packs that can be stored in the trailer at room temperature until needed. These are great for scrapes and bruises as well as reducing swelling on horses and people alike. Take a cell phone, even if you don't plan to carry it along on the ride, and don't forget a shovel and manure can. If possible, keep extra items, like clothes for riders, halters and leads, bridles, saddle pads, a shoe clencher, and grooming items for the horses, in the trailer permanently.

I am going to state the obvious because it is so important. Keep your trailer in good working condition, with the tires properly inflated. The trailer should be comfortable for the horses so they will not balk at getting in the trailer the next time. Be sure that the floorboards are in good condition and use rubber mats to cushion your horse's ride. If your horse urinates in the trailer, remove the rubber mats when you get home and wash and dry everything to prevent the floorboards from rotting. Wood shavings can help soak up some of the moisture, but they must be removed as well.

Open plenty of windows for ventilation, leaving a screen or bars over the opening to prevent the horses from being hit by flying objects, tree branches, etc. Even in wintertime, some ventilation is necessary. Each time you load up your trailer, including after the ride when the trailer has been unattended, double-check that the trailer is hooked up properly and that there is a pin in the hitch, and be sure that all of the lights and signals are working properly.

We feed our horses hay during the drive so they are not hungry or bored. A horse riding in a trailer is working just as hard as when you are riding him at a walk, so adjust the length of a ride accordingly. Start with short drive times if the horse is not used to traveling in your trailer for long periods of time. Horses should enter a trailer happily once they have been taught to go into it.

Getting our first horses to go into our trailer was a real production. I spent many frustrating sessions loading reticent horses, and reading books and articles devoted to trailer loading as well as using a trainer to teach them to load easily, all to no avail. One day I had to load a single horse into our trailer near a small airport, with a steady stream of airplanes flying low overhead. By the time I got the horse secured in the trailer he was extremely upset, so I decided to ride in the trailer with him down the long dirt driveway. What an eye opener! That old trailer rattled so loudly I could hardly stand the noise. No wonder our horses didn't want to get into it.

We bought a larger, brighter, and quieter slant-load trailer that horses get into it without hesitation. If your horses don't like your trailer, try to figure out why. If you can't make your trailer a pleasant environment for them, consider investing in one that is pleasant, so that you both enjoy the loading and the drive, and get to the trailhead ready to ride, instead of irritated and tired.

On the Trail

Sit relaxed when your mount is walking; riding as if in a show will cause you and your mount to become tired quite quickly. When you are relaxed, your mount is more apt to be calm, too. At a trot or a lope, adjust your center of balance forward so you are not falling behind the center of balance. To accomplish this, put more weight on your legs and feet and rotate slightly forward from the hips.

Staying balanced in the saddle makes it easier for your horse to carry you. In order for you to keep your balance when standing, your shoulders, hips, and heels are in line with each other and with gravity, and the same should be true when you are on your horse. Going up or down hills requires a slight forward or backward lean, just as when you are standing on a hill, to keep you upright. Since most trees grow in an upright direction regardless of the terrain, use them to judge your position by checking to see that your body is in a line that matches the truck of the tree.

On longer rides taking a lunch break is enjoyable for the rider and rejuvenates the horse. Loosen your mount's cinch or remove the saddle when dismounted. Hitching posts make convenient saddle racks. After your horse is cooled down and his or her vital signs are normal, you can feed the carrots or hay pellets you brought along, or let him or her graze a little if you are in an area that allows grazing.

Make sure your mount has plenty of plain water. Offer the horses water to drink before the drive home, especially on trails that do not have water for horses or if your horse won't drink water from streams. Providing horses with a salt block at home encourages drinking. Electrolytes are not necessary, or even desirable for this level of riding, and never should be given to a horse that is dehydrated. (See the *North American Trail Ride Conference's Riders Manual* for more information on electrolytes).

People drinking from a lake or stream can become infected with giardia, a parasite that has become prevalent in our mountain water sources, so riders should have adequate water for themselves too. You can assess your hydration level, as well as that of your horse, by pinching a small piece of skin between your thumb and forefinger and watching to see how long it takes to spring back. The longer it takes the skin to return to its normal position, the more dehydrated the person or horse is. Now that you are prepared, go out and have a great day in the mountains.

PART II.

TRAIL DESCRIPTIONS

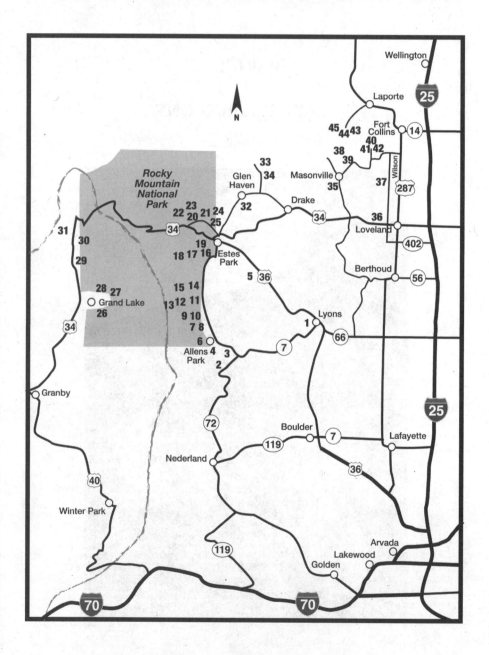

Map Legend

————	**Paved Road**
▬▬▬▬	**Dirt Road**
- - - - - - -	**Easy Trail**
· · · · · · · · · ·	**Moderate Trail**
-·-··-··-·-	**Advanced Trail**
♦ ♦ ♦ ♦ ♦ ♦ ♦	**Demanding Trail**
x x x x x x x x	**Closed to Horses**
▬▬▬▬	**Route Described**
* 2.2 mi. *	**Trail Mileage Between Two Points**

🅿	**Horse Trailer Parking**
🏇	**Trailhead**
🚻	**Restrooms**
🚰	**Water Faucet**
🚲	**Bicyclist Allowed**
⛱	**Picnic Area**
🐕	**Dogs Allowed**
$	**Fee Station**
⛺	**Camping**

Trails Overview
Trails are arranged below from the easiest to the most challenging

Easy Trails

Trail Number and Name	Total Distance	Elevation Gain (feet)	High Point
35. Valley Loop Trail	4.5 miles	300	5,800 feet
40. Nomad Trail	6.4 miles or less	100	5,600 feet
26. East Shore Trail, short option	1.0 mile to unlimited	100	8,600 feet
16. Moraine Park loop	5.0 miles	0	8,000 feet
43. Valley Trails	8.0 miles or less	100	5,600 feet
33. North Fork Trail, short option	4.2 miles or more	250	8,100 feet
12. Glacier Basin loop	5.0 miles	600	9,000 feet
28. North Inlet Trail, short option	6.0 miles or less	600	9,600 feet
21. North Deer Mountain Trail	9.4 to 12.6 miles	300	8,800 feet
31. Little Yellowstone	7.0 to 10 miles or less	900	9,900 feet
3. Bunce School Road	9.6 to 14 miles or less	600	8,800 feet
19. Beaver Meadows loop	9.0 miles or more	800	9,600 feet

Moderate Trails

42. Blue Sky Trail	13.4 miles or more	300	5,600 feet
17. Cub Lake	5.8 miles or more	550	8,700 feet
7. Calypso Cascades	6.0 miles or more	700	9,200 feet
37. Coyote Ridge	4.0 to 7.0 miles or more	578	5,600 feet
41. Stout Trail loop	6.5 miles	900	6,400 feet
29. Tonahutu Creek, south option	9.6 miles	400	9200 feet
36. Devil's Backbone trails	6.1 miles or more	320	5,400 feet
38. Wathen Trail	6.5 miles	1,000	6,900 feet
29. Green Mountain loop	7.5 miles	1,100	9,900 feet
1. Nighthawk Trail	8.0 miles or less	1,280	6,800 feet
14. Bierstadt Trail	7.0 miles or more	1,000	9,400 feet
13. Glacier Basin Creek	7.0 to 10 miles or more	1,000	9,800 feet
25. Black Canyon Trail, short option	7.2 miles or less	1,200	9,200 feet
39. Westridge Trail	8.8 miles	1,100	7,000 feet
32. Crosier Mountain	8.0 miles or less	1,250	9,250 feet

44. Mill Creek Trail	9.5 miles	1,400	6,900 feet
6. Finch Lake	7.2 miles	1,150	10,050 feet

Advanced Trails

5. Lion Gulch	5.0 miles or more	1,500	9,000 feet
20. Deer Mountain Trail	11 or 12.5 miles	1,500	10,000 feet
11. Storm Pass Trail	10 miles or more	1,600+	10,000 feet
1. Hall Ranch loop	9.0 miles	1,280	6,880 feet
45. Spring Creek Trail	12 miles	1,400	6,900 feet
10. Sandbeach Lake	9.5 miles	1,970	10,283 feet
6. Finch and Pear Lakes	11 miles	1,800	10,600 feet
30. Timber Lake	10.5 miles	2,060	11,000 feet
2. Peaceful Valley	15 miles or more	2,200	10,800 feet
26. East Shore Trail, long option	23 miles or less	100	8,600 feet
22. Lawn Lake	15.2 miles	2,500	11,000 feet
18. Fern and Odessa Lakes	9.2 or 10.6 miles	1,870	10.020 feet
8. Ouzel and Bluebird Lakes	13 or 14 miles	1,510	10,010 feet
24. Gem Lake loop	9.1 miles	1,600	9,100 feet

Demanding Trails

23. Ypsilon Lake	10 miles	2,100	10,700 feet
9. Thunder Lake	17 miles	1,290	10,590 feet
27. East Inlet Trail	14 miles or less	1,400	10,000 feet
4. Meadow Mountain	10 miles	2,760	11,360 feet
34. Signal Mountain	10 to 12 miles	3,362	11,262 feet
15. Hollowell Park loop	16 miles	2,800	10,800 feet
33. North Fork Trail to Lost Lake	19.4 miles	2,800	10,000 feet
29. Tonahutu Creek/ Flattop Mountain	22 miles or more	3,500	12,200 feet
28. North Inlet Trail, long option	24 miles or more	3,600	12,200 feet

Trailhead Ratings Legend

Drive Ratings:

Simple

Moderate

Difficult

Parking Ratings:

Good

Acceptable

Poor

Difficulty Ratings Legend

Trail Difficulty Ratings:

Easy - - - - - - - -

Moderate . . . .

Advanced . _ . _ . _ . _ .

Demanding ♦ ♦ ♦ ♦ ♦ ♦ ♦

Closed or
Dangerous x x x x x x x x

Terrain Ratings:

Mostly Smooth

Rocky or Steep

Steep Stairs
or Loose
Large Rocks

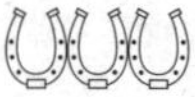

Extensive
Challenging
Footing

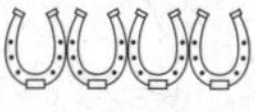

Training ability Ratings:

No Obstacles +

Some Obstacles + +

Lots of Obstacles + + +

Trails South and East of Rocky Mountain National Park

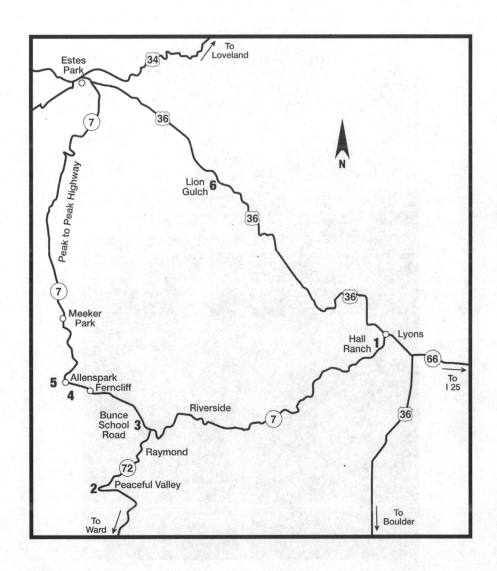

Trails accessed from Colorado State Highway 7

Hall Ranch Open Space Trailhead

Drive to the Trailhead	🗝 🗝 🗝
Parking	🅿 🅿 🅿
Amenities	Hitching posts, toilet
Fee Area?	No
Elevation	5,600 feet
Maps	Trails Illustrated 100: Boulder Golden, these trails are too new for USGS maps. An open space trail map is also available at the trailhead

Thank the Boulder County Open Space Department for this trailhead parking area, which is a dream come true for those of us pulling horse trailers, and also for the Nighthawk Trail which is the perfect trail to ride gaited horses up.

Directions from Boulder County and Interstate Highway 25.

Drive to the Hall Ranch Trailhead by traveling west toward the town of Lyons on Colorado State Highway 66 from north Longmont or Interstate Highway 25 (exit 243), or on U.S. Highway 36 from Boulder. A gas station that also sells diesel, and can accommodate a truck pulling a trailer is located in Lyons. Look for it on the south side of Colorado State Highway 66, shortly after the signal at the intersection of U.S. Highway 34 and Colorado State Highway 66.

Continue through Lyons on a one-way street, staying in the left-hand lane. At the west end of town, this street ends at a stop sign. Turn left and go straight through the traffic signal at the next street. You are now on Colorado State Highway 7. (On the way back turn right at the signal to go east on the road you came on.)

The trailhead can be difficult to see ahead of time. It is on the right after 1.5 miles, between mileage markers 32 and 31. Pull into the dirt driveway and continue straight to the upper parking lot, where hitching posts and roomy pull-through parking spaces for multiple horse trailers are provided. Pick up a trail map, which also lists the regulations for this area, at the information kiosk adjacent to the upper parking lot.

Trail #1
Hall Ranch Open Space trails

Trail rideable	All year as long as the ground is dry; snow and slippery mud can make this trail unsafe
Best time to ride	Spring and Fall
Maximum elevation	6,800 feet
Difficulty	**Moderate** to **Advanced** due to a steep hill on the Bitterbrush trail
Terrain	☘ to ☘☘☘ for one steep hill
Training ability	**+** to **+ +**
Length	9.0 miles round trip, with other combinations possible
Elevation gain	1,280 feet
Best features	Accessibility
Obstacles	An abundance of bicycles on some trails; two bridges and one steep, rocky hill
Special notes	The Nighthawk Trail is a great place for novice trail horses and riders, and barefoot horses; dogs are not allowed at Hall Ranch since it is designated as a wildlife preserve

This is a wonderful area to ride horses, especially during the cooler months, although the nice clay trail base on the Nighthawk Trail can turn into a slippery and dangerous path when wet. This route is described in a clockwise direction, going up

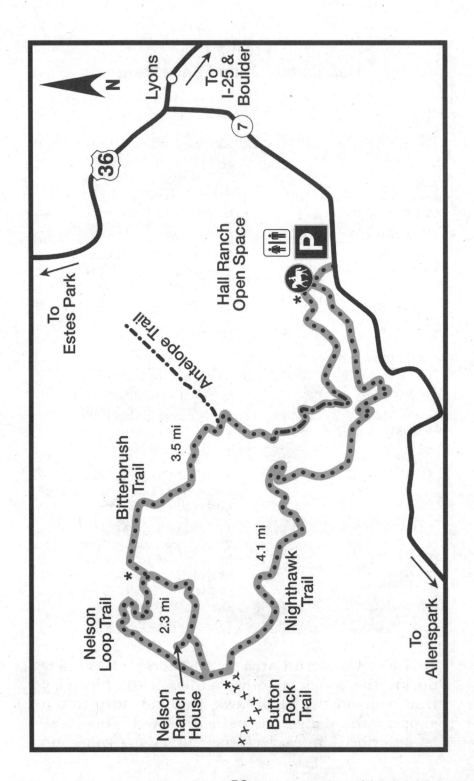

the long, gradual hill of the Nighthawk Trail that makes a great ride on a gaited horse. Riding up the challenging hill on the Bitterbrush Trail at the beginning of the ride may be slightly easier than riding down it at the end of the ride, which you can do by riding the trail in reverse.

The trailhead is west of the trailer parking area, near the restroom. The trail starts just past the information kiosk. This trail divides into two trails 50 feet from the trailhead. Stay left to follow the Nighthawk Trail, and step over a board lying across the trail that specifies this trail is not open to bicycles. Few hikers use the Nighthawk Trail because it is longer and less interesting than the Bitterbrush Trail. Follow this trail as it climbs steadily, but not too steeply for 4.1 miles. After the first switchback the trail crosses a small bridge over a gully. This route provides sweeping views of the red cliffs, and a working gravel quarry that can be heard on weekdays on the south side of Colorado State Highway 7. Many badly eroded dirt roads remain in this area from when the Hall family used it as a cattle ranch. The Boulder County Open Space Department has chosen to put in new trails, and to let the old roads revegetate. Please respect this decision and refrain from riding on the roads.

After passing the first of two stock tanks, which provide a welcome drink for horses on this otherwise dry ride, the trail continues into a ponderosa pine forest. In the wintertime, this area often remains covered with snow when the rest of the trail is clear. At the highest point of the trail enjoy the nice, if brief, view of Mount Meeker and Longs Peak. Shortly after breaking out of the trees, the trail passes a junction with the Button Rock Trail, which is only open to hikers. Button Rock Reservoir is the water supply for the City of Longmont.

Soon after that junction, the Nighthawk Trail ends at the Nelson Loop Trail. Up to this point the trail has no obstacles and the footing is good, although the elevation gain is enough to give many horses a good workout. On the Nelson Loop and the Bitterbrush Trail bicycles are frequently encountered. The round trip mileage for the Nighthawk Trail is 8.2 miles, and the Nelson Loop Trail is 2.3 miles. Riding the Nelson Loop Trail and returning to the trailhead on the Nighthawk Trail would total 10.5 miles. This is a good choice for a well-conditioned horse that has had little contact with bicycles. The horse can experience some bicycles without getting too much exposure at one time. Barefoot horses should turn around here as well.

Whichever direction you ride on the Nelson Loop Trail, it eventually comes to the junction with the Bitterbrush Trail. The left-hand option travels through the trees to the Bitterbrush Trail. In the wintertime, avoid this option because of the small stream that becomes a large ice flow where it crosses the trail. The right-hand option of the Nelson Loop Trail comes to another trail junction on the left after a few minutes. Turn left onto this short spur trail to visit the old homestead and silo, and the second stock tank. A sign tells about the homestead and gives some history of the area. Just north of the cabin are some nice rocks to sit on while taking a lunch break, free from the bicycles that are traveling on the loop trail. The junction with the Bitterbrush Trail is on the Nelson Loop Trail, a short distance past the junction for the homestead.

Returning to the trailhead on the Bitterbrush Trail is a 3.5-mile ride from the junction with the Nelson Loop Trail. The first part of this trail, which travels through ponderosa pine trees, can have snow on it and be slippery, even when the rest of the trail is clear. After crossing a bridge, the trail breaks out into the open. Bicycles can come up from behind quickly on this slightly downhill trail. While we have never had any trouble with cyclists, our horses are always quick to alert us to any movement behind them, so we ride them off the side of the trail and turn them so they can see the approaching two-wheeled contraptions.

Before long, this route skirts a valley that, not too many years ago, had a small prairie dog village in it. Today the prairie dog population has exploded. They have denuded the valley of grass and are spreading up the edges of the valley looking for food, so keep an eye out for prairie dog holes when riding through this area. While these rodents are cute and fun to listen to, this is a good example of the damage they have done to a once beautiful and green valley, as well as a formerly safe riding trail. Soon this route passes the junction for the Antelope Trail on the left. That 1.0-mile trail provides local access from Apple Valley. It is a steep and sometimes narrow trail with sharp switchbacks, so this guidebook does not recommend riding there.

At the far end of the valley, the trail climbs a short distance to the top of the hill, before it drops down steeply on the other side of the ridge. That hill is rocky and slippery, as bicycles have eroded most of the dirt away. It is also busy, with hikers, bicycles and horses trying to share a challenging piece of trail. Take your time getting down the many switchbacks, leading your mount if all the activity or the slippery surface is unsettling. Once off this hill, it is smooth riding back to the trailhead. After experiencing Hall Ranch on horseback, you will surely plan to come back again.

Drive to the Trailhead	
Parking	
Amenities	Hitching post and picnic table at the parking area, toilet in campground
Fee Area?	No
Elevation	8,600 feet
Maps	Trails Illustrated 200: Rocky Mountain National Park, USGS Allenspark; the approach to the trailhead through the campground is shown on the Trails Illustrated 100: Boulder Golden map, and the USGS Raymond map

This trailhead rates as very poor and this guidebook does not recommend using it on weekends.

Directions from Boulder County and Interstate Highway 25

Drive to the Peaceful Valley trailhead by traveling west toward the town of Lyons on Colorado State Highway 66 from north Longmont or Interstate Highway 25 (exit 243), or on U.S. Highway 36 from Boulder. A gas station that also sells diesel, and can accommodate a truck pulling a trailer is located in Lyons. Look for it on the south side of Colorado State Highway 66, shortly after the signal at the intersection of U.S. Highway 34 and Colorado State Highway 66.

Continue through Lyons on a one-way street, staying in the left-hand lane. At the west end of town, this street ends at a stop sign. Turn left and go straight through the traffic signal at the next street. (On the way back turn right at the signal to go east on the road you came on.)

You are now on Colorado State Highway 7. Follow this for 14 miles to the junction with Colorado State Highway 72, between mileage markers 20 and 19. Two signs mark the Riverside/Raymond turnoff, which is just before two signs marking the Colorado State Highway 72 junction. The first one is a large green sign indicating that Estes Park is straight ahead and that Nederland and Peaceful Valley are to the left. The second sign indicates that Colorado State Highway 7 is straight ahead, and Colorado State Highway 72 is to the left. Just past that sign, turn left onto Colorado State Highway 72.

Directions from Larimer County

From Loveland, drive to the Peaceful Valley Trailhead by traveling west on U.S. Highway 34 almost 30 miles to Estes Park. Turn left at the first traffic signal in Estes Park, and right at the next signal onto Colorado State Highway 7. Just before this signal is a right turn lane; vehicles in this lane do not have to stop at the light, as long as they yield to traffic coming through the signal. Moving into the right turn lane too soon will result in being forced onto a side street. If this happens, follow that road when it curves to the left and turn right at the stop sign. You will then be on Colorado State Highway 7.

Stay on this highway for 20 miles to Colorado State Highway 72. Past the turnoffs for Allenspark and Ferncliff, and between mileage markers 19 and 20, turn right onto Colorado State Highway 72, also signed as the Peak-to-Peak Highway.

Directions from the junction of Colorado State Highway 7 and Colorado State Highway 72

Follow Colorado State Highway 72 for 4.0 miles. Just after a sign pointing to the Peaceful Valley Lodge on the left, a green sign indicates that it is 8.0 miles to Ward and 20 miles to Nederland. Before long, near an old dirt road, a brown national forest campground sign for Peaceful Valley and Camp Dick campgrounds can be seen on the right. The turnoff, onto a paved road, is 300 feet past this sign. Mile marker 50 is on the left side of the road at that point. Drive through both campgrounds and over a multitude of abrupt speed bumps. Horses are not allowed in this area so do not plan to camp here. After what seems like an eternity, but is only 2.0 miles, the paved road ends at a small dirt parking lot.

Park on the outside of this loop, preferably on the south side of the lot where there is room for two or three trailers to park. To secure parking here come on weekdays or early on the weekends as this parking area is often full of ATV trailers. The parking lot can be chaotic with loose dogs and kids, and ATVs driven by those of all ages racing to and fro. Lead your horse to the start of the trail to avoid any mishaps. Fortunately, the ATVs are here to ride on the dirt road on the south side of the Middle St. Vrain River, so you will quickly leave them behind.

Another equally poor, but not busy, trailhead that could be used to access this trail is located at Beaver Reservoir. It is also on Colorado State Highway 72, just 2.5 miles south of the Camp Dick turnoff, and 6.5 total miles from the junction of Colorado State Highway 7. Driving south from the Camp Dick turnoff, a road to Jamestown on the left is followed by a sign for a Boy Scout Camp on the right, between mileage markers 46 and 47, where you turn right onto Boulder County Road 96. From Colorado State

Highway 72 to the Beaver Reservoir Dam is 2.0 miles on a reasonably good dirt road. From there it is another 1.0 mile to the trailhead.

From the highway the first 1.0 mile or so of the road belongs to a Scout Camp. Then it is on national forest land for 1.0 mile. The dam and the road after the dam are privately owned. Park alongside the road on national forest land, and ride on the road to the trailhead. A cement spillway just past the dam makes a good place to turn around, as long as no water is flowing over it. After the spillway, there are no areas to park trailers or opportunities to turn around.

Camping is allowed in undeveloped areas on national forest land. For camping, locate the road that forks off to the south with a gate that can be locked in the wintertime, but without any signs marking the road. It is only 1.0 mile long and ends at a peat bog, but it is a less busy place to camp than along the main road. This area is shown on the USGS map named Ward, the approach is on the Gold Hill map.

The trailhead is well marked on the right, not far past the spillway, and leads to a rocky 4-wheel drive road, which is a miserable by horse or vehicle. That road arrives at Coney Flats after 4.0 miles. However, 0.1 mile from the trailhead, a single track trail leaves the road to the right and travels through the trees for 1.5 miles, before passing a junction for the Sourdough Trail on the right and arriving at the Peaceful Valley Trailhead described previously. The Sourdough Trail can be accessed from CR96 as well and is a shorter route if you can find where it crosses CR96. It is a fairly flat trail rated **Easy** that travels through the trees for over 7.0 miles. Numerous other trails, including Mt. Audubon, Buchanan Pass Trail and trails headed towards Brainard Lake can be accessed from this area, although horses are not allowed on the trails that are south of here in the Indian Peaks Wilderness.

Trail #2
Peaceful Valley trails

Trail rideable	June through September
Best time to ride	September, because the trailhead is less busy after Labor Day
Maximum elevation	10,800 feet
Difficulty	**Advanced** due to mileage and elevation gain
Terrain	♘ ♘
Training ability	✛ ✛
Length	12 miles round trip to the rock slide
Elevation gain	1,500 feet
Best features	Scenery and the ability to vary the trail on the return
Obstacles	Busy parking lot, one bridge, and optional stream crossings
Special notes	Dogs are allowed in the Arapahoe National Forest, and on a leash in the Indian Peaks Wilderness area; Indian Peaks Wilderness requires a permit for overnight camping

This is a nice trail with a gentle grade that starts out as a forest trail, and then opens up to views of the Continental Divide. It travels old roads constructed by loggers over a hundred years ago and gives trail users the opportunity to visit some of the few remaining glaciers in Colorado on foot. By using a trail to a lake for a varied return to the trailhead, it can be ridden as a loop trail.

Starting at the far west end of this trail, the entire route of the South St. Vrain Creek can be traced in one day, starting with the headwaters at Lake Gibraltar, or the St. Vrain Glacier, and following it along the Peaceful Valley Trail and road. At the Peaceful Valley turnoff, the creek heads north along Colorado State Highway 72 and follows the highway bypass through Raymond and then continues to follow Colorado State Highway 7 to its confluence with the North St. Vrain Creek in Lyons. That is the end of the South St. Vrain Creek and the beginning of the St. Vrain Creek, which flows through Longmont before joining the South Platte River on its way to the Mississippi River.

To access the trail, follow the road that leaves from the west side of the parking lot, passing the gate and a campsite for the trail host. Then, 100 yards further, the trail leaves the road on the right, crosses the Middle St. Vrain River on a bridge with no ford for horses, goes up a few steps, and then parallels the river on the north side. This is shown as the St. Vrain Glacier Trail on the Trails Illustrated Rocky Mountain National Park map, which does not extend far enough to the east to show the parking lot. USGS maps do not show this trail, however the campgrounds and the trailhead, as well as the other trails in this area, are shown on the USGS Allenspark map.

The trail climbs at a slight but continuous grade. Watch for views of a small waterfall and the Middle St. Vrain River, which this route follows for its entire length. At one point the trail is built up to allow hikers to walk between a large rock and the river. A rather steep and rocky but more substantial horse trail has been built as a detour around this spot.

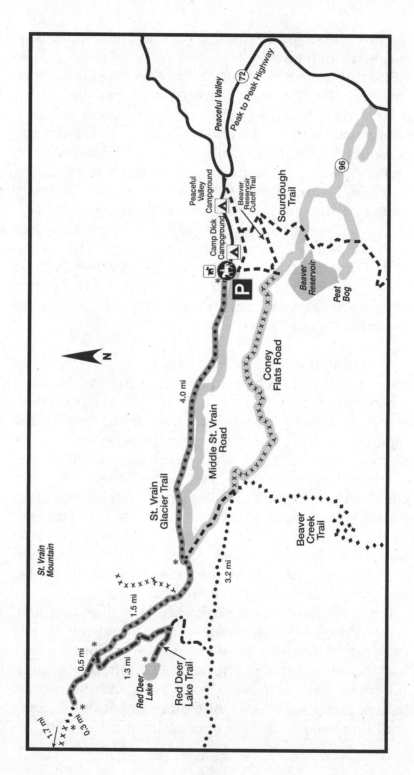

Peaceful Valley

Peak to Peak Highway

72

96

Sourdough Trail

Peaceful Valley Campground

Beaver Reservoir Cutoff Trail

Camp Dick Campground

Beaver Reservoir

Peat Bog

P

N

St. Vrain Glacier Trail

4.0 mi

Middle St. Vrain Road

Coney Flats Road

Beaver Creek Trail

3.2 mi

St. Vrain Mountain

1.5 mi

0.5 mi

1.3 mi

Red Deer Lake

Red Deer Lake Trail

0.3 mi

1.7 mi

This drainage has more moisture than many of the trails in this guidebook, resulting in somewhat different vegetation with fir, aspen, and willow predominating. When the trail breaks out of the trees, enjoy the splendid view of Buchanan Pass and Sawtooth Mountain. The first trail junction is 4.0 miles up the trail. The trail to the left leads to Coney Flats and eventually to Beaver Reservoir, and also to the dirt 4-wheel drive road south of the river, which becomes the Buchanan Pass Trail west of Coney Flats. This route turns right and continues north along the river. Make a note of this small trail junction signed only as "Camp Dick" to avoid missing it on the return trip.

A short distance further up the trail, a sign marks the boundary of the Indian Peaks Wilderness. In 1978, Congress decided to give this popular area wilderness status, which denied access to vehicles. Although this is the only trail in the Indian Peaks Wilderness that fits the parameters of this book, there are many interesting trails in this wilderness area, many of which are open to horses and also to camping, that requires a permit. (See Appendix B.)

Just beyond this sign is a junction for St. Vrain Mountain on the right, but the trail is steep and traverses rocky areas that are rated **Dangerous** for horses. The map also shows a trail on the left to Red Deer Lake there, but it has been rerouted. Remnants of former logging activity are evident along the main trail. Continue following the St. Vrain Glacier Trail, with the Middle St. Vrain River on the left and St. Vrain Mountain on the right. Ceran St. Vrain, a trader who came through here during the early days of settlement, put his name on everything in the area. This is a good spot to enjoy the view of the feature with the fitting name Elk Tooth. Continue following the river northwest, through a small meadow, and then through a larger clearing. It appears that this clearing burned at one time, and the remnants of a cabin can still be seen.

At the far end of the clearing, a trail to Red Deer Lake leaves the main trail and crosses the river on your left, 5.5 miles from the trailhead. To go to Red Deer Lake, ford the river, slightly upstream and to the right of a small bridge for hikers. Red Deer Lake is a charming gem of a lake 1.3 miles from this junction, and is well worth the visit. This can be a nice spur trail, returning the way you came, or continuing on to the Buchanan Pass Trail where turning left leads to Coney Flats. At that point head north, ford the river, and return to the trail junction previously ridden and signed "Camp Dick." It is 3.2 miles from Red Deer Lake to that signpost. It is another 4.0 miles back to the parking lot from that junction, making the round trip 13.5 miles, although if you are brave

enough to ride the 4-wheel drive road from Coney Flats, that option is a bit shorter.

This route continues on the St. Vrain Glacier Trail past the junction to Red Dear Lake for 0.5 mile, until the trail crosses a rockslide. This is probably a good place to turn around, although riders can continue another 0.3 mile up the trail. To avoid the rockslide, which is rated **Dangerous** for horses, an alternate trail descends a steep hill to the river. The river is not deep, but it is quite wide. This is not a good place for a training exercise as the riverbank is very steep, with no room to maneuver at the bottom before crossing the river. Before long, that trail crosses back to the north side of the river, and after a short distance comes to a small lake that has been created by beavers damming up the river in the 1990s. Horses cannot cross here, and in any case the trail becomes too rocky and narrow for horses soon after the river, so turn around here. If you want to hike to the end of the trail to see the St. Vrain Glaciers and Gibraltar Lake, cross on the footbridge, and continue 1.7 miles further up the trail on foot. This part of the trail is shown on the USGS map for Isolation Peak. Return the way you came, or via Red Deer Lake following the directions above.

Bunce School Road / Ironclads Trailhead

Drive to the Trailhead	🔑🔑🔑
Parking	🅿
Amenities	None
Fee Area?	No
Elevation	8,200 feet
Maps	Trails Illustrated 102: Indian Peaks, Gold Hill; USGS Raymond and Allenspark

This trailhead, at a historic one room schoolhouse, has little parking available and turning around requires backing your trailer, but driving to it is simple and on a paved highway.

Directions from Boulder County and Interstate Highway 25

Drive to the Bunce School Trailhead by traveling west toward the town of Lyons on Colorado State Highway 66 from north Longmont or Interstate Highway 25 (exit 243), or on U.S. Highway 36 from Boulder. A gas station that also sells diesel, and can accommodate a truck pulling a trailer is located in Lyons. Look for it on the south side of Colorado State Highway 66, shortly after the signal at the intersection of U.S. Highway 34 and Colorado State Highway 66.

Continue through Lyons on a one-way street, staying in the left-hand lane. At the west end of town, this street ends at a stop sign. Turn left there and drive south, continuing through the traffic signal at the next street. (On the way back turn right at the signal to go east on the road you came on.)

Continue on this road, Colorado State Highway 7, for 16 miles. The junction for Colorado State Highway 72 is just past the turnoff for the town of Riverside. Continue on Colorado State Highway 7 another 0.6 mile beyond this junction. A brown sign on the right indicates a Point of Interest on the left side of the road. Across the street from this sign is a cabin with two driveways and a sign with white lettering that says "Hilltop Guild". Just past this, also on the left, between mileage markers 19 and 18, is a dirt road with a street sign for Bunce School Road. Turn left onto this road.

Directions from Larimer County

From Loveland, drive to the Bunce School Trailhead by traveling west toward on U.S. Highway 34 almost 30 miles to Estes Park. Turn left at the first traffic signal in Estes Park, and right at the next signal onto Colorado State Highway 7. Just before this signal is a right turn lane; vehicles in this lane do not have to stop at the light, as long as they yield to traffic coming through the signal. Moving into the right turn lane too soon will result in being forced onto a side street. If this happens, follow that road when it curves to the left and turn right at the stop sign. You will then be on Colorado State Highway 7.

Stay on Colorado State Highway 7 for 18 miles. Just after a brown Point of Interest sign turn right onto Bunce School Road and park there. This is between mileage markers 18 and 19, just 3.6 miles after the turnoff for Allenspark and 2.4 miles after the turnoff for Ferncliff.

Directions from the turnoff

Proceed slowly onto this dirt road. One trailer can park across from the school. Do not park along the fence in front of the school. Another parking space that can accommodate a two-horse trailer is just uphill and toward the south from this. To park there, drive up Bunce School Road 50 feet and back your trailer into this space.

The first 1.0 mile of this trail is in the Roosevelt National Forest, where camping is allowed. While the road is probably too rugged to pull a trailer up it, the first two campsites are less than 0.3 mile from the schoolhouse. To camp there, leave your trailer at the trailhead and drive your truck to the campsites, or if the road looks good enough, unload your horses and pull the empty trailer to the campsite.

An alternate way to access this trail requires crossing a busy highway on foot. Drive east on Colorado State Highway 7 from Bunce School Road 0.6 mile to the junction with Colorado State Highway 72. Turn right onto Colorado State Highway 72, also signed as the Peak-to-Peak Highway. The parking area is the first large gravel area on the east side of Colorado State Highway 72, on a downhill stretch of road, 0.7 mile from the junction with Colorado State Highway 7. At the time of this writing, a sign on the right side of the highway asks, "Do you have defensible space?" You can park in the unmarked gravel area on the left side of the highway. Be extremely careful leading your horse across the highway. The trail is an old dirt road on the west side of the highway.

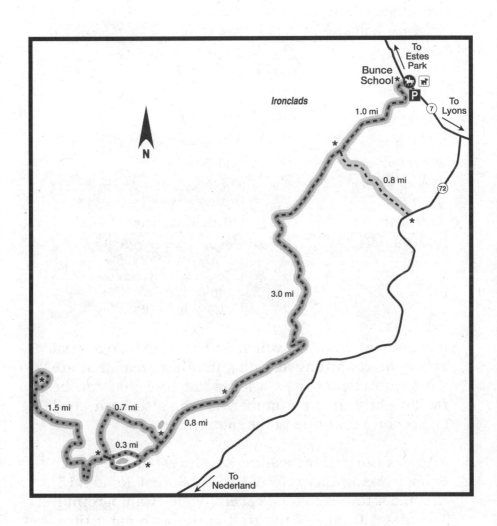

To
Estes
Park

Bunce
School*

To
Lyons

7

72

Ironclads

1.0 mi

0.8 mi

*

3.0 mi

*

1.5 mi

0.7 mi

0.8 mi

0.3 mi

*

*

*

To
Nederland

N

Trail #3
Bunce School Road/ Ironclads trails

Trail rideable	May through October
Best time to ride	June
Maximum elevation	8,800 feet
Difficulty	**Easy** to **Moderate** due to distance
Terrain	♘
Training ability	**+**
Length	9.6 miles round trip
Elevation gain	600 feet
Best features	The Ironclads, which are unusual rock formations
Obstacles	Off-road vehicles
Special notes	Good training ride for novice trail horses or riders; dogs are allowed as this trail is in the Roosevelt National Forest

I do not find this area, which suffers from recreational abuse, as rewarding as riding in other areas that are more natural, but it is a fairly flat trail that can be ridden early in the summer. It can also be a good choice for a first ride in the mountains.

Access the trail by heading southwest on the Bunce School Road, also referred to as Forest Road 115, which continues to the Peaceful Valley Campground. The first 1.0 mile of the trail is rife with campsites, their accompanying trash, and bogs that four-wheel drive vehicles have driven through. Rock climbers, four-wheelers, and in the fall, hunters heavily use this area. The trail is a dirt road, alternately rocky, rutted, and after a storm, full of puddles.

Just before the interesting Ironclads rock formations on the right, a trail junction on the left is marked as Forest Road number 217. This leads to Colorado State Highway 7 and the parking area described above, 0.8 mile away. Other smaller, but interesting rock formations can be seen near this road. To get closer to the larger rock formations, follow the road that heads uphill to the right from FR 115. After exploring this area, the route continues south on Bunce School Road. 1.0 mile later, the route comes to a sign stating that the road is on private property for the next 0.5 mile. Just past this sign, a stream passing under the road in a culvert is the only clean water along this ride, so offer the horses a drink at the side of the road both going in and on the return.

Much of the land the road crosses after this is also private, which explains the barbed wire laced along the sides of the road. This ride is fairly nondescript except for the abundance of fir and aspen trees growing among the other trees, the occasional view of Mount Audubon, and a splendid view of Sawtooth Mountain, Mount Audubon, and Piute Peak across a beautiful meadow 4.0 miles into the ride. After this meadow, the trail comes to a smaller, boggy meadow, which is shown as a small pond on the map. A jumble of roads made by off-road vehicles is just beyond this. One of these roads, which receives little use, is shown on the USGS map.

Continue on Forest Road 115 another 0.8 mile before arriving at a gate that is probably open. From there, the trail drops steeply into the Peaceful Valley Campground with no other trail leading out. Turn around at the gate, as horses are not allowed in the campground. Return to the trailhead from here, or to extend the ride, take one of two social trails that head west just before reaching the gate. These go up either side of a pond that is shown on the map, although the trails are not. Continue uphill after these trails merge, to the dirt road shown on the map. To the left, this road climbs 600 feet in 1.5 miles where it ends at 9,400 feet of elevation. This option extends the ride to 13.6 miles round trip, with an elevation gain of 1,200 feet. To the right, the road heads downhill where it intersects the main road, just south of the small meadow in 0.7 mile. After exploring this area return to the trailhead on the same road you came on.

Drive to the Trailhead	⚷
Parking	🅿
Amenities	None
Fee Area?	No
Elevation	8,600 feet
Maps	Trails Illustrated 200: Rocky Mountain National Park; USGS Allenspark

This parking area is rarely used but the parking is limited, so be prepared to go to one of the other nearby trailheads.

Directions from Boulder County and Interstate Highway 25

Drive to the Meadow Mountain Trailhead by traveling west toward the town of Lyons on Colorado State Highway 66 from north Longmont or Interstate Highway 25 (exit 243), or on U.S. Highway 36 from Boulder. A gas station that also sells diesel, and can accommodate a truck pulling a trailer is located in Lyons. Look for it on the south side of Colorado State Highway 66, shortly after the signal at the intersection of U.S. Highway 34 and Colorado State Highway 66.

Continue through Lyons on a one-way street, staying in the left-hand lane. At the west end of town, this street ends at a stop sign. Turn left there and drive south, continuing through the traffic signal at the next street. You are now on Colorado State Highway 7. (On the way back turn right at the signal to go east on the road you came on.)

Follow this highway for 18 miles and turn left at the sign for Ferncliff. This is 3.0 miles past the turnoff for Colorado State Highway 72, and between mileage markers 17 and 16. A sign indicates this is the turnoff for Colorado State Highway 7 business, and another sign indicates forest access. Just 0.1 mile before the turnoff to Ferncliff, a scenic overlook on the right side of the highway offers portable toilets and adequate parking for trailers. Continue through the miniscule town of Ferncliff to Allenspark. Then 0.8 mile from the highway turnoff, turn left onto Ski Road.

Directions from Larimer County

From Loveland, drive to the Meadow Mountain Trailhead by traveling west on U.S. Highway 34 almost 30 miles to Estes Park. Turn left at the first traffic signal in Estes Park, and right at the next signal, onto Colorado State Highway 7. Just before this signal is a right turn lane; vehicles in this lane do not have to stop at the light, as long as they yield to traffic coming through the signal. Moving into the right turn lane too soon will result in being forced onto a side street. If this happens, follow that road when it curves to the left and turn right at the stop sign. You will then be on Colorado State Highway 7.

Stay on Colorado State Highway 7 for 15 miles. After the town of Meeker Park and the Wild Basin area, start looking for a sign to Allenspark on the right, between mile markers 14 and 15. Turn right off the highway at Allenspark and then make an immediate left turn. After 0.4 mile and past the Meadow Mountain Cafe, turn right onto a dirt road labeled Ski Road. Two roads marked Ski Road exist, the other one is passed along the way to this turn. They both end up at the same place, but the first one is more winding and narrow than the one further east.

Directions from Ski Road

Follow Ski Road for 1.7 miles, staying left at the intersection with the other branch of Ski Road. An unsigned road on the right leads to the trailhead. This intersection is the only place to park, because the parking lot up the road will not accommodate a trailer. Turn around by backing up the road to the trailhead, and then park on the east side of Ski road. One trailer could also be parked on the south side of the road leading to the trailhead, near the junction with Ski Road.

Trail #4
St. Vrain Mountain/Meadow Mountain trails

Trail rideable	July through October
Best time to ride	August for wildflowers, September for Aspen
Maximum elevation	11,360 feet
Difficulty	**Demanding** due to the terrain and elevation gain, with an alternate route
Terrain	♘ ♘ ♘ ♘
Training ability	✚ ✚
Length	8.0 miles round trip
Elevation gain	2,760 feet
Best features	Amazing views above treeline
Obstacles	Challenging footing, no shade or shelter after the first part of the trail
Special notes	Dogs are allowed, as this trail is in the Roosevelt National Forest

This is a spectacular but challenging trail. Coming down a steep rocky hill is more difficult than going up one so if your mount is having a difficult time with the footing do not keep pushing on up the hill. Avoid this trail when the weather is threatening, as there is nowhere to seek shelter, and the trail becomes even more slippery when wet. I once reached the saddle between the two mountains as a thunderstorm was beginning to pass overhead, and scrambled to get below tree line before the lightening began crashing around me.

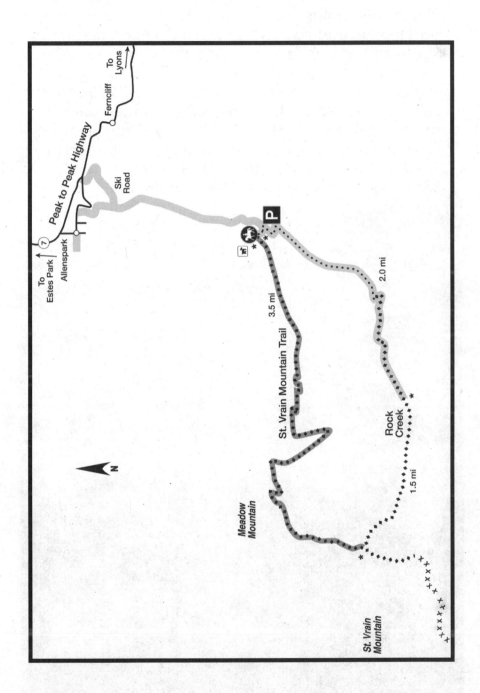

Access this trail from the trailer parking area by riding west along the dirt road 0.5 mile to the car parking lot, and go up three steps to get on the trail. The route travels for 1.0 mile through an extensive aspen grove with lush undergrowth, resulting in a fabulous ride whether it's summer or fall. The trail then climbs out of the trees and continues upward at a steep angle with footing consisting of good sized, smooth rocks that are challenging for horse's hooves. After 2.0 miles, the rocks give way to tundra, with spectacular views of Meadow Mountain to the

north and St. Vrain Mountain to the west, as well as close-up views of the Continental Divide. Panoramic views out to the plains are equally amazing. From this saddle, it is possible to peek into the Wild Basin area. Although trees block the view, Finch Lake is just below the saddle. A sign indicates that the trail passes briefly through the edge of Rocky Mountain National Park. This dividing line is shown quite clearly on the Trails Illustrated map; however, the park boundary on the USGS map is incorrect. From this point, the trail descends into the South St. Vrain Drainage, otherwise know as Peaceful Valley, but the trail is rated **Dangerous** for horses. So once you have enjoyed all the incredible views, turn around and return the way you came.

For those who do not mind riding on a 4-wheel drive road with no views, and slogging through some mud, this is the description of a second trail option. From the trailer parking area, continue south on Ski Road. This road continues a steady ascent through a thick lodgepole pine forest until it ends after 2.0 miles. This was once the site of a small ski area, thus the name of the road, but nothing remains today. At the end of the road, a faint trail continues to the west, along Rock Creek, for 1.0 mile. After crossing through some very wet, boggy areas, it heads up the hill and out of the trees. Look for the St. Vrain Mountain Trail above tree line, 0.5 mile further. The saddle described above is to the right. Finding this social trail from above may prove fruitless unless you have previously ridden it from below. The main trail is the only option available to hikers, because of the bogs on the second option.

Lion Gulch / Homestead Meadow / Pearson Park Trailhead

Drive to the Trailhead	🔑 🔑 🔑
Parking	P P
Amenities	Hitching rack and toilet
Fee Area?	No
Elevation	7,500 feet
Maps	Trails Illustrated 101: Cache La Poudre, Big Thompson; USGS Panorama Peak; the old roads are shown on this map, but the trails described here were put in after 1978 and are not marked on this map

This is a huge gravel parking lot on a busy highway. A hitching post and restroom are located at the trailhead.

Directions from Estes Park

From Estes Park, drive to the Lion Gulch Trailhead by traveling southeast on U.S. Highway 36 for 8.0 miles from the junction with U.S. Highway 34. The trailhead is on the right side of the road just past mile marker 8 and cars are usually parked there. Pull off the highway onto the gravel as soon as possible and continue driving east along the south side of the parking lot. Follow the fence line until the front of your vehicle faces the road. This arrangement makes it uncomplicated to exit the parking area, and accommodates many trailers. Although hikers generally prefer to park near the trailhead at the west end of the lot, pulling up close to the road deters cars from parking in front of your rig.

80

Directions from Boulder County and Interstate Highway 25

Drive to the Lion Gulch Trailhead by traveling west toward the town of Lyons on Colorado State Highway 66 from north Longmont or Interstate Highway 25 (exit 243), or on U.S. Highway 36 from Boulder. A gas station that also sells diesel, and can accommodate a truck pulling a trailer is located in Lyons. Look for it on the south side of Colorado State Highway 66, shortly after the signal at the intersection of U.S. Highway 34 and Colorado State Highway 66.

Continue through Lyons on a one-way street staying in the middle and then the right-hand lane but not in the left lane. At the west end of town turn right toward Estes Park on U.S. Highway 36. The parking lot is located 12.4 miles from this point and is marked only by a brown sign with the word trailhead on it. The National Park trail board can be seen from some distance down the road. The trailhead is on the left side of the highway and is best accessed by entering at the far (west) end of the parking lot and continuing to turn left until you are heading back toward the east. Following the south edge of the parking lot until the front of your vehicle faces the road makes it uncomplicated to exit the parking area and accommodates many trailers.

Trail #5
Lion Gulch/Homestead Meadows/Pearson Park trails

Trail rideable	June to September
Best time to ride	June
Maximum elevation	9,000 feet
Difficulty	**Advanced** due to challenging footing in Lion Gulch
Terrain	◡ ◡ ◡
Training ability	**+ +**
Length	Minimum 5.0 miles round trip, maximum unlimited
Elevation gain	1,500 feet
Best features	Many interesting trail options
Obstacles	Bridges and small streams crossed repeatedly
Special notes	Historical interest, dogs are allowed in the Roosevelt National Forest; beware of riding in Lion Gulch too early in the springtime or too late in the fall, due to ice

This is a fun trail with many options, which even include continuing on dirt roads to Estes Park or Meeker Park. Lion Gulch meets the dictionary definition of a gulch; a "deep, narrow ravine" so putting a trail there was a challenging undertaking. The trail crosses the stream many times to find anywhere flat enough to allow trail users to walk, and minor flash flooding occasionally damages the trail and crossings. The crossings are small, but your mount's hooves will

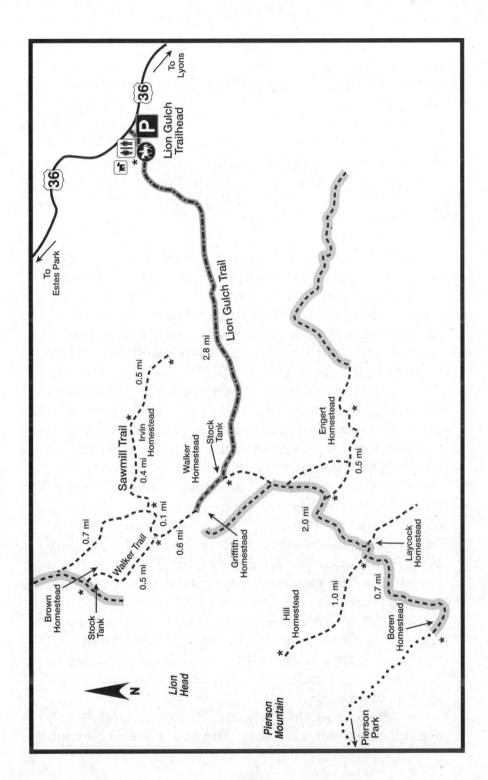

To Lyons

36

P

Lion Gulch
Trailhead

To Estes Park

36

Lion Gulch Trail

2.8 mi

Sawmill Trail

0.5 mi

Irvin
Homestead

0.4 mi

Walker
Homestead

Stock
Tank

0.1 mi

Walker Trail

0.6 mi

Griffith
Homestead

Engert
Homestead

0.5 mi

2.0 mi

0.7 mi

Brown
Homestead

Stock
Tank

0.5 mi

Laycock
Homestead

Hill
Homestead

1.0 mi

0.7 mi

Boren
Homestead

Pierson Park

Lion
Head

N

Pierson Mountain

get wet. The first 3.0 miles of trail are very popular and on summer weekends there can be a steady parade of hikers, many with children or loose dogs, as well as horses and bicycles. Sometimes it also has an abundance of bugs, including horseflies. Only one trail leaves the trailhead, but it divides into two trails upon reaching Homestead Meadows after 2.8 miles. Once past the challenging footing in Lion Gulch, the trails in Homestead Meadows are rated **Easy**.

To access this trail, lead your horse to the west end of the parking lot and around the gate to the trailhead. A hitching post and restroom are located there, near a sign listing the National Forest regulations. Another sign credits the Larimer County Horseman's Association for the trail maintenance activities it has done here for many years.

The first 2.8 miles of trail are in Lion Gulch. Access this trail by heading downhill past the hitching post. The trail descends quickly into the gulch and promptly crosses the Little Thompson River on a footbridge with a shallow ford for horses. In the summertime, the first part of this trail showcases many types of wildflowers. The trail continues along the south side of the stream, climbing slowly for some distance before going down several steps that can be slippery after it has snowed. Then make a right turn onto a bridge that horses must cross. Just after that bridge, a signpost directs horses to an alternate trail on the right. That trail climbs quickly for a short distance. When it reconnects to the main trail, turn right and continue uphill a little further before descending back into the gulch, and crossing the stream again by way of a bridge.

The shade and the babbling brook in Lion Gulch are refreshing on a hot day. The attractive vegetation there is a mixed forest of evergreens and aspen trees, with wild rose and red current bushes underneath the trees. Because the stream and surrounding areas rarely if ever get direct sun, this trail is rideable for a shorter season than might be expected at this elevation.

The sixth of the small stream crossings, which crosses from south to north, is tricky. Stepping immediately into the stream on the right is too far down for most horses to do safely. Instead, ask your mount to step over the large rock directly in front of you. This is somewhat difficult but not dangerous if the horse steps over, rather than on, the rock. Then turn right and cross the stream. Remember this crossing, because this large rock is much more difficult to step over from the opposite direction. On the way back, stay to the left (east) and cross through the deep part of the stream. From this direction, your horse will have to make a large step up to the solid bank, which he or she should be comfortable doing. Over the years this crossing changes, so always assess it before crossing. The last time I rode this trail, a flash flood had actually improved the crossing somewhat.

After crossing the stream, ride up a short, steep hill. At the top of the hill a well-worn social trail heads off to the north. Stay left, descending once again into the gulch and crossing the stream again. Continue up the trail, watching for areas on the ridges toward the south that were burned in the Big Elk fire. Before the final stream crossing, the trail climbs steeply up the south side of the gulch. Listening to the stream cascading down this steep spot adds to the enjoyment of this area. Notice the two large steps on the lower part of this hill, as they can be challenging for horses to step down when returning to the trailhead.

At the final stream crossing, the water is contained in a culvert. A rock usually covers the hole that is rusting in the culvert. Avoid this trail whenever the nighttime temperatures are below freezing, because the water in this culvert freezes, forcing the water to flow over the top. Then the water creates a large and perfectly smooth ice flow that is difficult for people to negotiate, and impossible for horses to cross.

Soon the gulch and the trail begin to widen and flatten out, and wild raspberries replace the red currant bushes. With sunshine again reaching the ground, wildflowers abound. These flowers are mostly different varieties from the ones lower down at the start of the trail. Before long, the trail enters the Homestead Meadows area and comes to a trail junction.

Numerous signs describe the historic significance of this area that was homesteaded by eight families. The Laycock Homestead was the first one in 1889, and the Griffith Homestead was the last one in 1923.

Each homestead has a sign that tells who lived there and gives interesting information about the residents and their homesteads. One family stayed a few months, one family stayed for thirty years. Each homestead was 160 acres and some families qualified for two homesteads, so the trails between them make a full day's ride if you visit each of their cabins. Eventually these homesteads became consolidated into one large ranch. The National Forest Service bought 2,240 acres here in 1978, and nominated it for acceptance to the National Register of Historic Places in 1990.

The shorter of the two trail options from this point continues straight, in a westerly direction. It passes a stock tank and the badly deteriorated Walker homestead. The next homestead along this route, the Griffeth homestead, is more extensive. Most hikers do not go beyond this meadow, so the crowd thins out considerably beyond this point.

The trail used to continue west from there, but now a fence blocks that trail, so turn right at the Griffeth cabin and head uphill until you reach an old road. Turn right there, and continue along the road to the next trail junction, which leads to the Brown homestead on a loop trail. This route turns left and follows the trail slightly downhill to that cabin. Just past the cabin is another spring-filled stock tank. After the horses have had a drink, continue downhill to a junction with another old road. To the left, this road eventually ends at a fenced property with a travel trailer parked on it. The meadow alongside this dead end road is a nice area to have lunch, because it is pleasant and few people come this way.

This route follows the loop road to the right, and returns to the main trail. Turn left at the main trail, and before long the trail arrives at the Irwin homestead in a lovely meadow. This is the most

87

extensive of all the homesteads. It was improved and used as a hunting camp until the 1960s, so the cabin has linoleum on the floors, asphalt shingles on the roofs, and a three-stall barn is nearby. A short trail leads to a former sawmill, parts of which are scattered around the area. A trail branching off of the Sawmill Trail leads to the lower cabins.

A little past the main homestead, two hitching posts are available near the meadow. This is a glorious place for lunch, and even a nap if you have it to yourself. The hitching posts are a logical place to turn around, making a 10-mile round trip ride. The trail, however, continues another 0.5 mile to the east, climbing the ridge parallel to Lion Gulch and eventually looking over the area from quite a height. The trail then becomes faint, leaving you to return the way you came.

The second option upon entering Homestead Meadows from Lion Gulch is to turn left at the first trail junction. This trail heads south from the main trail, east of the stock tank, and crosses a small meadow. You can turn right toward the west onto an old road at the next junction to enjoy a rousing trot or lope before the road ends at a fence. This route however continues straight, toward the south on the main road, and leads to several homesteads, and eventually to Pearson Park where it joins other roads. Ride to whichever homesteads you want to see, and as far as you want to go, returning on the main trail whenever you have gone far enough.

The next junction on this road used to be a very nice trail through a beautiful meadow to the Engert homestead. Sadly the cabin burned during the Big Elk fire in 2002, and the fire crews ripped up this trail to make a fire line. It has since been repaired and is rideable. Turn left and follow this trail to view more areas impacted by the fire. At the top of the meadow another junction comes into view. Turning right will take you back to the main trail and turning left will take you to the Engert Homestead.

If you want to see an example of a forest of lodgepole pine trees and aspen groves that burned, continue east on the old road, past the Engert cabin that burned down. A vehicle with a malfunctioning catalytic converter was the source of the fire. The car was parked on dry grass in Big Elk Meadows, which is southeast of Homestead Meadows, causing the grass to ignite.

It is fascinating to see the path the fire took and the forest growing back. Lodgepole pine trees grow close together, keeping the sun from reaching the ground and effectively preventing any new growth. During a fire, these trees burn very hot, killing them and sterilizing the dirt. The heat causes the lodgepole seeds to germinate, and starts a new forest of trees that are all the same age. Aspen trees are difficult to burn because they are high in water content, but since the fire was so hot here, the aspen trees burned completely. They started to grow back within weeks however, because aspens grow by means of a huge root system that survived the fire, and it was able to generate new tree growth. The ground cover came back sooner in these areas too, because the moisture in the trees cooled the fire and the ground wasn't sterilized as it was under the lodgepole pines.

Ponderosa pine trees and Douglas fir trees grow further apart than lodgepole pine trees, so the fire has a more difficult time jumping from tree to tree. As a result, the fire slowed down and cooled, and many of these trees that are somewhat burned still survived. It was in areas of ponderosa pine trees and in meadows that the Big Elk fire stopped, as can be seen when riding through this area.

Return to Lion Gulch the way you came or continue to more homesteads by staying left at the junction you passed on the way to the Engert Homestead. Once back at the main trail, turn left and continue south and downhill to a more extensive homestead, the Laycock homestead, just off the main trail to the left. This cabin is adjacent to a sizable meadow that is a pleasant spot for a lunch break. The Big Elk Ranch, a private operation that borders this area and is accessed from Meeker Park, occasionally brings horses into this area on trail rides, so you may notice an increased number of hoof-prints on the trails.

Continuing on the main trail, the Hill homestead is located on a 1.0-mile trail that veers off to the right. A short distance beyond this junction, the main trail comes to the Boren homestead, the final homestead on this route. This homestead is the end of this description, however the trail continues to the west, becoming rocky as it travels around the side of Pearson Mountain, before arriving at Pearson Park a couple miles further. At Pearson Park the trail connects with a 4-wheel drive road called Forest Road 119. That road goes north to Fish Creek Road in Estes Park or south to Meeker Park, where it connects to more dirt roads. A person who is adept at reading a map and does not mind sharing the dirt roads with motorized vehicles, could travel through this area for days, continuing as far south as Nederland.

The south end of Forest Road 119, near 82 Road, has several undeveloped campsites that are accessible to four-wheel drive vehicles, but the road is too rugged for trailers. The loop roads near Pearson Park also have campsites accessible by four-wheel drive from the Little Valley Road, off of Fish Creek Road, where Forest Road 119 begins. The gate across this road, where it enters the national forest, is locked in the wintertime, but the National Forest Service should be able to tell you whether it is open or not. The road becomes quite rugged past the gate. These are options for a one-way trip, or an overnight stay if someone brings in a four-wheel drive vehicle with camping equipment. Because Lion Gulch, Homestead Meadows and Forest Road 119 are in the Roosevelt National Forest, this entire area is open to camping and hunting. The roads and campsites here are rife with hunters in the fall.

Trails in Rocky Mountain National Park, East of the Continental Divide

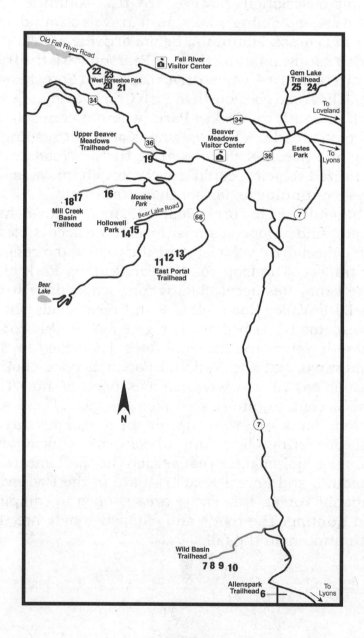

Trails accessed from Colorado State Highway 7

Drive to the Trailhead	🔑🔑
Parking	🅿
Amenities	None
Fee Area?	No, as the trailhead is just outside of the park boundary
Elevation	8,600 feet
Maps	Trails Illustrated: 200 Rocky Mountain National Park, USGS Allenspark

This trailhead accesses the trail to Finch and Pear Lakes. While the parking here is more challenging than at Wild Basin, it is not a fee area, and the trail to Finch and Pear Lakes is considerably more horse friendly than the route from Wild Basin.

Directions from Boulder County and Interstate 25

Drive to the Allenspark Trailhead by traveling west toward the town of Lyons on Colorado State Highway 66 from north Longmont or Interstate Highway 25 (exit 243), or on U.S. Highway 36 from Boulder. A gas station that also sells diesel, and can accommodate a truck pulling a trailer is located in Lyons. Look for it on the south side of Colorado State Highway 66, shortly after the signal at the intersection of U.S. Highway 34 and Colorado State Highway 66.

Continue through Lyons on a one-way street, staying in the left-hand lane. At the west end of town, this street ends at a stop sign. Turn left there and drive south. Continue through the traffic signal at the next street. (On the way back turn right at the signal to go east on the road you came on.)

You are now on Colorado State Highway 7, which you follow for 20 miles, driving straight through the intersection with Colorado State Highway 72. A scenic overlook with portable toilets and adequate parking for a trailer is on the right, 3.0 miles beyond that junction. The turnoff for the trail is on the left 2.0 miles past the overlook, at the sign for Allenspark, and between mileage markers 15 and 14. After turning left toward Allenspark make an immediate right turn onto Boulder County Road 90.

Directions from Larimer County

From Loveland, drive to the Allenspark Trailhead by traveling west on U.S. Highway 34 almost 30 miles to Estes Park. Turn left at the first traffic signal in Estes Park, and right at the next signal onto Colorado State Highway 7. Just before this signal is a right turn lane; vehicles in this lane do not have to stop at the light, as long as they yield to traffic coming through the signal. Moving into the right turn lane too soon will result in being forced onto a side street. If this happens, follow that road when it curves to the left and turn right at the stop sign. You will then be on Colorado State Highway 7.

Stay on Colorado State Highway 7 for 15 miles. After the town of Meeker Park, look for a sign to Allenspark on the right, between mile markers 14 and 15. Turn right off the highway toward Allenspark and then immediately right again onto Boulder County Road 90.

Directions from Boulder County Road 90

Follow this dirt road 1.4 miles to a road on the right that leads to the trailhead. Park on the side of the road there, or continue on that road 0.1 mile to the trailhead. Do not pull your trailer into the parking area, as it is too small for trailers. Back up into the parking area far enough to get turned around and park on the east side of the road.

Trail #6
Finch Lake and Pear Lake

Trail rideable	July and August
Best time to ride	July or August
Maximum elevation	10,050 to Finch Lake, 10,600 feet to Pear Lake
Difficulty	**Moderate** to Finch Lake due to river crossings, man-made steps, distance, and elevation gain; **Advanced** to Pear Lake for the same reasons
Terrain	♘ ♘
Training ability	✚ ✚ ✚
Length	7.2 miles round trip to Finch Lake, 11 miles round trip to Pear Lake
Elevation gain	1,150 feet to Finch Lake, and 1,800 to Pear Lake including elevation loss that is regained
Best features	Two nice lakes
Obstacles	Man-made steps, river crossings
Special notes	All Rocky Mountain National Park rules apply to this trail

This ride offers great views of two nice lakes on a shady trail. What more could one want when the temperature in Denver is over ninety degrees? Another bonus for this trail is that it descends to Finch Lake rather than climbing continuously upward, as many trails in the mountains do. Although this trail goes to Finch and Pear Lakes, it is called the Allenspark Trail, after its trailhead.

Ride through the parking lot to access the Allenspark Trail. After 1.0 mile of unbroken forest the trail comes to a junction. The trail to the right leads to Wild Basin via a steep and rocky hillside. I no longer ride that trail as one of our horses was slightly injured on it at the end of a ride. Part way down the steep and rocky trail, the horse slipped on the loose rock and went down on his knees. Fortunately, his wounds healed easily and the rider was not injured, but as a result of this incident I do not use the Wild Basin Trailhead when riding to Finch Lake.

This route continues to the left on the Allenspark Trail. The next 0.6 mile climbs more steeply to another trail junction that also leads to Wild Basin via a steep and rocky hillside. Neither of these trails is described in this guidebook, and they are rated **Advanced**. Continue on the trail to the left for 1.0 mile through a wooded area with a couple of small streams and less elevation gain. Up to this point, the trail has been rather nondescript because the thick forest has limited the views and the wildflowers, but the trees provide plenty of shade that is appreciated when the temperature is particularly warm.

At this point however, the trail crosses an area that was burned by a lightning strike. Enjoy the moisture and sunshine in this area, encouraging willow and wildflowers to grow, and helping the forest to grow back. The whirr of hummingbirds can often be heard as they fly among the flowers in pursuit of their lunch.

The impressive views of the mountains from this spot are especially appreciated for the former lack of views. The most obvious of these mountains is Mount Meeker at 13,911 feet. Peeking out from behind Meeker is the only fourteener in the park, Longs Peak that, aside from its 14,255-foot height,

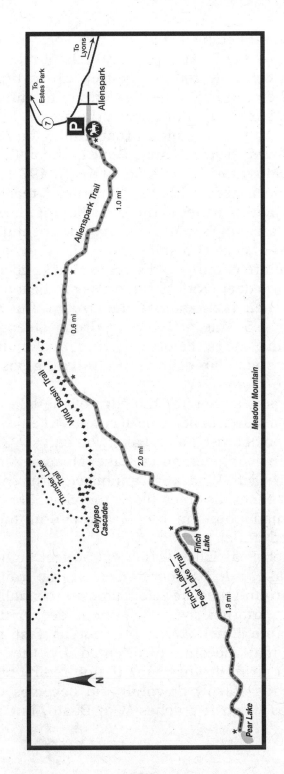

To Lyons

To Estes Park

Allenspark

7

P

Allenspark

Allenspark Trail

1.0 mi

0.6 mi

Wild Basin Trail

Thunder Lake Trail

Calypso Cascades

2.0 mi

Finch Lake — Pear Lake Trail

Finch Lake

1.9 mi

Pear Lake

Meadow Mountain

N

can be identified by its flat top and blocky profile. On an average day in August, hundreds of hikers make the fourteen-mile round trip trek up to this peak, where they can enjoy the views from its unusual flat summit. Luckily for our horses, the final 2,000 feet of elevation to the summit on that trail is too rocky for their hooves. Next to Longs Peak is the aptly named Pagoda Mountain at a formidable 13,497 feet, and then Chiefs Head with the Spearhead reaching up behind them. Further to the left is Mount Alice, which is 13,310 feet high, and is on the Continental Divide.

After the next 0.5 mile the trail returns to the forest before coming to a stream that is good sized, but not too deep. Riders can cross on the footbridge, leading their horse across the stream if necessary. The last 0.5 mile of the trail drops steeply down man-made steps before arriving at Finch Lake, where a stock campsite with a hitching post and a toilet are located.

The logs near here at the edge of the lake provide a nice view and make a perfect spot to enjoy lunch. As you look across Finch Lake, you can see St. Vrain Mountain rising behind the lake; Meadow Mountain is off to the left. What you cannot see is the saddle in-between them, as trees block the view. That saddle is the high point on the Meadow Mountain Trail described under trail #4.

To reach Pear Lake, which is 650 feet higher than Finch Lake, ride 1.9 more miles on this trail, which circles around the lake before crossing a small stream and then another river. This one is deeper than the river before Finch Lake, but not as fast moving. Horses may become disoriented by the current and can drift downstream if not redirected. This river heads steeply downhill and becomes Calypso Cascades when it reaches Wild Basin, but no trail follows the river.

From here, the trail climbs steadily for 1.0 mile before reaching a small pond in a boggy area. It climbs more steeply after this pond, and soon the route crosses a small stream coming from Pear Lake. Suddenly, the trail breaks out of the trees to a stunning view of the lake and mountains. Continue along the lakeshore to the hitching post.

Pear Lake is referred to on some maps as Pear Reservoir for reasons that are obvious when the lake comes into view. As with the other reservoirs in Rocky Mountain National Park, the former dam has been removed. Unfortunately, early in Colorado's history no one thought of the concept "leave no trace," and the legacy of these mountain reservoirs will last for many decades. Enjoy the view of Copeland Mountain at 13,176 feet, before returning the way you came.

Wild Basin

Drive to the Trailhead	🔑 🔑
Parking	🅿 🅿
Amenities	Picnic tables and hitching racks are available at the trailer parking area; toilets are available at both of the trailheads described
Fee Area?	Rocky Mountain National Park fees apply
Elevation	8,500 feet
Maps	Trails Illustrated 200: Rocky Mountain National Park; USGS Allenspark and Isolation Peak

The drive to this parking area is rather long, and the last 1.4 miles is on a dirt road, but it does have two designated horse trailer parking spaces. Several nice rides are accessible from this parking lot. On weekends, arrive early at this popular area and have an alternate trailhead in mind.

Directions from Boulder County and Interstate Highway 25

Drive to Wild Basin by traveling west toward the town of Lyons on Colorado State Highway 66 from north Longmont or Interstate Highway 25 (exit 243), or on U.S. Highway 36 from Boulder. A gas station that also sells diesel, and can accommodate a truck pulling a trailer is located in Lyons. Look for it on the south side of Colorado State Highway 66, shortly after the signal at the intersection of U.S. Highway 34 and Colorado State Highway 66.

Continue through Lyons on a one-way street, staying in the left-hand lane. At the west end of town, this street ends at a stop sign. Turn left there and drive south, continuing through the traffic signal at the next street. (On the way back, turn right at the signal to go east on the road you came on.)

You are now on Colorado State Highway 7. Follow this highway for 22 miles, driving straight through the intersection with Colorado State Highway 72. A scenic overlook, with portable toilets and adequate parking for a trailer, is 3.0 miles beyond this junction on the right. Pass the signs for Allenspark 2.0 miles beyond the overlook, and watch for signs to Wild Basin 2.3 miles further on the left. Just beyond the Wild Basin Livery, between mileage markers 13 and 12, a brown sign marks the turnoff.

Directions from Larimer County

To drive to Wild Basin from Larimer County, take U.S. Highway 34 west to Estes Park, 30 miles from Loveland, and turn left onto U.S. Highway 36 at the first traffic signal in Estes Park. Turn right at the next signal onto Colorado State Highway 7. Just before this signal is a right turn lane; vehicles in this lane do not have to stop at the light, as long as they yield to traffic coming through the signal. Moving into the right turn lane too soon will result in being forced onto a side street. If this happens, follow that road when it curves to the left and turn right at the stop sign. You will then be on Colorado State Highway 7.

Continue on Colorado State Highway 7 for 12 miles. After the town of Meeker Park, look for a sign to Wild Basin on the right, between mile markers 12 and 13. This sign can be difficult to see ahead of time.

Directions from the turnoff

Once you have turned off of Colorado State Highway 7, follow the paved road 0.3 mile beyond the intersection. Just after passing the Wild Basin Lodge, angle off to the right onto a dirt road where the Rocky Mountain National Park fee station is located. Automobile parking and the trailhead for Sandbeach Lake are on the right, near Copeland Lake. Designated parking reserved for two trailers is 1.3 miles past the fee station on the left. If these spots are full, you may be able to park in the large pullout on the north side of the dirt road between Copeland Lake and the trailer parking lot, 0.6 miles from the fee station.

The ranger at the fee station usually hands out a map of the trailer parking area and knows when the spaces are full. If so, he or she can help you find appropriate parking. The rangers are concerned about illegal parking and are often out on the road on weekends, so ask for their help. Do not drive beyond the trailer parking lot, as there is no place to park or turn around.

While it is possible to get to Pear and Finch Lakes from Wild Basin, both trail options are fairly steep and rocky. No descriptions for these trails are given, because it is prudent and more enjoyable to access these lakes from the trailhead near Allenspark. See trail description #6.

A bridle trail passes through the trailer parking area just north of the hitching racks. This trail parallels the road and is a safer option for riding to the various trailheads than riding on the road.

Trail #7
Calypso Cascades

Trail rideable	June through September
Best time to ride	June and September when the trail is less busy
Maximum elevation	9,200 feet
Difficulty	**Moderate** due to obstacles listed below
Terrain	♘
Training ability	✚ ✚
Length	6.0 to 8.0 miles round trip
Elevation gain	700 feet
Best features	Enjoyable waterfalls
Obstacles	Many hikers, some with small children; large bridges with noisy river below and some log steps
Special notes	Visit Copeland Falls

This is a fairly short ride, but it may be a good first high-elevation ride in the spring, or for a horse that has crossed small bridges but that needs experience with large bridges and around rushing water. The fairy slipper orchid (Calypso bulbosa) grows wild here in the springtime, hence the name of the falls.

To access this trail, follow the bridle trail west from the trailer parking area 0.2 mile to the trailhead, where a restroom is available. Along the way, this trail passes the junction for a trail to Copeland Falls that is nearby and fun to visit. The main trail can be quite busy; try to wait for hikers to exit the bridges before going over them. Ignore the trail junction on

105

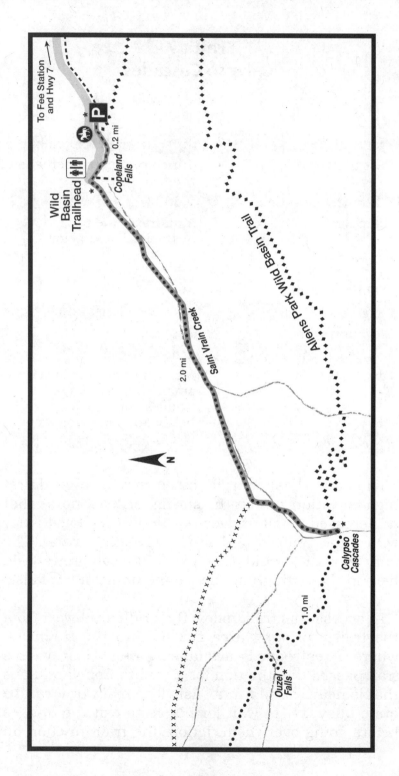

To Fee Station and Hwy 7 →

P *

Wild Basin Trailhead

0.2 mi

* Copeland Falls

Allens Park Wild Basin Trail

Saint Vrain Creek

2.0 mi

N

* Calypso Cascades

1.0 mi

Ouzel Falls *

the right that leads to campsites and is not open to horses. This trail is not shown on the USGS map.

Calypso Cascades is a congested area, with a trail junction for the challenging Allenspark Trail and hikers enjoying the falls. Turning around at this point creates a 6.0-mile ride round trip. If your horse is comfortable on the large bridges here and is not tired, the ride can be extended. Continue to Ouzel Creek and Falls 1.0 mile further along the main trail before returning the way you came, for an 8.0-mile round trip ride.

Trail #8
Ouzel and Bluebird Lakes

Trail rideable	July through August
Best time to ride	August is the only month Bluebird Lake is free of snow
Maximum elevation	Ouzel Lake is 10,010 feet; Bluebird lake is 10,978 feet
Difficulty	**Advanced** due to mileage and obstacles
Terrain	♘ ♘
Training ability	✚ ✚
Length	13 miles to Ouzel Lake round trip; 14 miles round trip to the hitching post before Bluebird Lake and 1.0 steep mile round trip on foot to the lake
Elevation gain	1,510 feet to Ouzel Lake; 1,700 feet to the hitching post before Bluebird Lake
Best features	Views
Obstacles	Many hikers near the beginning of the trail, some with small children; several large bridges to cross with noisy river below, and some log steps
Special notes	Horses are not allowed on the final part of the trail, so be prepared for a challenging 1.0 mile round trip hike with 800 feet of elevation gain if you want to see Bluebird Lake

This is a nice ride with varied terrain and many interesting sights. It is possible to turn around at several points along the way.

To access this trail, follow the bridle trail west from the trailer parking area 1.0 mile to the trailhead, passing a side trail to Copeland Falls along the way. The main trail can be quite busy; try to wait for hikers to exit the bridges before going over them. Ignore the trail junction on the right, which leads to campsites and is not open to horses. This trail is not shown on the USGS map.

Calypso Cascades is a congested area, with a trail junction for the **Advanced** Allenspark Trail and hikers enjoying the falls. Continue north on the same trail after the falls, and pass Ouzel Creek and Ouzel Falls in 1.0 mile. After a bridge, the trail climbs to a nice overlook, and then descends. The trail junction for Ouzel and Bluebird Lakes is on the left, 0.8 mile after crossing the last bridge. From this point it is 2.7 miles to Bluebird Lake. Turn left and follow the trail as it climbs to the west. After riding 1.5 mile along this trail, this route reaches the cutoff to Ouzel Lake on the left. The lake is quite close, and it has a hitching post for horses.

An ouzel is a fairly nondescript bird that plays in the water. You may see one diving into the water to find food on the bottom of the stream. Near Ouzel Lake is an area that was burned in 1978. This forest fire was started by lightning and burned only 1,000 acres, but Longs Peak and the Continental Divide can be seen clearly from here as a result.

To visit Bluebird Lake, continue along the main trail, which soon passes Chickadee Pond on the left. After 0.7 mile, a signpost near a hitching post states that horses are not allowed beyond this point. The final 0.5 mile is a steep hike up a hill, following a

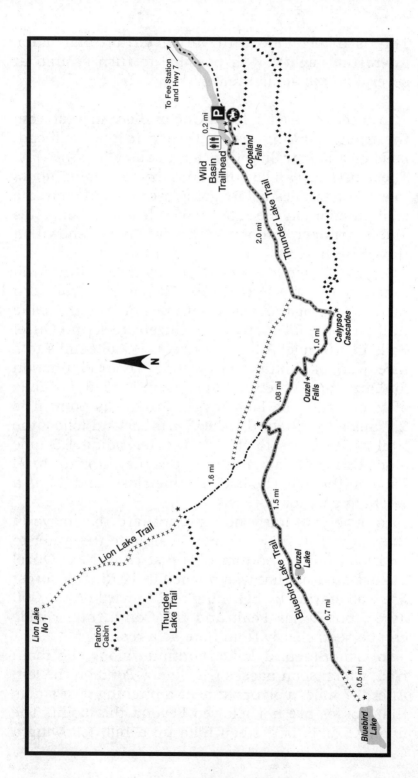

To Fee Station
and Hwy 7

Wild
Basin
Trailhead

P.

0.2 mi

Copeland
Falls

Thunder Lake Trail

2.0 mi

Calypso *
Cascades

1.0 mi

Ouzel *
Falls

.08 mi

N

1.6 mi

Lion Lake Trail

Thunder
Lake Trail

Lion Lake
No 1

Patrol
Cabin

Bluebird Lake Trail

1.5 mi

Ouzel
Lake

0.7 mi

0.5 mi

Bluebird
Lake

waterfall and sometimes crossing snowfields, before arriving at Bluebird Lake. This mountain lake was once used as a reservoir for the city of Longmont. Rocky Mountain National Park purchased this reservoir and two others in 1988 and removed the dams. Return the way you came.

Trail #9
Thunder Lake

Trail rideable	July through August
Best time to ride	August
Maximum elevation	10,590 feet
Difficulty	**Demanding** because of the mileage, elevation gain, and obstacles
Terrain	⊌ ⊌ ⊌
Training ability	✛ ✛
Length	17 miles round trip
Elevation gain	2,090 feet
Best features	Dramatic scenery and a gorgeous lake
Obstacles	Many hikers near the beginning of the trail, some with small children; several large bridges with noisy river below, and some log steps
Special notes	A steep drop-off below the trail on the side of a hill

Thunder Lake is one of the most beautiful lakes you will ever see. It is a long ride, but well worth it, if horse and rider are in excellent condition. Pick a day when it's not likely to rain, and get an early start.

To access this trail, follow the bridle trail west from the trailer parking area 1.0 mile to the trailhead, passing the trail to Copeland Falls along the way. The main trail can be quite busy; try to wait for hikers to exit the bridges before going over them. Ignore the trail junction on the right, which leads

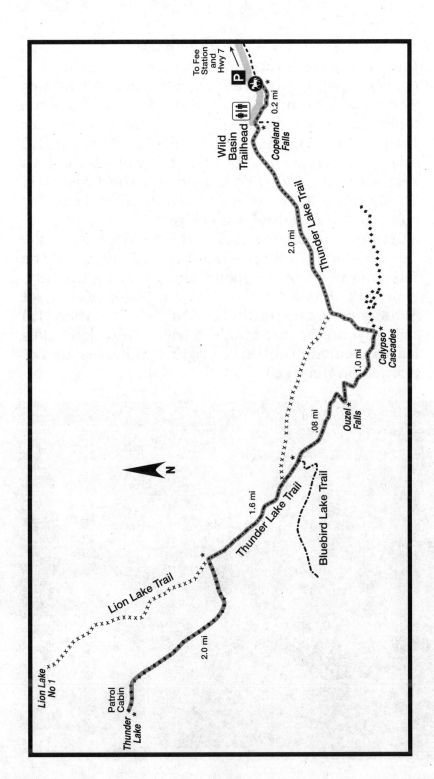

To Fee Station and Hwy 7

P

Wild Basin Trailhead

Copeland Falls

0.2 mi

Thunder Lake Trail

2.0 mi

Calypso* Cascades

1.0 mi

Ouzel * Falls

.08 mi

Thunder Lake Trail

Bluebird Lake Trail

1.6 mi

N

Lion Lake Trail

Lion Lake No 1

2.0 mi

Patrol Cabin

Thunder Lake *

to campsites and is not open to horses. The Calypso Cascades are 2.0 miles from the main trailhead, in a congested area with a trail junction for the Allenspark Trailhead, and hikers gazing at the falls from the large bridges. Continue north on the same trail after the falls, passing Ouzel Creek and Ouzel Falls in 1.0 mile. After crossing a bridge, the trail climbs to a nice overlook, and then descends a short distance. The junction to Ouzel and Bluebird Lakes is on the left, 0.8 mile from the last bridge.

Continue along the main trail to Thunder Lake. The final bridge on this trail is 0.5 mile further. The fabulous views of the mountains all along the way, especially Eagle's Beak, Tanima Peak, and Pilot Mountain, are captivating. A little more than 1.0 mile beyond the last bridge, a trail to the Lion Lakes leaves the main trail on the right, but horses are not allowed on that trail.

From there, it is just 2.0 more miles to Thunder Lake, but it is a steady climb, and part of the trail traverses a hillside that drops off steeply below the trail. Dismount if you are not comfortable riding this stretch of trail, especially on the return trip when your mount is going downhill. The end of the trail descends into Thunder Lake, which has a patrol cabin and corral used by the park service rangers. This is a good destination for camping overnight because it is so beautiful and one of the campsites here allows horses.

The view of Mount Alice From the lake, an impressive sight at 13,310 feet, is about as close as most people will ever get to the Continental Divide, except when driving over Trail Ridge Road. I find it amazing that all the rain and snow that falls on this side of Mount Alice runs east into the South Platte River, joining the North Platte River and then the Missouri River before becoming part of the Mississippi River, which empties into the Gulf of Mexico and eventually into the Atlantic Ocean. The rain and snow that falls on the other side of Mount Alice runs west into the Colorado River. That river eventually drains into the Gulf of California and then the Pacific Ocean. After you have had enough of the views, return the way you came.

Trail #10
Sandbeach Lake

Trail rideable	June through September
Best time to ride	July
Maximum elevation	10,283 feet
Difficulty	**Advanced** due to mileage and elevation gain
Terrain	♞ ♞
Training ability	✚
Length	9.5 miles round trip
Elevation gain	1,971 feet
Best features	This south-facing trail is free of snow early in the season, and the elevation gain makes this a good conditioning ride
Obstacles	Some small streams, and one large one that can be avoided, but is good for training; the entire trail is steep, and it is a narrow and rocky trail in some places
Special notes	Snowmelt runs down this trail in the springtime

This is a nice conditioning ride in the early summer because it is not too long, has a steady climb, and is free of snow earlier than many trails with higher elevations or northern exposures. The lake is also unusual as it does have a large sandy beach.

To access this trail from the trailer parking area, follow the bridle path east a little over 1.0 mile, paralleling the dirt road. There is one large stream to

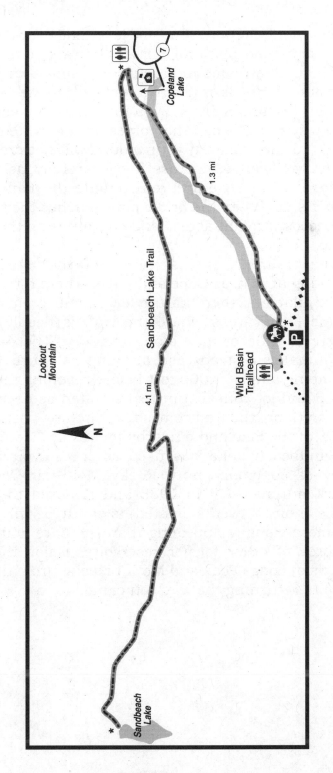

Copeland Lake

7

1.3 mi

Sandbeach Lake Trail

Lookout Mountain

N

4.1 mi

Wild Basin Trailhead

P

Sandbeach Lake

cross along the way. If no one is fishing near the ford, this is a good place for horses that are comfortable with small streams to practice crossing a large one. If your mount is reticent to get all four feet in the water, let him or her have a drink and try again on the way home, when the horses are motivated to get back to the trailer. If your mount will not cross the river, you can get across it by carefully using the bridge on the road and returning to the trail on the other side. When the bridle path reaches the road, it proceeds straight across and continues on the other side.

The trailhead is just north of the Sandbeach parking area near Copeland Lake, where a restroom is available. Other than a few small streams and some steep areas where the trail is deeply worn, there is little of note along the way. The 4.1-mile trail makes a steady ascent along its entire length, climbing almost 2,000 feet before reaching the lake. Stop and let your mount rest as often as necessary. Before long, the trail comes to a hitching post within view of the lake and a nearby toilet.

Sandbeach Lake was used as a reservoir by the city of Longmont until Rocky Mountain National Park purchased it in 1988 and removed the dam. This chain of events created its sandy beach, which is more visually appealing than the bare and rocky shores of other former reservoirs. Enjoy the nice views of Longs Peak and Mount Meeker from the lake before returning the way you came.

Trails accessed from U.S. Highway 34 and U.S. Highway 36

East Portal Trailhead

Drive to the Trailhead	🔑 🔑 🔑
Parking	P P
Amenities	Picnic tables and a toilet
Fee Area?	No, as this trailhead is just outside the park boundary
Elevation	8,400 feet
Maps	Trails Illustrated 200: Rocky Mountain National Park; USGS Longs Peak

This trailhead is simple to drive to and a loop at the end of the road makes it simple to turn around. The road by the parking area is not too busy. One or two trailers can park at this trailhead. Avoid using this area on Sundays, because cars that have been left overnight by backpackers can make it difficult for a trailer to find enough room to park. Automobile parking was allowed on the dam before 9/11. If the parking area on the dam reopens in the future, this trailhead would be upgraded to P P P.

Directions from Boulder County and Interstate Highway 25

Drive to the East Portal Trailhead by traveling west toward the town of Lyons on Colorado State Highway 66 from north Longmont or Interstate Highway 25 (exit 243), or on Colorado State Highway 36 from Boulder. A gas station that also sells diesel, and can accommodate a truck pulling a trailer is located in Lyons. Look for it on the south side of Colorado

State Highway 66, shortly after the signal at the intersection of Highways 34 and 66.

Continue through the town of Lyons on a one-way street, staying in the middle and then the right-hand lane. At the west end of town, this lane becomes a right-turn only lane; turn right toward Estes Park and drive 20 miles on U.S. Highway 36. Go straight through the first signal in Estes Park and turn left at the second signal, staying in the outside, or right, of the two left turn lanes. This is the junction with U.S. Highway 34. You are still on U.S. Highway 36, which you will follow through downtown Estes Park.

Directions from Larimer County

Drive to the East Portal Trailhead by traveling west on U.S. Highway 34 to Estes Park, almost 30 miles from Loveland. Drive straight through the first signal in Estes Park, which is the junction with U.S. Highway 36, staying in the right-hand lane. This is the junction with U.S. Highway 36, which you are now on. You will follow this highway through downtown Estes Park.

Directions from the intersection of Colorado State Highways 34 and 36 in Estes Park

After the scenery, Estes Park is best known for its awkward intersections, and this route drives through three of them in quick succession. At the third signal after the intersection, both lanes are left turn lanes. Stay in the right-hand lane and turn left onto Moraine Avenue, heading south. At the following intersection you will be in a right turn lane. Vehicles in this lane do not need to stop at that intersection. After making this right turn, you are headed west, toward the mountains again. A gas station, fast food restaurant and grocery store that can be accessed by a truck pulling a trailer are on the south side of this stretch of road, 1.7 miles from the intersection of Colorado State Highways 34 and 36.

Watch for a left turn lane after the next traffic signal. The main road curves to the right at this point, 2.0 miles from the intersection of Colorado State Highways 34 and 36. Left-turning traffic must stop at a stop sign before continuing to the west on Colorado State Highway 66. Follow this road that has a small loop at the end, 3.5 miles from this junction. Stay on the pavement at the end of the road; the dirt road leads to a campground and a dam. Park in the paved parking area on the south side of the loop, as far toward the east as possible, with your front wheels turned toward the road. If the paved parking area does not have enough space available for your rig, parallel park along the road, with the right side of your rig off the pavement.

The dam here collects water that comes under the mountains from Grand Lake in an amazing tunnel completed by the U.S. Bureau of Reclamation in 1947. This is the East Portal of the Alva B. Adams Tunnel, hence the name of the trailhead. From here, the water enters the Rams Horn Tunnel that goes under Rams Horn Mountain and empties into Marys Lake. Then it enters one more tunnel, the Prospect Mountain Tunnel, which empties into Lake Estes before it flows into the Big Thompson River, providing nonpolluting hydroelectric power and water for much of the region. Lake Estes is actually a reservoir, although most of us would not recognize Estes Park with the large meadow it was named after in place of its signature lake.

Trail #11
Storm Pass

Trail rideable	June through September
Best time to ride	August
Maximum elevation	10,000 feet at the hitching post
Difficulty	**Advanced**
Terrain	♘ ♘ ♘
Training ability	**+**
Length	10 miles round trip
Elevation gain	1,600 feet to the hitching post
Best features	Views of Mummy Mountains
Obstacles	One steep area, horses from rental stables use part of this trail
Special notes	All Rocky Mountain National Park rules apply on these trails

This is a nice trail that can be shortened or lengthened at will. It has nice views and adequate shade throughout the summer, and plenty of aspen trees at various elevations make it a good showcase for fall color as well.

To access this trail from the parking area, head to the north side of the paved loop where the trail starts near the picnic area. This route travels west, crossing a small stream running through a culvert and then traversing a small meadow before climbing a steep hill. Although short, this hot and unrelenting stretch of trail takes the edge off the horses by the time they have made it up to the first trail junction.

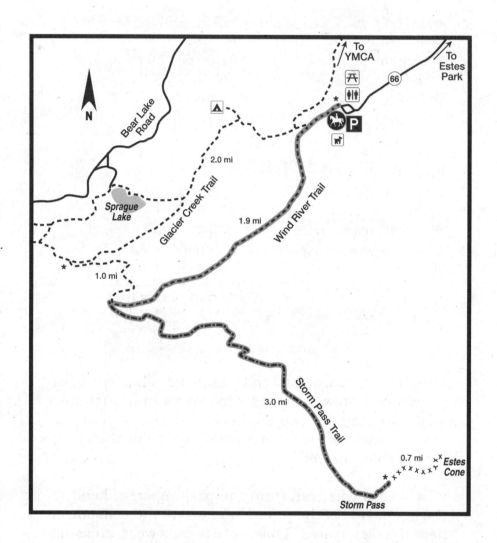

Halfway up the hill, a sign marks the Rocky Mountain National Park boundary. A little further up the hill, a signpost indicates that the Wind River Trail and East Portal is to the left, the YMCA is to the right and the Glacier Basin Campground is straight ahead. Turn left here, and follow this trail downhill until it intersects with the Wind River Trail after 0.2 mile. At that junction, the trail to the north, labeled East Portal, used to be a simple way to access this area, but since it leads to the dam, access has been restricted at the north end of the trail for Homeland Security. Notice that the trail you came on is labeled YMCA and Glacier Basin Campground. Since the signs were not updated when the trail was blocked off, this signpost can be confusing when returning to the trailhead.

Stay right and follow the Wind River for a few minutes before climbing up the side of a ridge. For a short distance, the trail travels through a lodgepole pine forest before returning to the river. Enjoy this delightful stretch of trail with aspen, willow, and other vegetation that prefers this wet environment to your left, and the shade provided by the lodgepole pines growing on the drier hillside to your right, for over 1.0 mile. Then the trail comes to a boggy area where it curves to the right to skirt the bog. This is a nice spot to take in the surroundings while letting the horses rest for a moment.

On the right, with a southern exposure, is a dry, rocky hillside where ponderosa pine trees eke out an existence. On the left, is a very wet meadow where willow and other water loving vegetation grow. Across the meadow, evergreen trees grow on the northern exposure, particularly spruce and fir trees that appreciate the extra moisture. To the southwest is Battle Mountain, which is covered with evergreen trees mixed with large groves of aspen trees that create a glorious sight in the fall. The Storm Pass Trail travels up this mountain to the Estes Cone, which can be seen sticking up on the left.

The trail junction for the Storm Pass Trail is just past this meadow. The signpost at the junction indicates that Bear and Sprague Lakes are to the right and Storm Pass is 3.0 miles to the left, as well as the Estes Cone at 3.7 miles. The trail you came on is labeled East Portal 1.9 miles. Make a left turn, to the south, and follow the trail as far as you want to. This trail works its way up Battle Mountain for 3.0 miles. Along the way, a place with nice views of the mountains to the north makes a good rest spot, or a place to turn around if your mount is tired.

A small meadow not far from Storm Pass, which has a hitching post for the horses and a nice view of the Estes Cone, is a pleasant setting for a lunch break. Turning around here results in a 9.0-mile

ride round trip. It is 0.5 mile further to Storm Pass and the Estes Cone trail junction. Since that trail is extremely rocky it is not open to horses. A hitching post is available at the trail junction for riders who want to hike the 0.7-mile trail to the top on foot. The main trail continues past Storm Pass to the Eugenia Mine and the Longs Peak Trail. Return the way you came, watching the trail signs. For variety, riders can return on the Glacier Basin Trail described in trail #12, without adding much mileage to the ride.

If your horse is in extremely good shape, well acclimated, and you get an early start, it is possible to make a loop that is long and difficult due to elevation gain, by following the Longs Peak Trail and continuing home on the North Longs Peak Trail as described in trail #13. Horses are not allowed on the Chasm Lake Trail, but a hitching post and restroom are available where this trail leaves the Longs Peak Trail. The Longs Peak Trail has a trailhead, but it usually fills up before daylight and is not appropriate for trailers.

Trail #12
Glacier Basin Loop

Trail rideable	June through October
Best time to ride	September, when the aspen trees are beautiful and the trails are less busy
Maximum elevation	9,000 feet
Difficulty	**Easy**
Terrain	♘ ♘ for one steep hill
Training ability	✛
Length	5.0 miles round trip for the basic loop, or longer
Elevation gain	600 feet
Best features	The ability to vary the route and aspen trees in the fall
Obstacles	Horses from rental stables use these trails
Special notes	Take a USGS map as the trail junction signs in this area can be confusing and the extra detail on this map is helpful; all Rocky Mountain National Park rules apply on these trails

This loop is a great little ride with little elevation gain and several options for more distance if desired.

To access this trail from the parking area, head to the north side of the paved loop where the trail starts near the picnic area. This route travels west, crossing a small stream running through a culvert and then traversing a small meadow before climbing

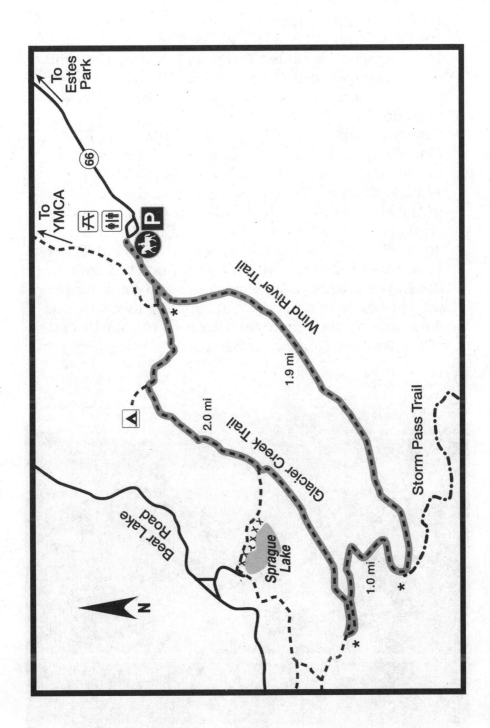

To Estes Park

66

To YMCA

P

Wind River Trail

1.9 mi

*

2.0 mi

Glacier Creek Trail

Storm Pass Trail

Bear Lake Road

Sprague Lake

1.0 mi

*

*

N

a steep hill. Although short, this hot and unrelenting stretch of trail is the most difficult part of this ride. This loop can be ridden in reverse, but by the time our horses get to the first trail junction they think they have worked hard enough, and they are ready to go downhill for awhile.

Halfway up the hill, a sign marks the Rocky Mountain National Park boundary. A little further up the hill, a signpost indicates that the Wind River Trail and East Portal is to the left, the YMCA is to the right and the Glacier Basin Campground is straight ahead. Turn left here, and follow this trail downhill until it intersects with the Wind River Trail after 0.2 mile. At that junction, the trail to the north labeled East Portal used to be a simple way to access this area, but since it leads to the dam, access has been restricted at the north end of the trail for Homeland Security.

Stay right and follow the Wind River for a few minutes before climbing up the side of a ridge. For a short distance, the trail travels through a lodgepole pine forest before returning to the river. Enjoy this delightful stretch of trail with aspen, willow, and other vegetation that prefers this wet environment to your left, and the shade provided by the lodgepole pines growing on the drier hillside to your right, for over 1.0 mile. Then the trail comes to a boggy area where it curves to the right to skirt the bog. This is a nice spot to take in the surroundings while letting the horses rest for a moment.

On the right, with a southern exposure, is a dry, rocky hillside where ponderosa pine trees eke out an existence. On the left is a very wet meadow where willow and other water loving vegetation grow. Across the meadow, evergreen trees grow on the northern exposure, particularly spruce and fir that appreciate the extra moisture. To the southwest is Battle Mountain, which is covered with evergreen trees mixed with large groves of aspen trees that create a glorious site in the fall. The Storm Pass Trail travels up this mountain to the Estes Cone, which can be seen sticking up on the left.

The trail junction for the Storm Pass Trail is just past this meadow. The signpost at the junction indicates that Bear and Sprague Lakes are to the right and Storm Pass and the Estes Cone are to the left. Turn right, toward the north, where this route soon heads downhill through a thick forest. Occasionally the lodgepole pines give way to groves of aspen. On a hot day the different scent given off by each type of tree is marvelous.

At the bottom of the hill is the next junction where riders can return to the trailhead by way of the Glacier Creek Trail on the right. The signpost here reads only that Glacier Basin Campground is this direction, but this is the correct trail. Ride eastward, passing trail junctions on the left to Sprague Lake and the Sprague Lake livery, and the campground along the way. Then this route passes a water tank and a junction with the trail to the YMCA livery. The trails in this area are frequented by the riding stables, so be prepared to get off the trail to let the dude strings pass. Continuing straight, this route soon heads downhill, providing a view of the West Portal of the tunnel and the trailhead at the bottom of the hill. This ride totals 5.0 miles round trip.

To make a longer ride, continue straight toward the north at the junction of the Glacier Gorge Trail with the Storm Pass Trail, until reaching the next junction. This junction has four trails coming into it. Continue straight on the Glacier Gorge Trail as described in trail #13.

For a shorter extension of the loop ride, or to use the restrooms in the Sprague Lake parking area, turn right. Stay right at the next junction as well; the trail on the left leads to Bear Lake Road. Ride by the Sprague Lake parking lot and old stables, and cross the road to access the trail to the north of Sprague Lake. Do not ride around the lakeshore on the footpath, but stay left on the trail that passes the new stables. Keep following the trail east, then southeast until reaching a trail junction with the Glacier Basin Trail. Turn left and continue riding eastward until reaching the trailhead.

The Sprague Lake area has several trails, and it can be fun to explore these flat, sandy trails. Read the trail signs at each junction, and use a map to get back to the trailhead. Sprague Lake has a trailhead, but no place to park a trailer.

Trail #13
Glacier Creek, Alberta Falls, and North Longs Peak trails

Trail rideable	June through October
Best time to ride	September, when the aspen trees are beautiful and the trails are less busy
Maximum elevation	9,800 feet
Difficulty	**Moderate**
Terrain	♘ ♘
Training ability	**+ +**
Length	10.5 miles round trip
Elevation gain	1,000 feet
Best features	The ability to vary the route and aspen trees in the fall
Obstacles	One small bridge by Galcier Gorge, noisy water and tourists at Alberta Falls, horses from rental stables use some of these trails
Special notes	Take a USGS map as the trail junction signs in this area can be confusing; all Rocky Mountain National Park rules apply on these trails

This trail is **Easy** to follow for a few miles with little elevation gain, as well as offering a **Demanding** all day ride. It exhibits some of the best views in Rocky Mountain National Park.

To access this trail from the parking area head to the north side of the paved loop where the trail starts near the picnic area. This route travels west, crossing a stream running through a culvert and then traversing a small meadow before climbing a steep hill. This hot and unrelenting stretch of trail is the most difficult part of this ride.

Halfway up the hill, a sign marks the Rocky Mountain National Park boundary. A little further up the hill, a signpost indicates that the Wind River Trail and East Portal are to the left, the YMCA is to the right, and the Glacier Basin Campground is straight ahead. The signpost is technically correct since the Glacier Creek Trail does pass the campground, however it is misleading because it leads many other places as well. For this ride, urge your horse to continue straight up this long steep hill. Ponderosa pine trees scattered along the hillside provide shady spots to rest along the way.

At the top of the hill, the trail comes to a junction for the YMCA livery on the right. The riding stables use these trails, so be prepared to get off the trail to let the dude strings pass you. Continue straight on this trail, and after the campground and a trail junction for Sprague Lake on the right, this route comes to another trail junction.

At this junction, the trail to the left leads to the Storm Pass and Wind River trails described in trail #11. Notice that the trail you are leaving is again marked only as the Glacier Gorge Campground. Stay right and soon the trail reaches a larger trail junction. To the left, is the Boulder Brook Trail that is not open to horses, and to the right, is a trail to Bear Lake Road and Sprague Lake that is described in trail #13. The trail you came on is labeled Glacier Basin Loop and the YMCA, as well as East Portal 1.7 miles. To continue on the Glacier Basin Trail, head up the trail straight ahead. This route is relatively flat, the scenery is splendid, and it is never very busy.

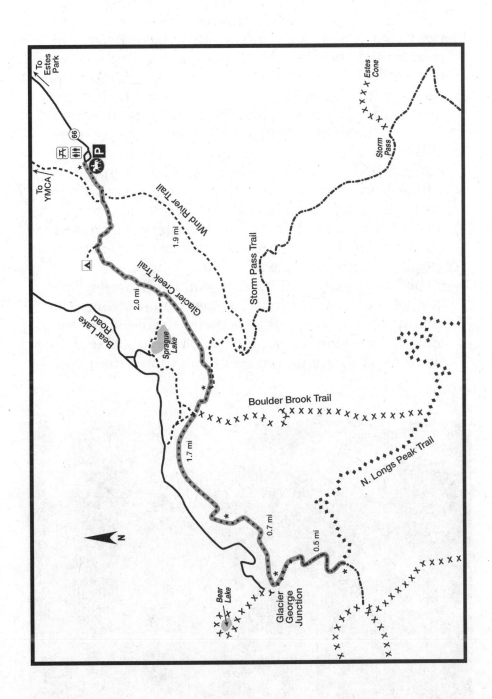

To Estes Park

66

To YMCA

Wind River Trail

1.9 mi

Glacier Creek Trail

2.0 mi

Bear Lake Road

Sprague Lake

Storm Pass Trail

Estes Cone

Storm Pass

1.7 mi

Boulder Brook Trail

N. Longs Peak Trail

0.7 mi

0.5 mi

N

Bear Lake

Glacier George Junction

As you ride along this trail, enjoy the views through the trees of the Bierstadt Moraine, the ridge off to the right that is just north of the Bear Lake Road. The road cannot be seen from here, but the traffic can be heard. A moraine is defined as a pile of rock and rubble left by a receding glacier. The east end of this moraine is rather bare and rocky. Toward the west, however, the slope is completely covered by aspen trees. This atypical situation is the result of a forest fire that burned this area 100 years ago. Aspen trees grow from a huge underground root system that is not destroyed during a forest fire, so it is the first vegetation to come back after afterward. It appears that these aspen trees grew back so densely that they left nowhere for slower growing evergreen trees to sprout.

This route arrives at a small pond with water lilies in it, about 1.5 miles from the last trail junction. The amazing thing about this pond is the view from it. This is an astounding place to have lunch and to sit so close to the mountains rising up in front you.

Hallett Peak is the most obvious one, with its angular sides that are favored by rock climbers. To its right is Tyndall Gorge, marked by the Tyndall Glacier, then further to the north, Flattop Mountain and Notchtop Mountain with more glaciers between them. It doesn't take much imagination to picture glaciers filling this drainage and scraping out the view. This is an obvious place to turn around and go back to the trailhead, making a 6.5-mile round trip ride.

The Glacier Creek Trail continues to the west, however, where it crosses Glacier Creek on a small bridge and then comes to the Glacier Gorge Junction. The trail straight ahead leads to Bear Lake. Horses are not allowed on any of the other trails near Bear Lake and although the parking lot is huge, it is extremely busy and does not offer trailer parking. Horses should turn left, heading up the steep hill to nearby Alberta Falls where this route becomes very busy for a short distance. The next trail junction, above the falls, has two options.

To the right, the Loch Vale Trail travels for 0.4 mile with nice views before reaching a hitching post and a signpost stating that horses are not allowed any further. The elevation at this point is 9,975 feet. Turn around there for a 10.5-mile ride round trip with an elevation gain of 1,175 feet. To the left at the junction, the North Longs Peak Trail continues to travel uphill 5.9 miles, where it joins the Longs Peak Trail at 12,100 feet of elevation. A spur trail to the summit of Longs Peak heads west and crosses the Boulder Field at that point, but horses cannot negotiate that natural feature. The main trail continues straight, heading downhill past the Boulder Field, and can be ridden as a loop with trail #11 if horse and rider are well prepared in advance. Whenever you have enjoyed yourself enough for one day, return the way you came.

Hollowell Park Trailhead

Drive to the Trailhead	🔑 🔑 🔑
Parking	🅿
Amenities	Picnic tables and a toilet
Fee Area?	Rocky Mountain National Park fees apply
Elevation	8,400 feet
Maps	Trails Illustrated 200: Rocky Mountain National Park; USGS Longs Peak and McHenrys Peak

This trailhead is just off Bear Lake Road on a short paved road, so it is simple to get to, but trailer parking is challenging. Rocky Mountain National Park is planning to add one or two trailer parking spots for trailers at this trailhead, which will be a big improvement to the current parking situation.

Directions from Boulder County and Interstate Highway 25.

Drive to the Hollowell Park Trailhead by traveling west toward the town of Lyons from north Longmont or Interstate Highway 25 (exit 243), or on U.S. Highway 36 from Boulder. A gas station that also sells diesel, and can accommodate a truck pulling a trailer is located in Lyons. Look for it on the south side of Colorado State Highway 66, shortly after the signal at the intersection of U.S. Highway 34 and Colorado State Highway 66.

Continue through Lyons on a one-way street, staying in the middle and then in the right-hand lane. At the west end of town, this lane becomes a right turn only lane; turn right toward Estes Park, and drive 20 miles on U.S. Highway 36. Go straight through the first signal in Estes Park, and turn left at the second signal, staying in the outside, or right, of the two left turn lanes. This is the junction with U.S. Highway 34. You are still on U.S. Highway 36, which you will follow through downtown Estes Park and the entrance station for the national park.

Directions from Larimer County

Drive to the Hollowell Park Trailhead by traveling west on U.S. Highway 34 to Estes Park, almost 30 miles from Loveland, and go straight through the first signal in Estes Park, staying in the right-hand lane. This is the junction with U.S. Highway 36, which you are now on. You will follow this highway through downtown Estes Park and the entrance station for the national park.

Directions from the intersection of Colorado State Highways 34 and 36 in Estes Park

After the scenery, Estes Park is best known for its awkward intersections, and this route drives through two of them in quick succession. At the third signal after the intersection of U.S. Highway 34 and 36 both lanes are left turn lanes. Stay in the right-hand lane and turn left onto Moraine Avenue, heading south. At the next intersection you will be in a right turn only lane. Vehicles in that lane do not need to stop at this intersection. After turning right, you are headed west, toward the mountains again. A gas station, fast food restaurant and grocery store that can be accessed by a truck pulling a trailer are on the south side of this stretch of road.

Continue straight through the next signal, 1.9 miles from the intersection of U.S. Highway 34 and 36, and around a curve to your right. The Beaver Meadows Visitor Center is on the left, less than 1.0 mile from the last signal. Stop here to talk to a ranger, obtain a copy of their *Horse and Pack Animals* brochure, apply for a backcountry camping permit, or to visit the restrooms, the gift shop or the bookstore. You can park in the bus parking area.

Continue west past the Visitor Center on the main road for another 1.0 mile to the fee station. Drivers who have a plastic park pass with a magnetic strip on the back, and who do not need to speak to a ranger, or to get a map or other information, can use the express lane on the right. Otherwise, use any of the other lanes where the rangers give out maps and current event information as well as collecting entrance fees.

Turn left onto Bear Lake Road 0.2 mile from the fee station. Follow this road 2.3 miles to the road marked Hollowell Park and turn right. Unless the park service has added trailer parking, park on the south side of the loop at the end of the road. Try to park in the parking place furthest to the east, with your windshield facing toward the north. If this spot is not available, head back toward Bear Lake Road and pull off of the right side of the road.

The only other parking option for this area is to continue up the Bear Lake Road. Across the road and 200 feet beyond the entrance to Hollowell Park, is a paved pullout large enough for one trailer. Because this pullout is on the left side of the road, continue up Bear Lake Road to the shuttle bus parking lot. This is a huge parking lot that would be great for horse trailers, but unfortunately the Park Service has chosen to keep the only trail that starts at this lot **Closed** to horses. So turn around and head back down the road to the pullout just before Hollowell Park. Carefully lead your horse across the road and walk alongside it to the Hollowell Park turnoff.

Trail #14
Bierstadt Lake

Trail rideable	June through September
Best time to ride	July
Maximum elevation	9,400 feet
Difficulty	**Moderate**
Terrain	♘♘
Training ability	✚
Length	7 miles round trip or longer
Elevation gain	1,000 feet
Best features	Varied trail that is lightly used
Obstacles	Large bridge and one river crossing
Special notes	Nice aspen trees in the fall

This is a nice ride that can be varied in two ways. This **Moderate** ride can become an **Advanced** 15 mile ride by following the trail description for trail #15 for up to 4.0 miles past Bierstadt Lake, passing two small lakes and ending at Odessa Lake. This extension has spectacular and unusual high altitude views of Bear Lake and Longs Peak as well as the Continental Divide. You can also refer to trail #15 if a 14 mile round trip ride to Flattop Mountain with more elevation gain appeals to you.

Or for a short 3.4 mile training ride, the Bierstadt Lake part of the trail can be left off. The creek on this route is wide and shallow with wide, gradual banks on both sides. The bridge is well built with hand railings and it has level footing before and after it, making both crossings excellent training opportunities on this lightly used trail. For additional practice, the small loop where these crossings are located could be ridden more than once in each direction.

This trail starts at the trail board on the west side of the parking area. Within 0.2 mile, a trail on the right, for Moraine Park and horses from the YMCA, joins the main trail. This route continues on the main trail, heads south and then parallels Mill Creek for a glorious 1.0 mile, before reaching the first trail junction. This junction is signed as Cub Lake to the right, and Bear and Bierstadt Lakes and Mill Creek Basin to the left. Go left across the creek on a sturdy bridge, arriving at another trail junction near the Mill Creek Basin campsite, 1.7 miles from the trailhead.

The signpost there indicates that Cub Lake and Mill Creek Basin campsite are to the right, and Bear and Bierstadt Lakes are to the left. To ride the 3.4-mile training loop, turn right and cross the river there. Stay right at each junction until you return to the bridge where you can ride the loop again, or turn left before the bridge to return to the trailhead.

Otherwise, to continue on this route to Bierstadt Lake, stay left at this trail junction heading south. The upper part of this trail travels on an old, rocky road for 0.5 mile before reaching another trail junction. The left-hand trail leads to Bierstadt Lake, a heavily treed and unremarkable lake. That trail continues around the lake with several trail junctions along the way. Two routes return to the main trail. Two other trails leave the lake; one goes south to the shuttle bus stop on the Bear Lake Road, but it is not open to horses. The other one heads east to the Bierstadt Lake Trailhead, which has no parking for trailers. To continue toward Bear Lake, use the description for ride #15, riding as far as you wish to before returning on the main trail.

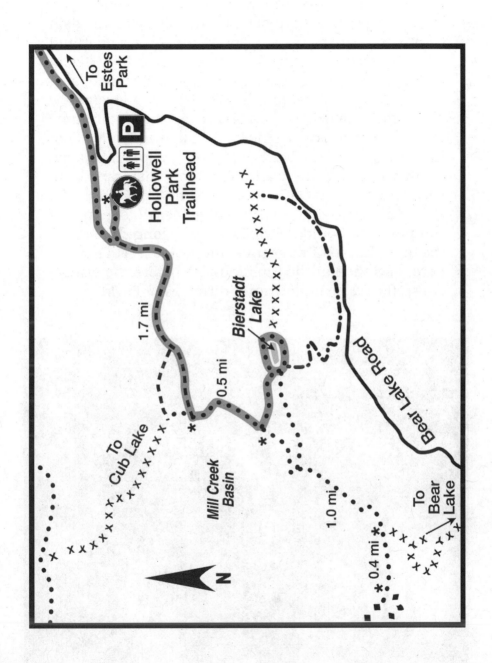

To Estes Park

P

Hollowell Park Trailhead

1.7 mi

0.5 mi

Bierstadt Lake

To Cub Lake

Mill Creek Basin

Bear Lake Road

1.0 mi

0.4 mi

To Bear Lake

N

When you are ready to return to the trailhead, head north on the main trail to return on the trail you came on. At the signpost for the Mill Creek Basin campsite, return the way you came, or stay left and ford the river. That trail continues into Mill Basin, a typical mountain meadow named because of a sawmill that was here in the late 1800s. A lovely view of the meadow ringed in aspen trees and mountains and a hitching post for horses make this a nice spot to enjoy your lunch before returning to the trailhead. Continue along this trail for a short distance, until you reach a trail junction leading to Cub Lake. Unfortunately, that trail becomes very steep and is composed of boulders, making for a long slide down the hill that is **Dangerous** for horses. Turn right here, and then at the junction just before the bridge, stay left and head downhill to Hollowell Park.

Trail #15
Hollowell Park/Moraine Park loop

Trail rideable	July through August
Best time to ride	August
Maximum elevation	10,800 feet
Difficulty	**Advanced** due to distance and elevation gain
Terrain	U U U
Training ability	+ + +
Length	16 miles round trip
Elevation gain	2,800 feet
Best features	This is a diverse, long loop trail with spectacular views
Obstacles	Parts of the trail are steep and rocky, and it fords several rivers
Special notes	This loop can be ridden in reverse, or started at Moraine Park

This trail is a full day's ride, with plenty of mileage and elevation for a well-conditioned horse. When ridden as described, the ride climbs before dropping into a nice lake for lunch, continuing downhill after lunch, and then ending the ride by gradually regaining elevation on a trail with good footing. Having the ascents and descents mixed-up is more enjoyable, for the horse and the rider, than the usual uphill before lunch and downhill afterwards.

This trail starts at the trail board on the west side of the parking area. Within 0.6 mile a trail from Moraine Park and horses from the YMCA join the

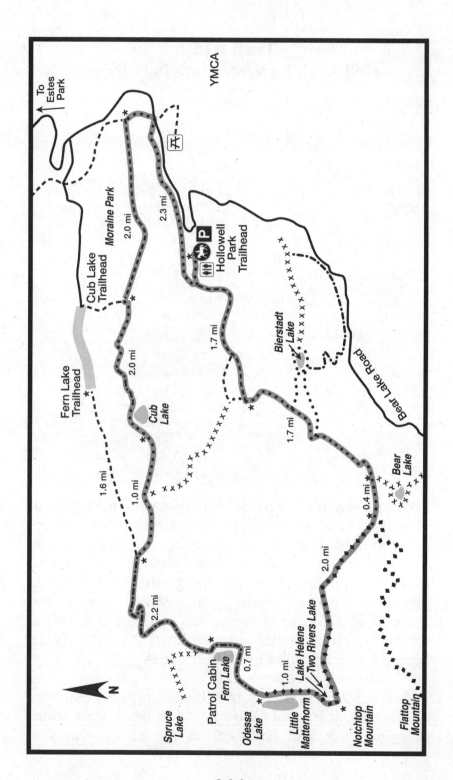

trail on the right. This route continues on the main trail, heading south and then paralleling Mill Creek for a glorious 1.0 mile, before reaching the first trail junction. The signpost there indicates that Cub Lake is to the right and Bear and Bierstadt Lakes and Mill Creek Basin are to the left. Go left across the creek on a sturdy bridge, arriving at another trail junction near the Mill Creek Basin campsite 1.7 miles from the trailhead. The signpost there is labeled Cub Lake and Mill Creek Basin campsite to the right, and Bear and Bierstadt Lakes to the left. Stay left at this trail junction, heading south. The upper part of this trail travels on an old, rocky road for 0.5 mile before reaching another trail junction in 1.0 mile. The left fork of the trail leads to Bierstadt Lake, a heavily treed and unremarkable lake. Continue straight toward Bear Lake for 0.7 mile. Horses are not allowed at Bear Lake, so at that junction, 3.4 miles from the trailhead, stay right and travel west and uphill, rather than descending down the hill to the left toward the lake.

This trail provides a spectacular view of Bear Lake with Longs Peak rising up behind it. When the aspen trees are turning gold in the fall, this makes an award-winning photo. The views of Hallett Peak and Glacier Gorge are spectacular too, as a result of a forest fire over a hundred years ago. In the future, as the trees grow thicker, the views will be obscured. Less than 0.5 mile from the Bear Lake junction, the trail comes to the trail junction for Flattop Mountain. This is one of the few mountains that are accessible by horseback, because it does not have a rocky summit. That trail travels 3.5 miles upward through the forest, continuing above tree line across tundra. Intrepid hikers follow this route over the Continental Divide and down the other side to Grand Lake, where they have a car bring them back over the divide. A horse and rider could plan to spend a night or two in Grand Lake and return by trail or horse trailer.

This route continues on the trail to the right, traveling steadily upward through the trees for another 2.0 miles before arriving at Two Rivers Lake and Lake Helene. This is the highest elevation point of this route, and it displays incredible views of Notchtop Mountain and Little Matterhorn. Ride 1.1 miles to the hitching post at Odessa Lake, and give your mount a break while taking the 0.2 mile walk to see the lake, which is not to be missed. Take a lunch stop here, or continue to Fern Lake, where the hitching post is within view of the lake.

Follow the main trail downhill, dropping 1,100 feet over the next 2.0 miles. Fern Lake is 0.7 mile from the hitching post near Odessa Lake, and has lovely views. Past the hitching post, ford the outlet river that is quite wide, but not deep or fast, and continue down the trail A little over 1.0 mile below Fern Lake, the trail passes Fern Falls, situated close to the trail at a switchback. Hikers stopped here, with their backs to the trail to enjoy the rushing water, may not see or hear horses approaching. Riders may want to dismount before approaching this turn. After another 1.0 mile the trail passes a toilet near a campsite and just minutes later drops into a busy trail junction at The Pool.

Turn right at this junction and continue 3.2 miles along this trail to Moraine Park with little elevation gain. This route passes a trail junction to Mill Creek Basin on the right. This is a steep trail covered with large rocks, making it a **Dangerous** option. Then this trail travels alongside Cub Lake, a small nondescript lake, except for the surprising lily pads growing in it. After Cub Lake, this route passes another camping area and toilet. Soon, beyond some beaver ponds, the trail descends into Moraine Park 2.0 miles from Cub Lake. Stay right at the junction, and follow the trail along the south side of the meadow.

From this junction it is 3.0 miles back to the Hollowell Park Trailhead. At the east end of Moraine Park, stay right and follow the trail up the hillside through the trees. This route curves to the right, following the curve of Bear Lake Road below. It passes a trail junction along the way for a trail that crosses the road, and continues across the river to the YMCA. Continue straight on this route and soon you will arrive at Hollowell Park. Stay on the trail until you reach the trail junction. Make a sharp left turn there to return to the trailhead.

Moraine Park

Drive to the Trailhead	🔑 🔑
Parking	🅿 🅿
Amenities	Picnic tables and toilets
Fee Area?	Rocky Mountain National Park fees apply
Elevation	8,150 feet
Maps	Trails Illustrated 200: Rocky Mountain National Park; USGS Longs Peak and McHenrys Peak

Two trailers can park at this parking lot. Otherwise some parking places are available alongside the road, but get an early start and have a second trailhead in mind, in the event no parking is available here.

Directions from Boulder County and Interstate Highway 25

Drive to Moraine Park by heading west toward the town of Lyons on Colorado State Highway 66 from north Longmont or Interstate Highway 25 (exit 243), or on U.S. Highway 36 from Boulder. A gas station that also sells diesel, and can accommodate a truck pulling a trailer is located in Lyons. Look for it on the south side of Colorado State Highway 66, shortly after the signal at the intersection of U.S. Highway 34 and Colorado State Highway 66.

Continue through Lyons on a one-way street, staying in the middle and then in the right-hand lane. At the west end of town, this lane becomes a right turn only lane; turn right toward Estes Park,

150

and drive 20 miles on U.S. Highway 36. Go straight through the first signal in Estes Park and turn left at the second signal staying in the outside, or right, of the two left turn lanes. This is the junction with U.S. Highway 34. You are still on U.S. Highway 36, which you will follow through downtown Estes Park and the entrance station for the national park.

Directions from Larimer County

Drive to Moraine Park by heading west on U.S. Highway 34, about 30 miles past Loveland, and go straight through the first signal in Estes Park, staying in the right-hand lane. This is the junction with U.S. Highway 36, which you are now on. You will follow this highway through downtown Estes Park and the entrance station for the national park.

Directions from the intersection of Colorado State Highways 34 and 36 in Estes Park

After the scenery, Estes Park is best known for its awkward intersections, and this route drives through two of them in quick succession. At the third signal after the intersection of U.S. Highway 34 and U.S. Highway 36, both lanes are left turn lanes. Stay in the right-hand lane and turn left onto Moraine Avenue, heading south. At the next intersection you will be in a right turn only lane. Vehicles in that lane do not need to stop at the intersection. After this turn, you are headed west, toward the mountains again. A gas station, fast food restaurant and grocery store that can be accessed by a truck pulling a trailer are on the south side of this stretch of road.

Continue straight through the next signal, 1.9 miles from the intersection of U.S. Highway 34 and 36, and around a curve to your right. The Beaver Meadows Visitor Center is on the left, less than 1.0 mile from the last signal. Stop here to talk to a ranger, obtain a copy of their *Horse and Pack Animals* brochure, apply for a backcountry camping permit, or visit the restrooms, gift shop or book store. You can park in the bus parking area.

Continue west past the Visitor Center on the main road for another 1.0 mile to the fee station. Drivers who have a plastic park pass with a magnetic strip on the back, and who do not need to speak to a ranger, or to get a map or other information, can use the express lane on the right. Otherwise, use any of the other lanes where the rangers give out maps and current event information as well as collecting entrance fees.

Turn left onto Bear Lake Road 0.2 mile past the fee station. Follow Bear Lake Road 1.3 miles to the museum on the left, and turn right onto the road marked Moraine Park. Follow this road 0.5 mile, where it makes a ninety-degree turn to the left; the straight route leads to a campground. (Make sure to turn right here when leaving.)

After turning left, continue following this road another 1.5 miles, noticing possible parking spots along the way. Wherever you park, stay on the gravel and keep your tires off the grass. The pavement ends near the Cub Lake Trailhead, 1.5 miles from the Bear Lake Road. From there, it is 0.5 mile further to the loop parking area. Drive around the loop, and park parallel on the right side of the road on the south side of the loop. A sign limits this to horse trailers but only two trailers can park here, and it is rather narrow. The cars backing out of their spaces are a concern as well as not having much room to tack up your horse. Do not continue to drive west past this loop, through the open gate, as there is no place to park or turn a trailer around. In the event that no parking is available here, or if you feel uncomfortable with the lack of space, go back the way you came, and park alongside the road east of the Cub Lake Trailhead.

Trail #16
Moraine Park loop

Trail rideable	May through October
Best time to ride	June or September
Maximum elevation	8,000 feet
Difficulty	**Easy**
Terrain	♘
Training ability	✚
Length	5.0 miles round trip
Elevation gain	Negligible
Best features	Short, simple, tune-up or trailing ride
Obstacles	Two small bridges, cars on the road
Special notes	Popular elk viewing area in fall

This is a ride that can be done as an **Easy** ride for a novice horse or rider. It could be lengthened without adding much elevation by combining it with other trails, such as Cub Lake or Beaver Meadows.

This can also be a fun ride in the latter park of September and early in October, when the elk come down from the mountains and put on their mating displays. Rocky Mountain National Park is known for its elk that can be seen and heard bugling in the autumn, during the afternoon and early evening hours. Take a dependable horse and, while riding around this area after noon, you should come upon one or more small bands. The best sightings and largest herds appear around dusk, but don't let the elk entice you into staying beyond 5:00, when the road gets really busy.

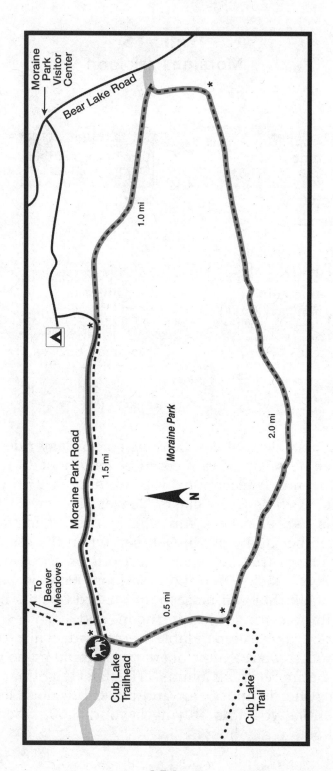

Moraine Park Visitor Center

Bear Lake Road

*

1.0 mi

Moraine Park Road

1.5 mi

Moraine Park

N

2.0 mi

To Beaver Meadows

0.5 mi

*

Cub Lake Trailhead

*

Cub Lake Trail

For this trail, park alongside the Moraine Park Road wherever it is convenient, rather than the parking lot described above for Moraine Park. To access this trail, ride alongside the road, heading west until reaching the Cub Lake Trailhead that has a small auto parking area. Cross the bridge into the meadow on the south. The trail junction for Cub Lake is on the right, 0.5 mile from the trailhead. Turn left there, and ride along the south side of Moraine Park. After 2.0 miles the trail splits again. Stay left, traveling by some cabins and through a parking area, eventually arriving at another trail that runs along the east side of the meadow before paralleling the paved road. When the trail intersects Moraine Park Road, ride alongside it back to your trailer, or cross the road and continue along the trail.

On the north side of the road are several little trails leading to the riding stables and the campground. To return to the Cub Lake Trailhead, turn left each time you come to a trail junction. This is a small area and it would be difficult to get lost, so feel free to wander around the trails here. For a full day's ride head north to the Beaver Meadows area, using a map to navigate.

Trail #17
Cub Lake loop

Trail rideable	June through September
Best time to ride	September, when the tourists are gone and the aspen are glorious
Maximum elevation	8,700 feet
Difficulty	**Moderate**, with an **Advanced** piece of trail
Terrain	♘ ♘ to ♘ ♘ ♘
Training ability	✚ ✚
Length	5.8 miles round trip or longer
Elevation gain	550 feet
Best features	Unique lake in an area of mixed forest and many aspen trees
Obstacles	Cars on the road, small streams, five bridges, and scores of hikers
Special notes	This ride can be combined with the Moraine Park Trail #17 above

Due to the low elevation, this trail is accessible earlier in the summer than many other trails in Rocky Mountain National Park. As it is fairly short, it can be ridden in two hours. The route is more challenging than it appears however, since it has five bridges and some small streams to cross, a short hill to climb, part of the trail is busy, and part of it has difficult footing. The **Advanced** portion of the trail can be avoided. I describe this trail in a counterclockwise direction for those choosing the **Moderate** option; however, for those who want to ride the entire loop,

156

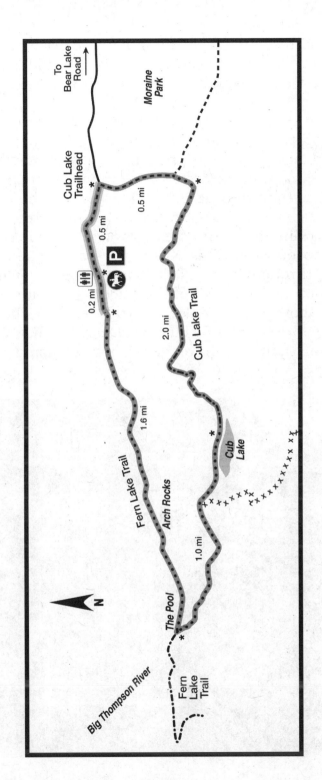

To
Bear Lake
Road

Moraine
Park

Cub Lake
Trailhead

0.5 mi

0.5 mi

P

0.2 mi

Cub Lake Trail

2.0 mi

1.6 mi

Fern Lake Trail

Arch Rocks

Cub
Lake

1.0 mi

N

The Pool

Big Thompson River

Fern
Lake
Trail

I would recommend riding it in a clockwise direction so that the difficult part of the trail is ridden uphill rather than downhill.

From the loop parking area, ride west through the open gate on the dirt road watching for cars. When the gate is locked to prevent vehicles from driving on the road, horses can go around it. After the road reaches the trailhead in 0.8 mile, access the trail on the west side of the parking lot. Continue west on the trail, riding through aspen groves alongside the Big Thompson River. This part of the trail is often busy. Pass through Arch Rock, watching your mount's reaction to the sound of their hooves echoing on the rock above. In 1.7 miles the trail reaches The Pool, where it encounters a large bridge over a fast moving stream that may have many hikers gazing at the water.

Once you are over the bridge, stay left to follow the trail 1.2 miles to Cub Lake. This piece of trail has some of the largest aspen trees I have ever seen. After a short rocky ascent and two bridges, the trail passes a junction to Mill Creek Basin on the right. That trail is quite steep and covered with large rocks, making it a **Dangerous** option for horses. This trail soon skirts the north side of Cub Lake, a fairly unremarkable lake, except for the surprising fact that it is filled with water lilies. Past the lake, the trail arrives at a hitching post and a toilet. This is a nice spot to stop and is the turnaround spot for the **Moderate** option. For the next 1.0 mile the route quickly loses 500 feet of elevation on a rocky and slippery trail. Then for the following 1.0 mile it travels alongside multiple beaver ponds, before descending into Moraine Park 2.0 miles past Cub Lake. Turn left at the trail junction and follow the trail north 0.5 mile to the bridge that crosses over to the road and the Cub Lake Trailhead. Turn left onto the road and ride another 0.5 mile to your trailer.

To extend your ride to 11 miles, stay right after the beaver ponds and follow the trail around Moraine Park as described in trail #16.

Trail #18
Fern and Odessa Lakes

Trail rideable	July through August
Best time to ride	August
Maximum elevation	10,020 feet
Difficulty	**Advanced**
Terrain	♘ ♘ ♘
Training ability	**+ +**
Length	10.6 miles round trip
Elevation gain	1,870 feet
Best features	Views of two beautiful and very different high altitude lakes
Obstacles	Cars on the road, one bridge, a waterfall, and a river crossing
Special notes	Turning around at Fern Lake saves 2.0 miles and 500 feet of elevation

This is a great ride. While the parking area and the first part of the trail can be fairly busy, two fabulous lakes and views of the mountains make it well worth the trouble.

From the loop parking area, ride west through the open gate on the dirt road watching for cars. When the gate is locked to prevent vehicles from driving on the road, horses can go around it. After the road reaches the trailhead in 0.8 mile, access the trail on the west side of the parking lot. Continue west on the trail riding through aspen groves alongside the Big Thompson River. This part of the trail is often busy.

160

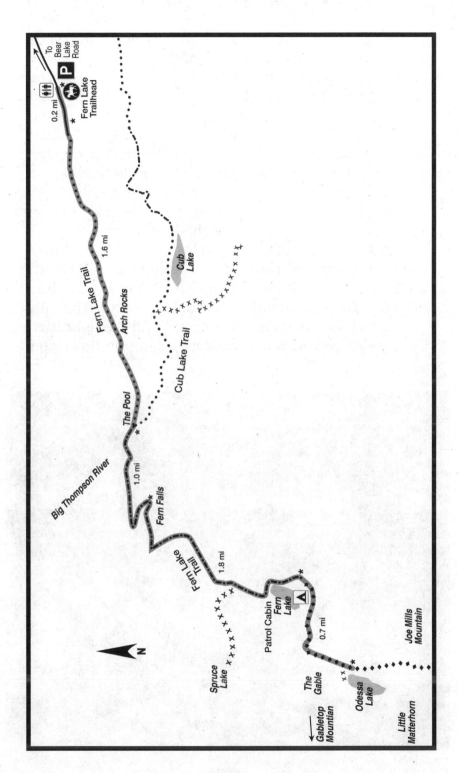

To
Bear
Lake
Road

Fern Lake Trailhead

P

0.2 mi

Fern Lake Trail

1.6 mi

Arch Rocks

Cub Lake

Cub Lake Trail

The Pool

Big Thompson River

1.0 mi

Fern Falls

Fern Lake Trail

1.8 mi

Spruce Lake

Patrol Cabin

Fern Lake

The Gable

0.7 mi

Odessa Lake

Gabletop Mountian

Joe Mills Mountain

Little Matterhorn

N

When passing through Arch Rock, watching your mount's reaction to the sound of their hooves echoing on the rock above. In 1.6 miles the trail reaches The Pool, where it encounters a large bridge over a fast moving stream, and many hikers gazing at the water.

Cross the bridge as soon as it is safe, and then immediately ride up the trail that veers up the hill to the right. Before long, this trail levels out near a campsite and a toilet. It then crosses Fern Creek and travels along the south side of Spruce Creek for a short distance before heading south. From this point the trail climbs at a steady rate. A little less than 1.0 mile past The Pool, the route comes suddenly upon Fern Falls at a switchback, where hikers stop with their backs to the trail to enjoy the rushing water. The falls are very noisy and close to the trail, and the tight turn is usually crowded with hikers gazing at the water

who may not see or hear approaching horses. Riders may want to dismount before approaching this turn.

After the falls, the trail continues its upward ascent on a narrow, rocky trail for another 1.0 mile before leveling out somewhat. It then passes a junction for Spruce Lake on the right, which is not open to horses because it is not maintained adequately. After traversing a grassy area and crossing a small stream, a view of Fern Lake appears. A cabin and a horse corral, which are used by park rangers, are on the right. This route continues along the east side of the lake, crosses Fern Creek, which is wide but not deep, and then comes to an open area near a stock campsite. When no one is using this campsite, horses can be tied to the hitching post while you enjoy a lunch break. It is only another 0.7 mile to Odessa Lake, but it is a steep trail, so your horse will appreciate the break now. Stopping here also gives you more time to enjoy the lovely view of Fern Lake and The Gable rising behind it.

Continue riding up the trail 0.7 mile to a signpost indicating that a hitching post is on a trail to the left. Turn left and tie the horses there, hiking the last 0.25 mile to Odessa Lake. Walk west from the hitching post until this trail ends at the main trail. Turn right for a very short distance, and then left at the spur trail headed west toward Odessa Lake. Take in the arresting views of Notchtop Mountain, Tabletop Mountain, and Little Matterhorn that are definitely a photo opportunity. Return the way you came.

Upper Beaver Meadows Road and Loop

Drive to the Trailhead	🗝 🗝 🗝
Parking	🅿
Amenities	A toilet and picnic table
Fee Area?	Rocky Mountain National Park fees apply
Elevation	8,400 feet
Maps	Trails Illustrated 200: Rocky Mountain National Park; USGS Longs Peak.

This is a simple place to drive to and to park. Unfortunately, only one car or trailer can park here, and the adjacent road is fairly busy. This trail is especially nice when the road to Upper Beaver Meadows is locked to prevent vehicles from driving on the road for the winter, generally from mid October through May. You can call visitor information to ask if the gate is open. See Appendix B for contact information.

Directions from Boulder County and Interstate Highway 25.

Drive to the Beaver Meadows parking area by heading west toward the town of Lyons on Colorado State Highway 66 from north Longmont or Interstate Highway 25 (exit 243), or on U.S. Highway 36 from Boulder. A gas station that also sells diesel, and can accommodate a truck pulling a trailer is located in Lyons. Look for it on the south side of Colorado

State Highway 66, shortly after the signal at the intersection of U.S. Highway 34 and Colorado State Highway 66.

Continue through Lyons on a one-way street, staying in the middle and then in the right-hand lane. At the west end of town, this lane becomes a right turn only lane; turn right toward Estes Park, and drive 20 miles on U.S. Highway 36. Go straight through the first signal in Estes Park, and turn left at the second signal, staying in the outside, or right, of the two left turn lanes. This is the junction with U.S. Highway 34. You are still on U.S. Highway 36, which you will follow through downtown Estes Park and the entrance station for the national park.

Directions from Larimer County
Drive to the Beaver Meadows parking area by heading west on U.S. Highway 34, about 30 miles past Loveland, and go straight through the first signal in Estes Park, staying in the right-hand lane. You are now on U.S. Highway 36, which you will follow through downtown Estes Park and the entrance station for the national park.

Directions from the intersection of Colorado State Highways 34 and 36 in Estes Park
After the scenery, Estes Park is best known for its awkward intersections, and this route drives through two of them in quick succession. At the third signal after the intersection of U.S. Highway 34 and U.S. Highway 36, both lanes are left turn lanes. Stay in the right-hand lane and turn left onto Moraine Avenue, heading south. At the next intersection you will be in a right turn lane. Vehicles in this lane do not need to stop at the intersection. Now you are headed west, toward the mountains, again. A gas station, fast food restaurant and grocery store that can be accessed by

a truck pulling a trailer are on the south side of this stretch of road.

Continue straight through the next signal, 1.9 miles from the intersection of U.S. Highway 34 and 36, and around a curve to your right. The Beaver Meadows Visitor Center is on the left, less than 1.0 mile from the last signal. Stop here to talk to a ranger, obtain a copy of their *Horse and Pack Animals* brochure, apply for a backcountry camping permit, or to visit the restrooms, the gift shop or the bookstore. You can park in the bus parking area.

Continue west past the Visitor Center on the main road for another 1.0 mile to the fee station. Drivers who have a plastic park pass with a magnetic strip on the back, and who do not need to speak to a ranger, or get a map or other information, can use the express lane on the right. Otherwise use any of the other lanes, where the rangers give out maps and current event information and collect entrance fees.

After the fee station, follow the road around a curve in the road to the right, until reaching a dirt road on the left for Beaver Meadows, 0.7 mile from the entrance station. Trailers can park in the pullout on the right side of the main road, across from the Beaver Meadows road.

Trail #19
Upper Beaver Meadows Road and Loop

Trail rideable	May through October
Best time to ride	Late October
Maximum elevation	9,600 feet
Difficulty	**Easy**
Terrain	♞
Training ability	✚
Length	9 miles round trip
Elevation gain	800 feet
Best features	Elk viewing
Obstacles	Vehicles on the Beaver Meadows Road, when the gate is open
Special notes	This ride can be extended with little additional elevation gain

This trail is just a short loop, but following other trails to the Moraine Park area can extend the ride. It is a lower elevation trail, which can be ridden when higher trails are still snowbound. This is also a popular elk viewing area in the fall. To see and hear the elk bugling here, come after noon in the latter part of September or early October, and you should be able to find some small bands near the trail. This loop is described in a counterclockwise direction, but it can be ridden in either direction.

From the trailer parking area, lead your horse across the paved road onto the dirt road, passing through or around the gate. Then ride 1.5 miles on the Beaver Meadows Road toward the small car parking area and trailhead. To access this trail, turn right

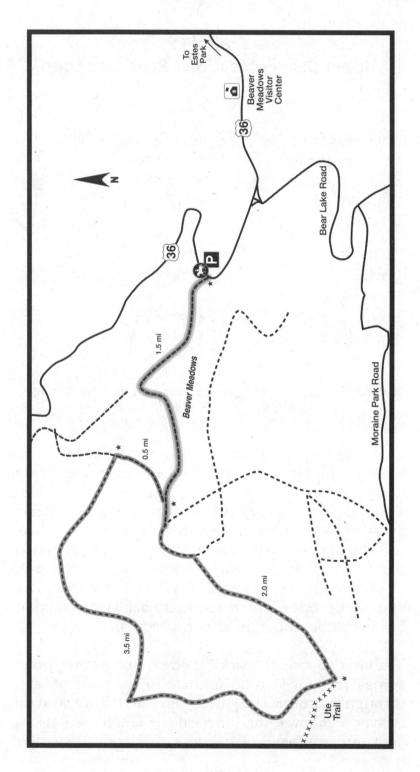

from the road onto a trail headed north, just before reaching the parking area. At the first trail junction turn left; the right-hand option goes to the highway. This route climbs 300 feet and passes less than 0.5 mile below the Many Parks Overlook on Trail Ridge Road. Then it levels off before making another ascent along the side of Beaver Mountain. The trail begins to lose elevation before the next junction where this route turns left. The Windy Gulch Trail to the right leads to Trail Ridge Road, but this trail is not open to horses. After 1.0 mile the trail encounters another junction. That trail is the first of two small loops in Upper Beaver meadows. The second one connects to a large loop around Beaver Meadows and the campground at Moraine Park. If you are interested in riding these loops, or the other small trails in this area, get out a map and start exploring.

This route stays left at each of the next two junctions, returning to the trailhead in 1.0 mile. Cross a very small stream just before the parking lot and return to your trailer by way of the road.

West Horseshoe Park

Drive to the parking lot	🔑 🔑 🔑
Parking	P P P
Amenities	None
Fee Area?	Rocky Mountain National Park fees apply
Elevation	8,500 feet
Maps	Trails Illustrated 200: Rocky Mountain National Park; USGS Estes Park and Trail Ridge

This is a huge pull-through parking lot, used chiefly in autumn for watching the elk bugling in the adjacent meadows, since it has no trails of interest to hikers. It does, however, have trails that lead to two other areas, making this paved lot perfect for parking horse trailers. This parking area is most easily reached from the Fall River entrance on the north side of the park.

Directions from Boulder County and Interstate Highway 25

Drive to West Horseshoe Park by heading west toward the town of Lyons on Colorado State Highway 66 from north Longmont or Interstate Highway 25 (exit 243), or on U.S. Highway 36 from Boulder. A gas station that also sells diesel, and can accommodate a truck pulling a trailer is located in Lyons. Look for it on the south side of Colorado State Highway 66, shortly after the signal at the intersection of U.S. Highway 34 and Colorado State Highway 66.

Continue through Lyons on a one-way street, staying in the middle and then in the right-hand lane. At the west end of town, this lane becomes a right turn only lane; turn right toward Estes Park, and drive 20 miles on U.S. Highway 36. Go straight through the first two signals in Estes Park. You are now on U.S. Highway 34, which you follow to the parking area.

Directions from Larimer County

Drive to West Horseshoe Park by heading west on U.S. Highway 34, about 30 miles past Loveland, and turn right at the first signal in Estes Park. This is the intersection of U.S. Highway 34 and U.S. Highway 36.

Directions from the intersection of U.S. Highways 34 and 36 in Estes Park

Stay on U.S. Highway 34, otherwise know as the Fall River Road, 4.7 miles to the fee station, passing the Gateway Visitor center on the left after 4.4 miles. This building is marked by a brown Visitors Center sign and another one for the Gateway Visitor Center, which are the same place. Stop here to talk to a ranger, to obtain a copy of their *Horse and Pack Animals* brochure, or to visit the restrooms, the gift shop or the bookstore. You can park in the bus parking area.

After the Fall River fee station, continue on this road for 2.6 more miles. Drive slowly as you pass through the mountain sheep viewing area. A large number of tourists, who may not be paying much attention to traffic, are usually looking for somewhat elusive sheep here. Continue around a left curve, passing a sign for Fall River Road and the Lawn Lake parking area on the right and a small parking area on the left. Then, after crossing a bridge over the Fall River, turn

171

left into a large parking area. A small sign indicates that this area is West Horseshoe Park. The lot is designed for cars to pull into the log barriers, but parking spaces are not marked and trailers will not fit that way, so park parallel to the logs on the right side. When leaving this parking area after the ride, drive straight toward the south end of the parking lot, then make a right turn onto the road and return the way you came.

The Fall River entrance to the park is the shorter way to this trailhead, and it is also a good way to drive to Trail Ridge Road, because it avoids the congestion in Estes Park. If you prefer to use the Beaver Meadows entrance, stay on the main road for 3.0 miles after leaving that fee station. The road starts to climb before the junction of Trail Ridge Road and U.S. Highway 34, which is the road into the Horseshoe Park area. Turn right at this junction and follow this road as it descends into Horseshoe Park. The large parking area is on the right, 1.5 miles from that junction, and is marked by a small sign for West Horseshoe Park.

Trail #20
Deer Mountain

Trail rideable	Late June through September
Best time to ride	July
Maximum elevation	10,000 feet
Difficulty	**Advanced** for mileage and elevation gain
Terrain	♘ ♘
Training ability	**+**
Length	11 miles round trip, or 12.5 miles round trip
Elevation gain	1,500 feet
Best features	Outstanding views of the mountains
Obstacles	A small boggy area, and dude horses on the lower part of the trail; small streams at the start of the trail offer the only water along this route
Special notes	A great, simple ride

This is a great ride that is not too long or complicated. The snow seems to melt off this trail rather early, considering its elevation. It can be ridden as an out and back, turning around at any point, or as a loop if you return on an alternate trail.

To access this trail, ride to the south end of the West Horseshoe Park parking area. A short distance down the trail, a signpost on the left indicates that it is 2.0 miles straight ahead to Deer Ridge Junction. Follow this route, passing through a somewhat boggy

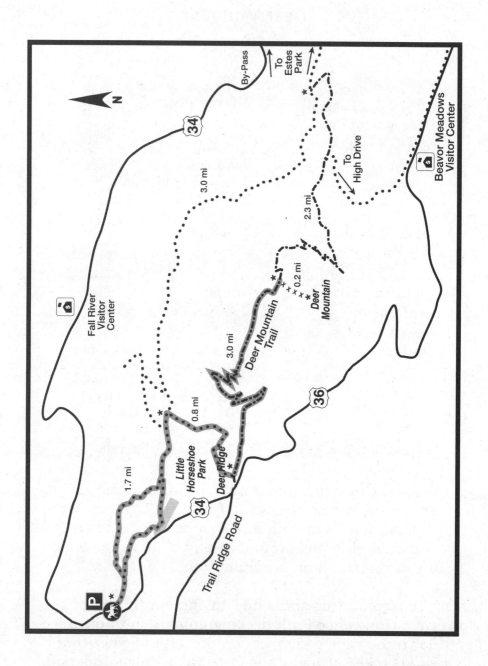

area. Stay on the trail to avoid doing more damage to the vegetation than is necessary. Along the next 0.5 mile are half a dozen small streams, followed by several trail junctions. These trails are all loops that eventually lead to the route described here, or to a dead end.

A signpost at the first junction indicates that the Aspenglen Campground is 1.2 miles straight ahead, Deer Ridge Junction is 1.7 miles to the right, and the loop trail goes both directions. The trail straight ahead is described first. Before long, this route comes to another signpost, which shows it is 1.0 mile from here to Horseshoe Park to the left, and the loop trail shortcut and North Deer Mountain Trail is straight ahead. Continue straight on this trail too, traversing up a ridge through a stand of lodgepole pine trees, until you reach the top of the ridge and another trail junction. A signpost there indicates the trail to the left leads to Deer Ridge Junction and the North Deer Mountain Trail, so turn left.

For the other option at the loop trail, make a right turn at the signpost that indicates Deer Ridge Junction is 1.7 miles to the right. That trail leads to a dirt road with an old camp at the end of it. Follow that road for a very short distance. The trail veers to the left, marked by a sign, before it reaches the camp. After this turnoff, the route runs along a ridge for a short distance before merging with the trail described above. On the ride back, the description uses this trail option.

After these trails merge, the route descends into a wonderful meadow before arriving at another trail junction. This one has a signpost showing Aspenglen Campground to the left, North Deer Mountain Trail and Deer Ridge Junction straight ahead, and Horseshoe Park back the way you came. The trail to the campground is one of the trails used by the Gateway Riding Stable. It can be ridden as a loop and has attractive scenery, but the trail is very dusty and is not well maintained by the riding stable.

This route goes straight through this junction, and when the trail heads up the far side of this meadow another signpost comes into view. This reads 0.9 mile straight ahead to the Deer Mountain Junction, 1.7 miles back to Horseshoe Park, and 4.6 miles to Estes Park on the left trail option.

Stay right, heading toward the south, and across the bottom of Deer Mountain. After 1.0 more mile, this route merges with a trail on the right, which leads to the trailhead for hikers. Stay left at this junction. The next 3.0 miles of trail to Deer Ridge Summit has an abundance of hikers. Follow this route, riding up a gradual incline and then through a meadow scattered with ponderosa pine trees. Stop to enjoy the incredible views to the south of Beaver Meadows and the mountains, including Meeker Mountain and Longs Peak as well as Chiefs

Head Peak, McHenrys Peak, Hallett Peak and Flattop Mountain. Longs Peak is the highest point in Rocky Mountain National Park at 14,259 feet. Mount Meeker is a close second at 13,911 feet. Even without the views, this is an attractive area with grass, wildflowers, and aspen trees.

The trail then makes numerous switchbacks across the west side of the mountain. As the trail travels from south to north and back again, the views just keep getting better and better. The vista starts at Longs Peak and Chiefs Head to the south, and along the Continental Divide to the west. Then the Mummy Range to the North, including Mounts Chapin and Chiquita, Ypsilon Mountain, and Mummy Mountain comes into view. Ypsilon Mountain can be identified by its couloirs in the shape of a "Y" that hold the snow until late in the summer, showing a white outline of its namesake. Below, in the valley, is a nice view of the West Horseshoe Park area. Although this mountain is a steep climb for horses, the captivating views make it simple to stop often for them to rest.

The mixed evergreen and aspen forest here is unremarkable except for its diversity, having fir, spruce, and pine trees. As the trail climbs up the mountain, the switchbacks become shorter and steeper. Where the trail levels out and heads west, some trees show evidence of old fires started by lightning. This is not a good place to be when the weather is threatening, as intense storms can form suddenly near the summit of Deer Mountain, even when the trail below is pleasant. From here the trail is almost level for 0.5 mile, before reaching a junction with the trail to the summit. This last 0.2 mile of the trail is not open to horses, but a hitching post is straight ahead. Estes Park, the YMCA, and other areas that are not usually seen from above can be viewed from the summit and are worth the stiff hike. Because this trail is popular with tourists and the hitching post is within view of the trail, take turns watching the horses and hiking up the trail to enjoy the interesting view.

Return the way you came, turning right at the first trail junction, toward Aspenglen Campground, and left at the second one, toward Horseshoe Park. At each subsequent trail junction, follow the signs to Horseshoe Park. This route returns to the parking lot a slightly different way, making the ride more interesting and simplifying the route finding. After the boggy area, ride straight toward the parking area, at the last junction.

To increase the total ride mileage to 12.5 miles and leave the crowds behind, continue to the east from the hitching post. Connect with the North Deer Mountain Trail by heading down the mountain from the junction near the hitching post, on the trail labeled Estes Park. The trail descends steeply at first, switchbacking along the east side of the mountain. While somewhat rockier than the route up the mountain, the footing soon improves. This trail swings toward the south with delightful views of Twin Sisters Mountain, Longs Peak, Meeker Mountain, and an interesting perspective of the Beaver Meadows Entrance Station and Marys Lake.

After 2.5 miles, a trail junction comes into view on the right. That trail leads to a residential area called High Drive, so continue straight ahead, following the signs to Estes Park. After that junction, this route heads northward with views of Estes Park and Lake Estes. It is impossible not to notice the power lines that take hydroelectric power produced here, with water brought by tunnel from Grand Lake, to the Front Range. Before long, the trail comes to another junction. Going straight leads to the Elkhorn stables in Estes Park, but to head back to Horseshoe Park and your horse trailer, turn left onto the North Deer Mountain Trail.

This trail traverses the side of Deer Mountain for its entire length. The forest is interesting, as it changes periodically from mixed evergreen and aspen trees, to lodgepole pine trees. The Park Service has done some thinning of the lodgepole pine trees, which grow close together and burn very hot and fast when ignited. This is nature's way of starting fresh, as the fire opens up the forest floor to the sun and allows the lodgepole's seeds to germinate. However, when a forest fire starts this close to a town, it is preferable if it burns at a slower rate.

After 4.0 miles this route comes to a trail junction it passed on the way in. Follow the signs to Horseshoe Park at each trail junction. This route returns to the trailhead a slightly different way, making the ride more interesting and simplifying the route finding. After the boggy area, go straight at the last junction to the parking area.

Trail #21
North Deer Mountain

Trail rideable	July to August
Best time to ride	August, when the shady trail is appreciated
Maximum elevation	8,800 feet
Difficulty	**Moderate** for mileage
Terrain	♘
Training ability	✚
Length	9.4 miles or up to 12.5 miles, round trip
Elevation gain	300 feet
Best features	This route has little elevation gain; even on the busiest of weekends the trail is lightly used and has plenty of shade
Obstacles	A small boggy area, and dude horses on the lower part of the trail; small streams at the start of the trail offer the only water along this route
Special notes	This is a summertime ride only, due to northern exposure

This route travels along the north side of Deer Mountain. It is not a particularly memorable trail, as it is mostly in the trees, but it is a nice training ride, as it has little elevation change and no obstacles other than some mud and small streams in the first 0.5 mile. Because this trail is on the north side of the mountain and continually in the shade, avoid it early in the year and after the first snowfall in autumn. During the summer it is a nice respite from the sun and the crowds.

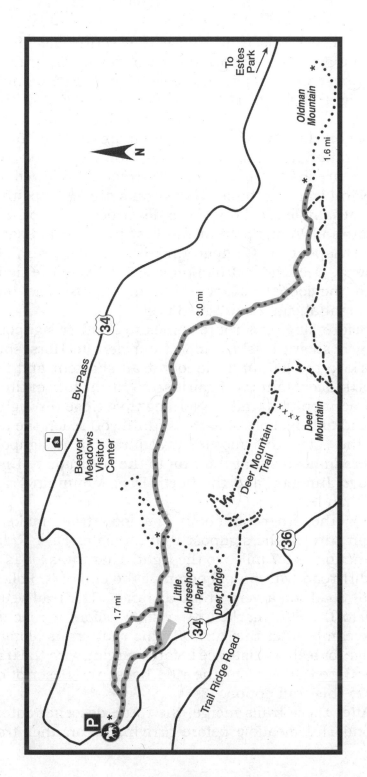

To Estes Park

Oldman
Mountain

*

1.6 mi

N

*

3.0 mi

34
By-Pass

Beaver
Meadows
Visitor
Center

Deer
Mountain

Deer Mountain Trail

x x x

36

1.7 mi

Little
Horseshoe
Park

Deer Ridge

*

34

Trail Ridge Road

P

*

181

To access this trail, ride to the south end of the parking area. A short distance down the trail, a signpost on the left indicates that it is 2.0 miles straight ahead to Deer Ridge Junction. Follow this route, passing through a somewhat boggy area. Stay on the trail to avoid doing more damage to the vegetation than is necessary. Along the next 0.5 mile are half a dozen small streams, followed by several trail junctions. These trails are all loops that eventually lead to the route described here, or to a dead end. A signpost at the first junction indicates that Aspenglen Campground is 1.2 miles straight ahead, Deer Ridge Junction is 1.7 miles to the right, and the loop trail goes both directions. The trail straight ahead is described first.

Before long, this route comes to another signpost, which shows it is 1.0 mile from here to Horseshoe Park to the left, and the loop trail shortcut and the North Deer Mountain Trail is straight ahead. Continue straight on this trail, traversing up a ridge through a stand of lodgepole pine trees, until you reach the top of the ridge and another trail junction. A signpost there indicates that the trail to the left leads to Deer Ridge Junction and the North Deer Mountain Trail, so turn left.

For the other option at the loop trail, make a right turn at the signpost that indicates Deer Ridge Junction is 1.7 miles to the right. That trails leads to a dirt road with an old camp at the end of it. Follow that road for a very short distance. The trail veers off to the left, marked by a sign, before it reaches the camp. After this turnoff, this route runs along a ridge for a short distance before merging with the trail described above. On the ride back, the description uses this trail option.

After these trails merge, the route descends into a wonderful meadow before arriving at another trail junction. This one has a signpost showing Aspenglen Campground to the left, North Deer Mountain Trail and Deer Ridge Junction straight ahead, and Horseshoe Park back the way you came. The trail to the campground is one of the trails used by the Gateway Riding Stable. It can be ridden as a loop and has attractive scenery, but the trail is very dusty and not well maintained by the riding stable.

This route goes straight through that junction and when the trail heads up the far side of the meadow another signpost comes into view. This reads 0.9 mile straight ahead to the Deer Mountain Junction, 1.7 miles back to Horseshoe Park, and 4.6 miles to Estes Park on the left trail option, which is the one this route takes.

This trail traverses the side of Deer Mountain for its entire length. The forest here is interesting as it changes periodically from mixed evergreen and aspen trees, to lodgepole pine trees. The Park Service has done some thinning of the lodgepole pines trees, which grow close together and burn very hot and fast when ignited. This is nature's way of starting fresh, as the fire opens up the forest floor to the sun and allows the lodgepole's seeds to germinate, but when a forest fire starts this close to a town, it is preferable if it burns at a slower rate.

After 3.0 miles the trail comes to a junction at a grassy knoll. This open area is a nice place to have lunch before turning around. Continuing on the trail to Estes Park from this junction increases this route's mileage to 13 miles round trip. Return the way you came, following the signs to Horseshoe Park at each trail junction. This route returns to the trailhead a slightly different way, making the ride more interesting and simplifying the route finding. After the boggy area, ride straight toward the parking area, at the last junction.

Trail #22
Lawn Lake

Trail rideable	July to August
Best time to ride	July
Maximum elevation	11,000 feet
Difficulty	**Advanced** due to mileage and elevation gain
Terrain	♘ ♘
Training ability	**+**
Length	15.2 miles round trip
Elevation gain	2,500 feet
Best features	The dramatic display of the force of water
Obstacles	One shallow river to ford that is a good training opportunity
Special notes	Do not attempt this trail in June, due to ice on the trail

This is a nice straightforward trail, which gets up high enough that the temperature is comfortable on even the hottest day. It is also interesting due to historical and geological features. This trail has more mileage than Ypsilon Lake, but it is not as steep and has better footing.

Water has always been a precious resource in Colorado, and in the early part of the century many mountain lakes were dammed so they could collect more water and be used as reservoirs. In the early 1900s a dam was built at the outlet of Lawn Lake, allowing it to hold a substantial amount of additional water. In 1982 this dam collapsed,

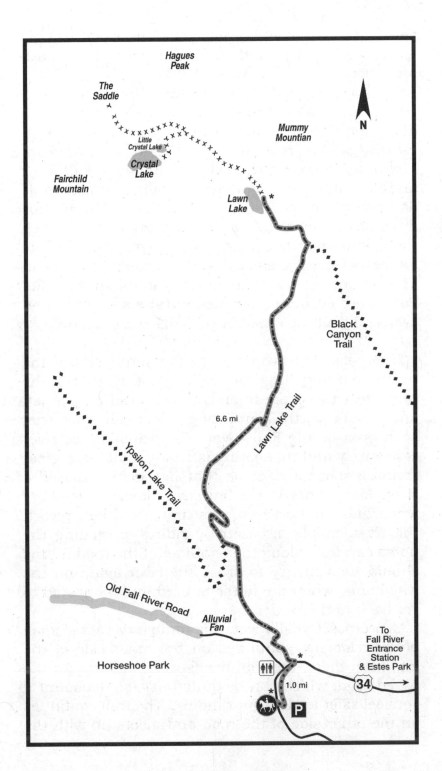

Hagues
Peak

The
Saddle

Little
Crystal Lake

Crystal
Lake

Fairchild
Mountain

Mummy
Mountian

Lawn
Lake

Black
Canyon
Trail

Lawn Lake Trail

6.6 mi

Ypsilon Lake Trail

Old Fall River Road

Alluvial
Fan

Horseshoe Park

To
Fall River
Entrance
Station
& Estes Park

34

1.0 mi

N

sending a wall of water down the mountain, taking trees, rocks, dirt and anything else in its path along with it.

The water slowed upon reaching Horseshoe Park, where the land levels out. Some of the debris was left at the mouth of the canyon that the river carved out, creating what is referred to today as the Alluvial Fan. The water, however, rushed on, joining the Fall River and continuing to surge down the valley. Considerable damage was done to the town of Estes Park by this flash flood, since the Fall River runs right through the middle of town. The need to remove obsolete dams was made clear from this catastrophic event. The remaining dams in Rocky Mountain National Park were evaluated for structural soundness, and eventually all the dams in the park were removed.

To access this trail, ride to the south end of the trailer parking area. After a short distance, the route to Lawn Lake intersects this trail on the left and heads north, paralleling the road. This trail soon crosses the Fall River. The water in the river is leisurely and the footing is sandy, making a great training spot for a horse that has never crossed a river. Many horses will happily splash across here when another horse crosses first. As a last resort, the river can be crossed by riding or leading the horse carefully along the shoulder of the road. If this should happen, try to cross the river again on the way home, when the horse is tired and motivated to get back to the trailer.

After crossing Fall River, this route traverses a small parking lot and continues on the other side of the lot. From there, the trail heads west and crosses the paved road, which can be quite busy, so dismount if you feel safer leading your mount. The trail continues on the other side of the road and meets up with the main trail in 0.2 miles, just above a parking lot that serves as the Lawn Lake Trailhead. The restroom here is the only one available along this route, but it is not particularly convenient when on horseback. The trail then traverses up the hill, passing a trail on the left that is used by the riding stables, whose riders then dismount and walk to the Alluvial Fan area.

This route continues to switchback steeply up the sunny hillside for a short distance, before heading west to the canyon carved out by the Roaring River when it came sweeping down the mountain. The trail follows this canyon for another 5.0 miles to the Lawn Lake, affording interesting views. Before long, the trail junction for Ypsilon Lake comes into view on the left. That trail crosses the river shortly after leaving the Lawn Lake Trail, and provides the only opportunity for horses to have a drink on this trail.

Continue up the trail, gradually but steadily gaining elevation. At one point, the trail crosses a tiny stream in a north facing area. In the summertime this stream is barely noticeable, but in the winter it becomes a small ice flow, which remains long after all the snow on the trail has disappeared in the spring, making the trail impassable to horses until it melts. Further up, the trail opens out and the vegetation becomes astonishingly lush. 6.0 miles from the trailer parking area, this route passes the Black Canyon trail heading up Mummy Mountain, on the right. That is a rocky and steep trail, and while not treacherous, there seems little reason to clamber up it.

Continuing straight, the trail arrives at the lake within 0.5 mile. The patrol cabin and corral located here are for the use of park rangers; a hitching post on the shore of the lake and the restroom are for public use. Lawn Lake has an imposing backdrop of Mummy Mountain on the north, and Fairchild Mountain on the west. The lake itself is rather barren, since the shores have not recovered their vegetation after being under water for over seventy years.

The trail continues to two lakes on Fairchild Mountain and to the saddle between Fairchild and Mummy Mountains, but horses are not allowed past the hitching post. The Saddle, where the hiking trail ends, is 0.5 mile further and another 600 feet of elevation gain; Crystal Lake, which may be the deepest lake in the park, is 1.0 mile away with 600 feet of elevation gain. Return to the parking lot the way you came.

Trail #23
Ypsilon Lake

Trail rideable	July to August
Best time to ride	July
Maximum elevation	10,700 feet
Difficulty	**Demanding** due to the footing and elevation gain
Terrain	♘ ♘ ♘ ♘
Training ability	**+ +**
Length	10 miles round trip
Elevation gain	2,100 feet
Best features	Historical and geological interest
Obstacles	Two rivers to ford
Special notes	This trail can be ridden earlier than the Lawn Lake Trail

While this trail has the advantage of being shorter and has less elevation gain than the Lawn Lake Trail, it is a more difficult trail because it is steeper and the footing is challenging. I find this a less enjoyable ride due to the rocky trail, lack of views, and the fact that the lake is much less attractive than Lawn Lake.

To access this trail, ride to the south end of the parking area. After a short distance, the route to Ypsilon Lake intersects this trail on the left and heads north, paralleling the road. Before long, the trail crosses the Fall River.

After the river, this route traverses a small parking lot, continuing on the other side. From there, the trail heads west and crosses the paved road, which can

189

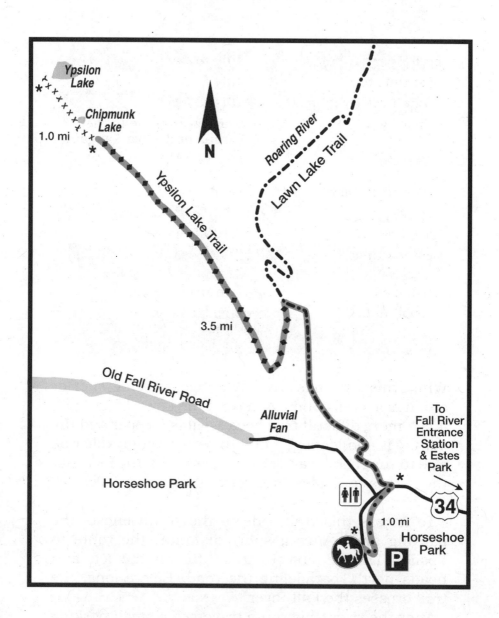

Ypsilon Lake

Chipmunk Lake

1.0 mi

Ypsilon Lake Trail

N

Roaring River

Lawn Lake Trail

3.5 mi

Old Fall River Road

Alluvial Fan

Horseshoe Park

To Fall River Entrance Station & Estes Park

34

1.0 mi

Horseshoe Park

P

be quite busy, so dismount if you feel safer leading your mount. The trail continues on the other side of the road and meets up with the main trail in 0.25 mile, just above the parking lot that serves as the Ypsilon Lake Trailhead. This restroom is the only one available along this route, but it is not particularly convenient to access when on horseback. The trail then traverses up the hill, passing a trail on the left that is used by the riding stables, whose riders then dismount and walk to the Alluvial Fan area.

This route continues to switchback steeply up the sunny hillside for a short distance, then heads west to the canyon carved out by the Roaring River when it came sweeping down the mountain. Before long, the trail junction for Ypsilon Lake comes into view on the left. This trail crosses the river shortly after leaving the Lawn Lake Trail, and provides the only opportunity for horses to have a drink on this route.

A footbridge is provided for hikers, but horses are expected to ford the river, which is wide but not too deep, and somewhat fast and rocky.

After the river, this trail ascends steadily upward over rocky footing. For the next 3.0 miles this route travels through a lodgepole pine forest, with occasional glimpses of Ypsilon Peak. Then the trail descends towards the lake. Early in the season this north facing spot can be icy. It is a 1.0 mile ride to the lake that passes an overgrown pond called Chipmunk Lake, with Fairchild Mountain as a backdrop, along the way. The trail then accesses Ypsilon Lake at its west end, denying trail users a view of the lake with mountains behind it. The small waterfall on the stream coming into the lake is more attractive than the lake itself. A hitching post is available here. Return the way you came.

Lumpy Ridge / Cow Creek Trailhead

Drive to the trailhead	🔑 🔑 🔑
Parking	P
Amenities	None
Fee Area?	No
Elevation	7,800 feet
Maps	Trails Illustrated 200: Rocky Mountain National Park; USGS Estes Park and Glen Haven

All Rocky Mountain National Park rules apply to this trail

This wonderful area of Rocky Mountain National Park has had no parking for horse trailers for many years. A new parking lot opened here in 2007. It literally took an act of Congress to accomplish this feat, as it involved a land exchange between the national park and McGregor Ranch, to provide an appropriate place to put the parking lot. It provides parking for two horse trailers. However, it is questionable if one could pull far enough off the road to keep from being hit by passing cars. The person on the passenger side of the tow vehicle has to exit on the driver's side, as the area on the right side of the road has a steep drop-off. The horses have to be tied to the back of the trailer and if the tack room is on the right side of the trailer, it cannot be accessed due the steep drop-off. We had to pass on this parking lot for that reason. No fee station is planned here. If enough of us express concern about the safety issues of this parking area, perhaps it could be changed.

Equally challenging parking options exist at Cow Creek to access this area. Directions for that trailhead continue below from this parking area.

Directions from Boulder County and Interstate Highway 25.

Drive to the Lumpy Ridge Trailhead by traveling west toward the town of Lyons on Colorado State Highway 66 from north Longmont or Interstate Highway 25 (exit 243), or on U.S. Highway 36 from Boulder. A gas station that also sells diesel, and can accommodate a truck pulling a trailer is located in Lyons. Look for it on the south side of Colorado State Highway 66, shortly after the signal at the intersection of U.S. Highway 34 and Colorado State Highway 66.

Continue through Lyons on a one-way street, staying in the middle and then in the right-hand lane. At the west end of town, this lane becomes a right turn only lane; turn right toward Estes Park, and drive 20 miles on U.S. Highway 36. Go straight through the first and second signals in Estes Park. The second signal is the junction with U.S. Highway 34.

Directions from Larimer County

Drive to the Lumpy Ridge Trailhead by traveling west on U.S. Highway 34 about 30 miles from Loveland, and turn right at the first signal in Estes Park. This is the junction with U.S. Highway 36.

Directions from the intersection of Colorado State Highways 34 and 36 in Estes Park

Follow this highway 0.4 mile, driving by the Stanley Hotel, and make a right turn onto MacGregor Avenue. Follow this road for 1.3 miles. After 0.8 mile the road makes a 90-degree turn at the entrance to MacGregor Ranch. After turning east, look for the parking lot on the left. It is well signed and the trailer parking, which is on the right side of the road before reaching the auto parking area, is signed as well.

Trailers used to be able to park at the Cow Creek Trailhead at McGraw Ranch, but the parking at this privately owned area with no fee station has been severely limited in the last few years, effectively barring trailers from using it. Parking here has been downsized to seventeen spaces on the west side of the road. A very early arrival is required to find enough room for a trailer. McGraw Ranch is, however, a nice access point to this area.

To access the Cow Creek Trailhead, continue east on MacGregor Avenue. A dirt road to McGraw Ranch veers off to the left after 2.2 miles, between mileage markers 3 and 4. An electronic sign there shows "full" most of the time, but I have not found it to be particularly accurate. The Cow Creek Trailhead is 2.2 miles further on a dirt road, coming to an area near the ranch buildings where trailers can pull off the road and back around to get headed in the opposite direction.

If you are lucky enough to secure parking here, ride down the road and through the turnaround area near the cabins, continuing past the cabins and riding up the trail, passing the Taj Mahal of pit toilets along the way. The North Boundary Trail, also known as the North Fork Trail intersects this trail on the right, and connects with the Lost Lake Trail. That trail is outside the park boundaries, and is popular with hunters. It is a north–south trail over several east–west ridges. As a result, the entire trail is very steep up and down repeatedly, with treacherous river crossings at the bottom of each descent, so it is rated **Dangerous**.

Continue west, paralleling Cow Creek for 1.0 mile, where the Gem Lake Trail joins it on the left. From here, follow the directions for the Gem Lake loop description below.

Trail #24
Gem Lake loop

Trail rideable	June through October
Best time to ride	Late September
Maximum elevation	9,100 feet
Difficulty	**Advanced** due to the terrain and mileage
Terrain	♘ ♘ ♘ due to one steep rocky area and steep stepped areas
Training ability	**+ +**
Length	9.1 miles round trip
Elevation gain	1,600 feet
Best features	Aspen trees in autumn
Obstacles	Steep stair stepped trails, two small streams and two gates
Special notes	The trail passes through the McGregor Ranch pasture

This is a great and varied little loop trail, without too much altitude gain. The ascents and descents are mixed up some, making it a good conditioning ride.

To access this trail from the trailer parking area, lead your horse up the road to the auto parking lot, where the trail starts, to mount your horse. After 0.3 mile, this route intersects the main trail. Turn right toward Gem Lake. Watch for unusual rock formations, especially the one named "Paul Bunyan's Boot," which is just off the main trail with a well-worn trail to and around it. It is on a flat area between two sets of switchbacks, and can be easily spotted because of the hole in the "sole" of the boot.

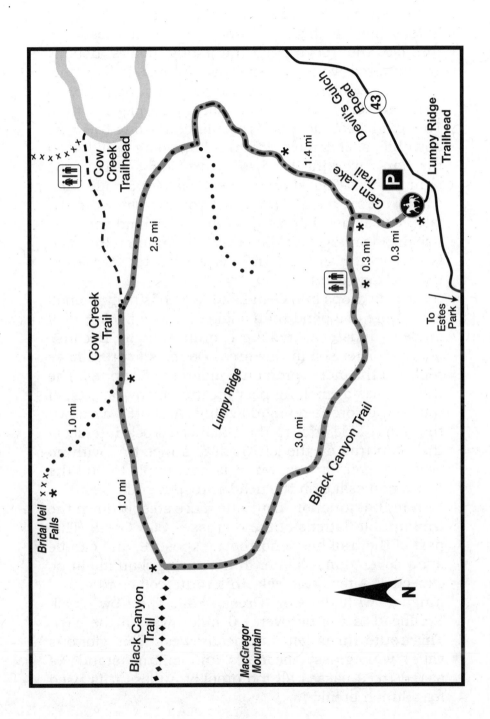

Cow Creek Trailhead

Cow Creek Trail

2.5 mi

Bridal Veil Falls

1.0 mi

1.0 mi

Black Canyon Trail

MacGregor Mountain

Lumpy Ridge

Black Canyon Trail

3.0 mi

Gem Lake Trail

Devil's Gulch Road

43

Lumpy Ridge Trailhead

1.4 mi

0.3 mi

0.3 mi

To Estes Park

P

N

The trail twists and turns up a rock stairway, and horses have to pay attention to find the best way through the rocks and the many hikers usually encountered working their way up and down it too. You may want to dismount if your mount is not in shape to carry you up this challenging piece of trail. This guidebook does not recommend riding this trail downhill, as it is more difficult than going uphill, with the horse working hard to control his speed in the tight turns. This stairway only lasts 0.5 mile, and when you see a sign for a toilet you are almost to the lake. Once past that sign, try to look behind you. The one disadvantage to riding this loop counterclockwise is that you miss the terrific view of Estes Park from this vantage point.

The trail drops into Gem Lake, which is truly a small gem. More of a pond than a lake, it has a backdrop of eroded sandstone, making it quite unique. Because of the moister soil in this area, Douglas fir trees have replaced the more common ponderosa pine trees. The trail passes a hitching post on the northwest side of the lake before heading downhill. A short way down the hill, a side trail to the Balanced Rock intersects the main trail on the left. That is a nice trail with no elevation gain or loss, but it is not simple to find the trail's namesake on the dead end spur trail.

From that junction, continue more steeply down the trail until it flattens out and crosses Cow Creek. This part of the trail has a northern exposure, and can be snow covered much later in the spring than might be expected. After the creek, this route comes to a trail junction with the Cow Creek Trail. The Cow Creek Trailhead is a little over 1.0 mile away to the east. This route turns left and heads west. This glorious valley with grassy meadows and mature stands of aspen trees passes all too quickly, unless it is used for a lunch break.

A trail to Bridal Veil Falls leaves the main trail on the right, 0.5 mile from the Gem Lake Trail junction. That popular destination for hikers is less than 1.0 mile away with little elevation gain or loss. Although that trail is fairly wide at the beginning, it becomes more and more narrow until reaching a hitching post. From there it is a short distance to a nice little waterfall on foot.

Just past that junction this route crosses Cow Creek again. This stream is the last time horses have an opportunity for a drink on this loop. Soon, the trail changes character as it becomes drier and rockier and starts a slow but distinct ascent. After some rocky spots, the trail leaves the aspen groves for a dense evergreen forest, where it switchbacks up a steep and sometimes stair-stepped ridge as it makes its way out of the Cow Creek drainage. This hill is also on a northern exposure, and remains slippery long after the snow has melted off the other trails at this altitude. A trail junction is encountered at the top of the hill, only 1.0 mile from the Bridal Veil Trail junction. Turn left there, following the Black Canyon Trail as it makes a gentle descent for 3.0 miles to Twin Owls. Along the way, the dramatic rock formations of Lumpy Ridge can be seen on the left. At this popular rock climbing area, people can usually be seen climbing the rock faces, but they are tiny unless binoculars are used for a better view.

This route passes through a recently installed gate that replaced a large, heavy gate. The trail crosses a pasture belonging to the MacGregor Ranch, which has been in operation since 1874. Their Hereford cattle and horses graze this meadow much of the year. Please keep your horses on the trail, and do not approach their livestock as they have generously made this trail available to Rocky Mountain National Park trail users. The ranch has a museum and hosts living history days to allow the public to see more of it.

Before long, the trail comes to another fence with a new horse-friendly gate. The old gate is still there for hikers, and is a nice reminder for equestrians to be thankful they no longer have to get their horses through it! Make sure you securely close and latch both gates after using them. You may have to dismount to do this, since the latches are quite low, but they are a huge improvement from the previous gates.

Soon the trail arrives at the Twin Owls, named for the rock formation that towers over this area. In the summertime, a drinking fountain is available there. Then the trail heads up one last hill 0.5 mile long before reaching the junction for the trail back to the Lumpy Ridge parking lot. Turn right and follow this trail that you rode in on 0.3 mile to the parking lot, where you can dismount and lead your horse back to your trailer.

Trail #25
Black Canyon Trail

Trail rideable	June through October
Best time to ride	July
Maximum elevation	Up to 11,000 feet
Difficulty	**Moderate** to **Demanding** due to the distance and elevation gain
Terrain	♘ ♘
Training ability	**+**
Length	7.2 to 17.2 miles round trip
Elevation gain	1,200 to 3,200 feet
Best features	The lower part of this trail is accessible year round
Obstacles	Two gates
Special notes	Turn around at any point, no water for horses to drink; Rocky Mountain National Park rules apply

This makes a great conditioning ride, as it is a continuous but not steep climb as far up the mountain as you are willing to go; riders can turn around at any point. Since the trail is mostly sunny the snow melts quickly, making the first 4.0 miles rideable most of the year. In the springtime, the rest of the trail can be ridden until a snowdrift stops you.

To access this trail from the trailer parking area, lead your horse up the road to the auto parking lot. Mount your horse at the trailhead. After 0.3 mile, this route intersects the main trail. Turn left toward the Twin Owls. This trail drops gently for another 0.5

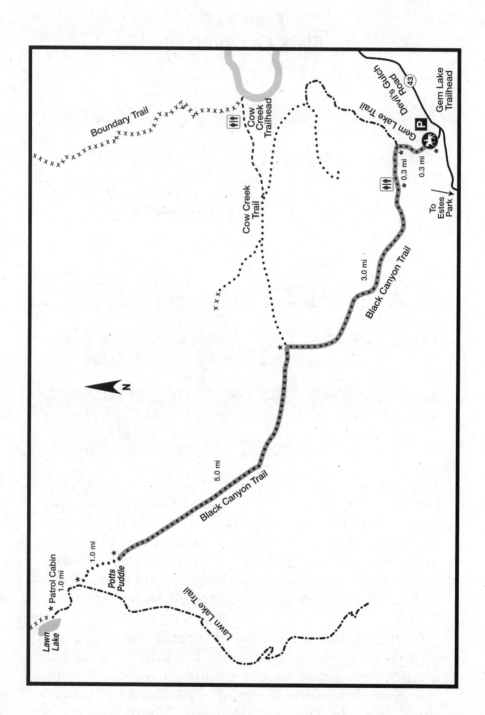

mile, before arriving at the area named for the rock formation that towers over it. A drinking fountain that is usable in the summertime is located here. Continue on the trail 0.2 mile, and go through a new horse friendly gate in a fence.

The trail then crosses the pasture for the MacGregor Ranch, which has been in operation since 1874. Their Hereford cattle and horses graze this meadow much of the year. Please keep your horses on the trail, and do not approach their livestock as they have generously made this trail available to Rocky Mountain National Park trail users. The ranch has a museum and hosts living history days to allow the public to see more of it.

Along the way, enjoy the dramatic rock formations of Lumpy Ridge on your right. At this popular rock climbing area, people can usually be seen climbing the rock faces, but they are tiny unless binoculars are used for a better view. When leaving the MacGregor Ranch, the trail passes through another recently installed gate that replaced a large, heavy gate. Make sure to securely close and latch both gates after using them. This requires dismounting because the latches are quite low, but they are a huge improvement from the previous gates. The trail makes a gentle ascent for 3.0 miles to the junction with the Cow Creek Trail. This junction is the turnaround point for this route in the wintertime, making a 7.2-mile ride round trip from the Lumpy Ridge parking lot.

Turn left to continue on the Black Canyon Trail, which drops down a small incline before climbing continuously again. After 1.0 mile, the trail passes the MacGregor Mountain campsite at around 9,000 feet elevation. The Big Horn campsite, which is approved for groups and livestock, is 3.0 miles further on the left at around 10,000 feet elevation. Along the way, the trail passes through meadows and forests. Two more campsites and an area of meadows lie beyond the Big Horn stock site, as well as a small pond appropriately named Potts Puddle. The description of this ride ends there, although the trail continues 2.0 miles to Lawn Lake down a steep and rocky trail. Turn around near Potts Puddle and congratulate your horse for a long day's ride, as you are still 8.6 miles from the Lumpy Ridge parking area.

Trails in Rocky Mountain National Park, West of the Continental Divide

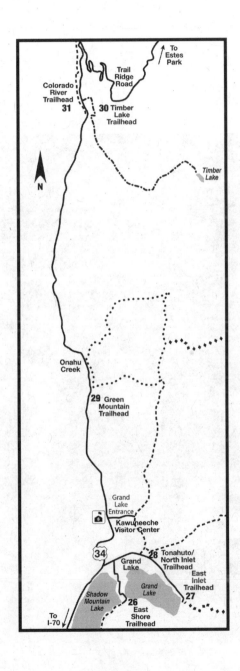

Trails accessed from U.S. Highway 34 near Grand Lake

East Shore Trailhead

Drive to the trailhead	🗝🗝
Parking	🅿 🅿
Amenities	None
Fee Area?	No, because the trailhead is outside the park boundary
Elevation	7,800 feet
Maps	Trails Illustrated 200: Rocky Mountain National Park; USGS Grand Lake and Shadow Mountain

The directions to this trailhead have lots of turns, but it is close to Grand Lake, and has adequate parking. If you go into town without your trailer, drive the route ahead of time. The trailhead is near the spit of land that separates Grand Lake from Shadow Mountain Lake.

Directions from U.S. Highway 34 in Grand County

From U.S. Highway 34 drive to the East Shore Trailhead by turning east at the sign for Grand Lake onto Colorado State Highway 278. After 0.2 mile, turn right onto Center Drive. Turn left after another 0.2 mile onto Marina Drive, and turn right one block later onto Shadow Mountain Drive. Turn right again after 0.3 mile, onto Jericho Road. Cross the bridge, drive 0.5 mile, and turn left onto Shoreline Landing at the stop sign. Parking for the trailhead is in the lot just ahead.

This trail can also be accessed from the south end of Shadow Mountain Lake, a few miles to the south of Grand Lake. To drive there from U.S. Highway 34, turn east at the sign for the Green Mountain Campground area, and park near the dam. From there, cross the dam and decide whether to ride north, a maximum of 6.0 miles round trip, or south, a maximum of 17 miles round trip.

Trail #26
East Shore Trail

Trail rideable	June through September
Best time to ride	June or September
Maximum elevation	8,600 feet
Difficulty	**Easy** to **Advanced** depending on mileage
Terrain	♘ this trail could be ridden barefoot
Training ability	✛
Length	1.0 to 23 miles round trip
Elevation gain	Negligible
Best features	Nice training or acclimatization ride
Obstacles	Up to seven stream crossings
Special notes	Plenty of shade on sunny days, all Rocky Mountain National Park rules apply to this trail except in areas that are outside of the park boundaries

This nice **Easy** trail can be accessed at both ends as well as in the middle, and riders can turn around at any point. It follows the eastern shoreline of Shadow Mountain Lake and Lake Granby, which are obviously not lakes at all, but reservoirs created by damming the Colorado River. The entire route has signposts indicating that it is part of the Continental Divide Trail that runs from Mexico to Canada.

Access the trail from the east side of the parking lot. Then turn right, proceeding south. After 0.7 mile, a signboard marks the boundary for Rocky Mountain

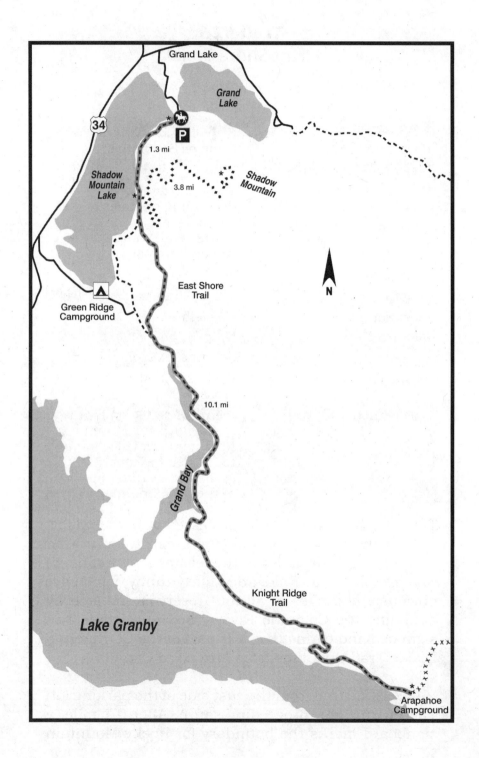

Grand Lake

Grand Lake

34

1.3 mi

Shadow Mountain Lake

3.8 mi

Shadow Mountain

East Shore Trail

N

Green Ridge Campground

10.1 mi

Grand Bay

Knight Ridge Trail

Lake Granby

Arapahoe Campground

210

National Park. After another 0.6 mile of riding along the shoreline of Shadow Mountain Reservoir, a trail for the Shadow Mountain Trail climbs uphill, on the left. Horses can only go up part of the 3.8 miles to the summit before it becomes too steep and rocky for their hooves.

Stay to the right, and before long the route comes to a fork in the trail. The trail on the right follows the shoreline through a marshy area and past a busy marina and campground. This is the alternate parking area mentioned in the trailhead description.

The trail on the left heads inland and bypasses that busy area before the trails reunite 1.5 miles south of the dam. This route follows the trail to the left, crossing Ranger Creek after 0.7 mile. After this creek, the trail comes to an area of meadows where it becomes faint, making it difficult to follow. Cross the 0.2-mile long meadow, and then enter the forest again for a short distance before coming to another meadow. The trail skirts this meadow on the east side for another 0.2 mile, before heading back into the trees for a short distance, and then reaching another small meadow. From here, the trail heads west, entering a lodgepole pine and aspen forest. After another 0.2 mile the trail crosses yet another meadow. The trail from the marina joins this route on the right, 0.2 mile from the end of that meadow. Another trail from the marina joins this one 0.2 mile further down the trail on the right. Stay left both times, and before long this trail crosses Pole Creek. When the trail reaches the Colorado River, it follows it southward. This beautiful area makes a nice lunch stop. The route to here is 7.5 miles round trip.

The river begins to widen 1.5 miles south of the marina, due to another dam downstream. After passing Columbine Bay, the trail follows the banks of Grand Bay, which is an arm of the massive Lake Granby.

This route leaves Rocky Mountain National Park 2.5 miles and 3 stream crossings further down the trail. Over the next 5.5 miles, the trail travels back and forth several times, crossing the boundary between the Arapahoe National Forest and the Indian Peaks Wilderness. It passes through meadows, lodgepole pine forests, and a stand of aspen trees along the way, as well as crossing several ridges. Blazes on the trees mark the route. This trail description ends at the south end of Lake Granby, near the scenic Arapahoe Bay Campground, but this campground is not open to horses. The Roaring Forks Trail starts here as well, but it is too steep for horses. Return the way you came, unless you have a trailer at this trailhead.

East Inlet Trailhead

Drive to the trailhead	🔑🔑
Parking	🅿 🅿 🅿
Amenities	Toilet
Fee Area?	No, because the parking area is outside the park boundary
Elevation	8,400 feet
Maps	Trails Illustrated 200: Rocky Mountain National Park; USGS Shadow Mountain and Isolation Peak

It is a short drive to this huge parking lot that is used for the marina, and therefore provides ample trailer parking.

Directions from U.S. Highway 34 in Grand County

From U.S. Highway 34, drive to the East Inlet Trailhead, at the east end of Grand Lake, by turning east on Colorado State Highway 278 at the sign for Grand Lake. The road forks after 0.3 mile; Colorado State Highway 278 continues straight to the town of Grand Lake. The West Portal Road veers off to the left and ends after 2.5 miles at a large paved parking area for the marina and the trailhead.

This area is called the West Portal because it is near the West Portal of the 13 mile long Alva B. Adams Tunnel, which was completed by the U.S. Department of Reclamation in 1947. This tunnel takes water from west of the Continental Divide to

Estes Park, where hydroelectric power is generated for Front Range communities. Some of the water is then released into the Big Thompson River, and some goes to Pinewood Reservoir by way of another tunnel. The trail, and the stream it follows, are named East Inlet, because the stream brings water into Grand Lake from the east.

Trail #27
East Inlet Trail

Trail rideable	July and August
Best time to ride	July
Maximum elevation	10,200 feet at Lake Verna
Difficulty	**Advanced** due to the terrain and mileage
Terrain	♘ ♘ ♘ due to areas of steep rocky trail
Training ability	**+ +**
Length	14 miles round trip to Lake Verna
Elevation gain	1,800 feet
Best features	A waterfall near the start of the trail and a beautiful lake at the end of the trail
Obstacles	This trail is steep and narrow in spots, and it has one bridge to cross and four streams to ford
Special notes	All Rocky Mountain National Park rules apply on this trail

The first 0.3 mile of this trail are perpetually busy, as it is a short distance to walk to see a waterfall. Few hikers continue up this trail beyond Adams Falls. The trail follows the East Inlet to its headwaters at Lake Verna.

To access this trail, find the trailhead at the southeast end of the parking lot. Before long, the trail crosses the East Inlet stream on a bridge. After climbing a small ridge, it passes a junction with the

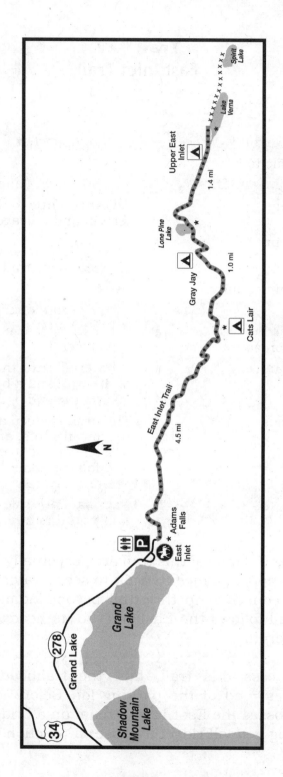

Spirit Lake

Lake Verna

Upper East Inlet

1.4 mi

Lone Pine Lake

Gray Jay

1.0 mi

Cats Lair

East Inlet Trail

4.5 mi

N

Adams Falls

East Inlet

P

Grand Lake

278

Grand Lake

34

Shadow Mountain Lake

short, loop trail to Adams Falls. When the trail is busy, stay left to avoid the crowds at the falls. The next 2.0 miles are on a pleasant trail that skirts the north edge of several meadows. This area affords nice views of Mount Craig to the east before it starts to climb and crosses a small stream. At this point, Mount Cairns is on the left and Mount Westcott is on the right, with Mount Craig situated farther west. After these meadows, the trail traverses steeply across the side of a hill. Since the trail is rather narrow here, you may want to dismount to negotiate this part of the trail, particularly on the return.

Beyond this steep portion, the trail becomes more rolling but still rocky for the next 1.0 mile. Several campsites have been established along this trail. The third one, Cats Lair, is 4.5 miles up the trail and has a toilet nearby. After this campsite the trail crosses a side stream, and then the East Inlet itself. It climbs steadily up to the next campsite at 5.3 miles; a stock site on the north side of the East Inlet named the Gray Jay. The small, but attractive Lone Pine Lake is just past this campsite, 5.5 miles from the start of the trail.

From there, the trail is 1.5 miles with little elevation gain and one stream crossing before you reach Lake Verna. This route travels along the south side of Lone Pine Lake, and once again crosses the East Inlet, before climbing up a steep and rocky section of trail. Then the trail flattens out and passes three more campsites and a pond along the way to Lake Verna. Horses are not allowed beyond the lake, although hikers can continue on the trail to a smaller lake just past Lake Verna. Follow this route back to the trailhead.

North Inlet Trailhead

Drive to the trailhead	🔑🔑
Parking	🅿
Amenities	None
Fee Area?	No, the parking area is outside the park boundaries
Elevation	8,600 feet
Maps	Trails Illustrated 200: Rocky Mountain National Park; USGS Grand Lake and McHenrys Peak

Trailers cannot park at the main trailhead, so horse trailer parking here is limited to on-street parking. The Green Mountain trailhead, the Visitor Center near the entrance station, and the West Portal parking areas all have trails that can be used to access this trailhead, but doing this adds to the mileage ridden.

Directions from U.S. Highway 34 in Grand County

From U.S. Highway 34 drive to this parking area by turning east on Colorado State Highway 278, at the sign for Grand Lake. The road forks after 0.3 mile; Colorado State Highway 278 continues straight to the town of Grand Lake and the West Portal Road veers off to the left. Stay left, and drive 0.7 mile to reach a road on the left that has signs to the Tonahutu/North Inlet Trailhead. The parking lot at the trailhead is quite small, so park along the side of the West Portal Road. When leaving, either turn around here, or continue to the large marina parking lot at the end of the road, less than 2.0 miles ahead to turn around.

Trail #28
North Inlet Trail

Trail rideable	July and August
Best time to ride	July
Maximum elevation	9,600 to 12,200 feet
Difficulty	**Easy** to **Demanding** due to mileage and elevation gain
Terrain	♘ to ♘♘♘♘ for steep rocky trail
Training ability	✚ to ✚✚
Length	6 miles to Cascade Falls 14.4 miles round trip to the first trail junction 20 miles round trip to Lake Nanita 23 miles round trip to Flattop Mountain
Elevation gain	600 feet to 3,600 feet
Best features	No specific turnaround spot; the trail travels through several ecological zones, from meadows to forest to tundra
Obstacles	Six stream crossings, and steep, rocky switchbacks after the first 6.0 miles
Special notes	All Rocky Mountain National Park rules apply on this trail

The name, North Inlet Trail, comes from the stream it follows, which enters Grand Lake from the north. This trail starts out as an **Easy** stroll in the mountains, and becomes a **Demanding** ascent, continuing over the Continental Divide to Bear Lake, 16 miles away. While this route would make a good training ride for the Tevis Cup endurance ride, a 100 mile competition that crosses over the Sierra Nevada Mountains, even novice horses and riders can enjoy the lower part of the trail.

To access this trail from the West Portal Road, ride north following the signs to the Tonahutu car parking area. From that parking area ride east to the North Inlet Trailhead, 1.5 miles from your trailer, on an old road until reaching the Summerland Park campsite. A stock campsite is also located here. From here, the trail follows the North Inlet for almost 6.0 miles. The first 1.3 miles of this trail are **Easy**, skirting a valley on the north side. Then the trail climbs up a short, steep hill by Cascade Falls. Two campsites, a toilet, and a hitching post are located nearby.

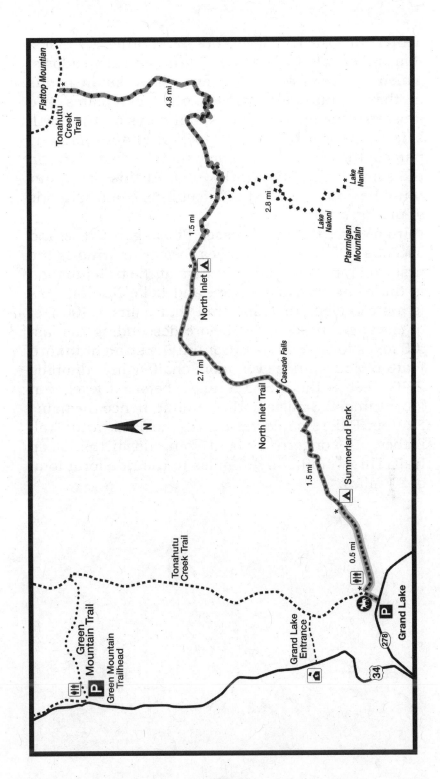

After this, the trail levels out for another 2.7 miles. It meanders along the north side of several meadows, which are very wet; some even have small ponds in them. This route passes more campsites and crosses some small streams, but stays on the north side of the North Inlet. A stock site, appropriately named the North Inlet campsite, is near here on the south side of the North Inlet. At this point, our route has only climbed 600 feet in 5.7 miles, and is a full day's ride.

From here, the trail crosses Ptarmigan Creek and ascends 300 feet in 1.5 miles, before arriving at the first trail junction. The right turn at the trail junction is the route to Lake Nakoni and Lake Nanita. This is a steep switchbacking trail that gains 1,400 feet of elevation in 2.3 miles before descending the last .05 miles to Lake Nanita. Continuing straight toward Flattop Mountain is even more challenging, climbing 2,400 feet in the first 2.5 miles, before it levels out for the final 2.3 miles to the summit, hence the name Flattop. Riders could return on the Tonahutu Trail if they are concerned about going down this steep trail. This would add 4.0 miles to the ride for a total of 27 miles.

Green Mountain Trailhead

Drive to the trailhead	🔑🔑🔑
Parking	🅿️🅿️
Amenities	Toilet
Fee Area?	Rocky Mountain National Park fees apply
Elevation	8,800 feet
Maps	Trails Illustrated 200: Rocky Mountain National Park; USGS Grand Lake and McHenrys Peak

This trailhead is simple to get to and is a simple place to park a trailer. Several trail options exist from here.

Directions from U.S. Highway 34 in Grand County

Drive to the Green Mountain Trailhead by heading north from Grand Lake on U.S. Highway 34. The Green Mountain Trailhead is the first trailhead inside the park boundaries. Look for it on the right, 4.5 miles past the entrance station. If you have already paid the park fee, this route is also the best way to access the Tonahutu Trail (which is an **Easy** trail that is not described), as the parking is better here than at the Tonahutu Trailhead. People staying at the Winding River Resort can ride the 3.0 miles to the trailhead on a well-maintained trail, and leave their trailer parked in the campground. Ask at the campground for directions to the start of the trail. The Onahu Trailhead, 0.5 mile further, does not have adequate parking for trailers, but a trail connects the two trailheads.

Trail #29
Green Mountain/Onahu/Tonahutu Creek trails

Trail rideable	July and August
Best time to ride	July
Maximum elevation	9,900 feet for the loop trail, 12,200 for Flattop Mountain
Difficulty	**Moderate** to **Demanding** due to the distance and elevation gain
Terrain	♘ to ♘ ♘ ♘ for steep rocky trail
Training ability	**✦** to **✦ ✦**
Length	7.5 miles round trip for the loop trail, 22 miles round trip to Flattop Mountain, 19 miles one way to Hollowell Park
Elevation gain	1,100 feet for the loop trail, 3,500 to Flattop Mountain
Best features	Various trail options are available
Obstacles	Each trail option has four stream crossings
Special notes	None

This nice trail has various options, from manageable to marathon. The loop described is the **Moderate** option with notes about the other trails in the area.

Access the trail at the trailhead sign adjacent to the parking lot, by riding up the trail to the right, which is 2.0 miles long. The first 1.0 mile ascends through a dense evergreen forest following a stream.

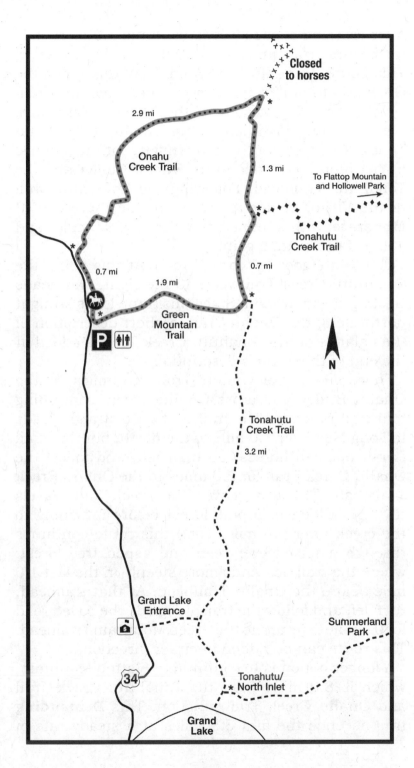

Closed
to horses

2.9 mi

Onahu
Creek Trail

1.3 mi

To Flattop Mountain
and Hollowell Park

Tonahutu
Creek Trail

0.7 mi

1.9 mi

0.7 mi

Green
Mountain
Trail

N

Tonahutu
Creek Trail

3.2 mi

Grand Lake
Entrance

Summerland
Park

34

Tonahutu/
North Inlet

Grand
Lake

After crossing a side stream, continue 1.0 more mile to the first trail junction located in a big meadow. This route goes left for 0.7 mile. At this point the Green Mountain Trail intersects the Tonahutu Trail, which means Big Meadow in the Arapahoe language. The trail to the right follows the Tonahutu Trail and Tonahutu Creek south for 3.5 miles, with no change in elevation, and leads to the Visitor Center and the Tonahutu Trailhead. Following the Tonahutu Trail to the Visitor center results in a ride that is rated **Moderate**, with a round trip mileage of 9.2 miles and 400 feet of elevation gain.

This route goes left for 0.7 mile. At this point, the Tonahutu Creek Trail veers to the right, and heads west up the mountain. Since this route leads straight north along the Onahu Trail, a short description of the balance of the Tonahutu Creek Trail is added at the end of this route's description.

Travel along the Onahu Trail 1.3 miles to the Onahu Bridge and cross Onahu Creek, continuing to a trail junction. The trail that goes straight leads to Long Meadows 1.0 mile to the north, but that trail is not open to horses. So turn left, and follow the Onahu Creek Trail for 2.0 miles to the Onahu Creek Trailhead. The trail leaves the creek and travels through a lodgepole pine forest before returning to the creek after 0.5 mile. Then this route continues through a mixed evergreen and aspen tree forest, where the trail descends more steeply in the last 1.0 mile before the Onahu Trailhead. At that trailhead, turn left and follow the trail alongside the paved road for 0.5 mile to return to the Green Mountain Trailhead. This route can be ridden in either direction.

A longer option is to continue to Flattop Mountain, which is 8.0 miles from the Tonahutu Creek Trail and Onahu Creek Trail junction. This **Demanding** trail ascends the first 3.5 miles at a steady rate of

300 feet per mile. It climbs more steeply the next 0.5 mile, passing two stock campsites, the Tonahutu and Timberline sites, and a trail junction on the left in quick succession. That trail leads to the Haynach Lakes in 2.0 miles, but it is not open to horses. Flattop Mountain is another 4.0 miles from here on the main trail. This route climbs 800 feet in the next 1.0 mile, then it leaves the trees behind and ascends at a more reasonable but still steep pitch to the summit, gaining 1,000 feet over 3.0 miles.

This trail is the easier of the two possible routes to ride a horse from the east side of Rocky Mountain National Park to the west side, which although long, is a hike that is not uncommonly done by adventurous hikers. The nearest place to park a trailer is Hollowell Park and the ride is 19 miles to the Green Mountain Trailhead, and another 3.0 miles to the Winding River Resort to spend a night or two with advance reservations. This is a challenging undertaking in either direction.

Another marathon ride entails starting at the Tonahutu/North Inlet Trailhead, ascending the North Inlet Trail to Flattop Mountain, and descending the Tonahutu Creek Trail, to make a large loop returning to the same trailhead. This route should not be ridden in reverse, due to the steepness of the North Inlet Trail. This results in a ride that is 27 miles long with 3,500 feet of elevation gain.

Timber Lake Trailhead

Drive to the trailhead	🔑🔑🔑
Parking	🅿️🅿️🅿️
Amenities	A toilet and a picnic table
Fee Area?	Rocky Mountain National Park fees apply
Elevation	9,000 feet
Maps	Trails Illustrated 200: Rocky Mountain National Park; USGS Grand Lake and Fall River Pass

This easily accessible parking lot is on U.S. Highway 34, otherwise known as Trail Ridge Road when it is in Rocky Mountain National Park. Additional parking is available across the street.

Directions from U.S. Highway 34 in Grand County

Drive to the Timber Lake Trailhead by driving north on U.S. Highway 34 from Grand Lake, continuing 9.6 miles past the Rocky Mountain National Park entrance station. The parking area for Timber Lake is a good-sized paved lot on the right side of the road. In the event that no trailer parking is available, try to park across the street and slightly further north, at the Colorado River Trailhead.

Trail #30
Timber Lake

Trail rideable	July and August
Best time to ride	July
Maximum elevation	11,000 feet
Difficulty	**Advanced** due to mileage and elevation gain
Terrain	♘ ♘
Training ability	✚
Length	10.5 miles round trip
Elevation gain	2,060 feet
Best features	This easy-to-follow trail has a nice lake at the end
Obstacles	None
Special notes	None

This is a convenient trailhead, and although the trail is steep, its final destination is a nice lake that is not too far away. It could be the perfect mountain ride. The trail starts at the northeast side of Jackstraw Mountain, and contours around to the southwest side, steadily gaining elevation before heading south for the last 0.5 mile to reach Timber Lake. Jackstraw Mountain acquired its name from the fallen trees on the western side of the mountain that are vestiges of an 1872 forest fire.

Access the trail for Timber Lake at the trailhead adjacent to the parking area. The first 3.5 miles of the trail travel through the forest around the side of Jackstraw Mountain. A trail junction on the right, just past the Timber Creek campsite, leads to a small pond at the north end of Long Meadows, but that

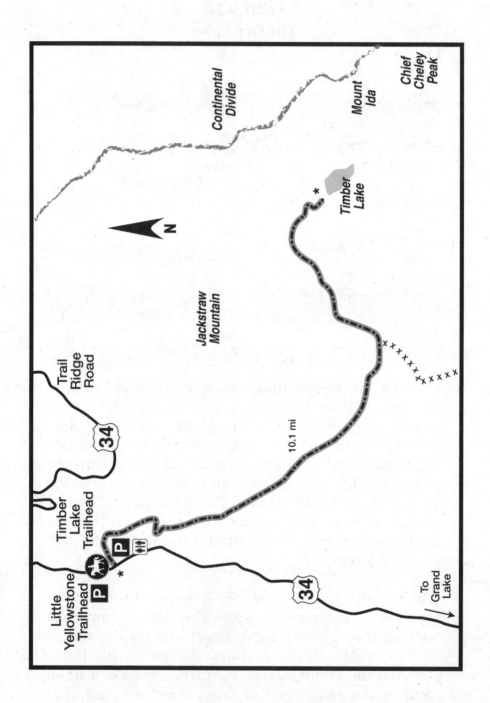

Continental Divide

Mount Ida

Chief Cheley Peak

Timber Lake

*

N

Jackstraw Mountain

Trail Ridge Road

34

10.1 mi

Timber Lake Trailhead

P

Little Yellowstone Trailhead

P

*

34

To Grand Lake

trail is not open to horses, so this route continues up the main trail. After that junction, the trail becomes noticeably steeper, switchbacking its way up the mountain for 0.5 mile before regaining a more comfortable grade and reaching the next campsite. Then the trail follows Timber Creek the last 1.0 mile to Timber Lake, passing three more campsites along the way.

This alpine lake at the base of Mount Ida is a pleasant spot to have lunch and give your mount a rest. Timber Lake is less than 1.0 mile from the Continental Divide, which runs from the summit of Chief Cheley Peak, just south of the lake, and the summit of Mount Ida, at 12,889 feet, continuing north to Milner Pass on Trail Ridge Road. When you have had enough of the views, return to the parking lot the way you came.

Lulu City, Little Yellowstone Trailhead
Colorado River Trailhead

Drive to the trailhead	🔑 🔑 🔑
Parking	🅿 🅿
Amenities	A toilet and a picnic table
Fee Area?	Rocky Mountain National Park fees apply
Elevation	9,000 feet
Maps	Trails Illustrated 200: Rocky Mountain National Park; USGS Fall River Pass

The Colorado River Trailhead is the northernmost of the trailheads described on the west side of the Continental Divide. This trailhead is across the street and just north of the Timber Lake Trailhead. Beyond this, Trail Ridge Road begins to climb, and the trails that leave from the road after this point, such as the Poudre River Trail, the trail from Milner Pass to the Alpine Visitor Center, and the Ute Trail, are not open to horses.

Directions from U.S. Highway 34 in Grand County

Drive to the Colorado River Trailhead by heading north on U.S. Highway 34 from Grand Lake, continuing 9.6 miles past the Rocky Mountain National Park entrance station. The parking area for the Colorado River trailhead is a good-sized paved lot on the left side of the road. In the event that no trailer parking is available, try to park across the street and slightly further south, at the Timber Lake Trailhead.

Trail #31
Lulu City/ Little Yellowstone
Colorado River Trail

Trail rideable	June through September
Best time to ride	July
Maximum elevation	9,900 feet
Difficulty	**Easy,** could be ridden barefoot
Terrain	⊔
Training ability	+
Length	7.5 to 10 miles round trip or longer
Elevation gain	900 feet
Best features	This **Easy** valley trail is surrounded by mountains
Obstacles	The trail crosses five streams
Special notes	Moose may be seen here, especially early in the day

This trail is commonly referred to by a variety of names. In addition to the names used above, the Trails Illustrated map labels it the La Poudre Pass Trail. The first 3.5 miles of the trail wander along the Kawuneeche Valley, paralleling the Colorado River, with only 300 feet of elevation gain. It is possible to turn around at any point in the ride, and other options for longer rides are available. Directly west of here are Mounts Stratus, Nimbus, Cumulus and Cirrus, which, along with Baker Mountain, are at the south end of the Never Summer Range.

Access the Colorado River Trail at the trailhead adjacent to the parking area, and head north, with the Never Summer Range on the left. Within 0.2 mile

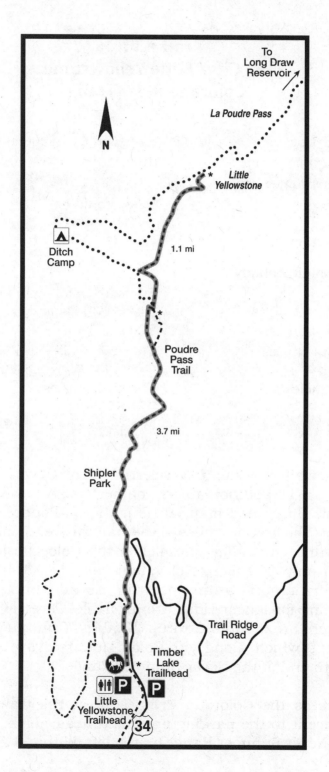

To
Long Draw
Reservoir

La Poudre Pass

* *Little*
Yellowstone

1.1 mi

Ditch
Camp

Poudre
Pass
Trail

3.7 mi

Shipler
Park

Trail Ridge
Road

Timber
Lake
Trailhead

*

Little
Yellowstone
Trailhead

34

of the trailhead, the Red Mountain Trail intersects the main trail on the left. That trail climbs over 1,000 feet in 3.0 miles to end at a campsite near the Grand Ditch. This route continues north on the Colorado River Trail, passing the Shipler Park area, which was the site of a mine and some cabins, 1.5 miles up the trail. Continue on the main trail until you reach a side trail on the left, 3.7 miles from the trailhead, which leads to Lulu City. Follow that trail to the site of the ghost town.

There were great hopes for this mining town when it was founded in 1879. It was laid out from the start to have 100 blocks, and connected to Fort Collins via the Old Flowers Road, much of which still exists and can be traveled on horseback. The ore proved to be too low grade to maintain operations, and within four years the town was largely abandoned. At its height Lulu City had only 500 residents. Little remains to be seen now, except a beautiful valley with Lulu Mountain as a backdrop.

Mountains border this area on three sides. The Continental Divide crosses Trail Ridge Road at Milner Pass. It continues north to the summit of Specimen Mountain, directly to the east of Lulu City. After Specimen Mountain, the Divide curves to the west, and crosses the Colorado River Trail at La Poudre Pass, then continues across the summit of Lulu Mountain. After that, it runs west to the summit of Mount Richthofen, and turns south to follow the Never Summer Range as far as Mount Nimbus. This valley may be the only place in North America that is surrounded on three sides by the Continental Divide, and it is where much of the water in the Colorado River originates. From Mount Nimbus, the Divide runs west along the Rabbit Ears Range for 35 miles to Rabbit Ears Pass, before continuing in its usual northerly direction.

This route continues to the north. Within 0.5 mile from Lulu City, it reaches a trail junction. The Thunder Pass Trail heads off to the left, crossing the Colorado River and following Skeleton Gulch along Lulu Creek a short distance to a stock campsite near the Grand Ditch. The ditch, started in the 1890s and completed in 1929, carries water to the Long Draw Reservoir. That trail continues further up Skeleton Gulch, but it is not open to horses beyond the stock site. The other trail from the Ditch Camp crosses the Continental Divide at Thunder Pass and leads to the Michigan Lakes, eventually connecting to Colorado State Highway 14. Although this trail is open to horses, it is steep and rocky. To the west of Skeleton Gulch, you can identify the tallest mountain in the Never Summer Range, Mount Richthofen, at 12,940 feet.

This route rejoins the main trail by turning right at the Thunder Pass junction, and climbs uphill for a short distance before coming to another junction. Turning right here will return you to the trailhead, making a 7.5 mile round trip ride. Turn left to continue along the main trail, which descends to cross the Colorado River that is just a stream this close to its headwaters. Then climb steadily up on the far side, before leveling out for the final 0.5 mile at the area referred to as Little Yellowstone, due to the yellow colored rock there. This area is 4.5 miles from the trailhead and is the turnaround spot for this route. The trail continues 1.0 more mile, on a gravel road following the Grand Ditch and passing a ranger station before traversing La Poudre Pass and the Continental Divide at 10,180 feet. It leaves Rocky Mountain National Park 0.5 mile further down the trail and ends on a dirt road to the Long Draw Reservoir. Return the way you came.

Trails North and East of Rocky Mountain National Park

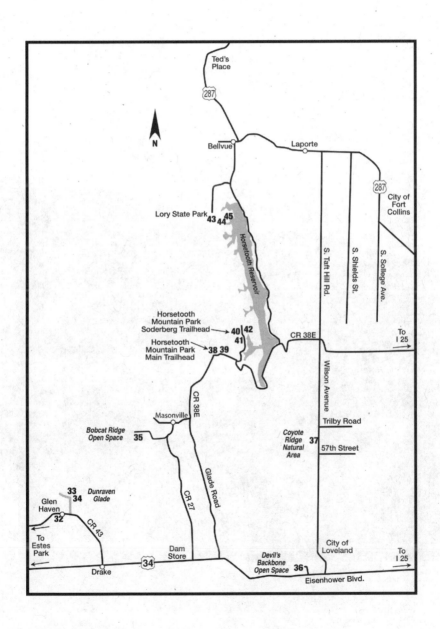

Trails accessed from Larimer County Road 43, near the town of Drake

Crosier Mountain Trailhead

Drive to the trailhead	𝗉 𝗉 𝗉
Parking	**P**
Amenities	None
Fee Area?	No
Elevation	7,000 feet
Maps	Trails Illustrated 101: Cache La Poudre Big Thompson, USGS Glen Haven

Although this is a trailhead, it has no parking lot. Two trailers can park alongside the road and still have enough room to tack up horses. From Loveland, the drive to this trailhead is slightly shorter than driving from Loveland to Estes Park. From Boulder County it requires first driving to Loveland, making a long drive.

Directions from Estes Park

Drive to the Croiser Mountain Trailhead by heading north on U.S. Highway 34 from the junction with U.S. Highway 36, passing the Stanley Hotel. Turn right 1.0 mile past that junction onto MacGregor Avenue. That road makes a ninety-degree turn to the right after 1.0 mile, becoming Devil's Gulch Road, also known as Larimer County Road 43. After 3.0 more miles, the road comes to four very sharp and very steep switchbacks. I do not recommend driving this road with a large rig. Continue 2.0 miles past the swithchbacks to the small town of Glen Haven.

The first building in this tiny town is a Post Office on the right, and the second one is a riding stable, also on the right. Turn around wherever you can, and park on the north side of the road, across the street from the stable.

Directions from Larimer County and Interstate Highway 25

Drive to the Croiser Mountain Trailhead from Interstate Highway 25, by taking exit 257B. Drive west 18 miles on U.S. Highway 34 through Loveland, following the Big Thompson River. From the Dam Store, at the base of the Big Thompson Canyon, it is 8.0 miles to the town of Drake. Turn right just past this miniscule town, between mileage markers 76 and 75, onto Larimer County Road 43, also known as Devil's Gulch Road. Follow this road along the North Fork of the Big Thompson River for 8.0 miles through the tiny town of Glen Haven. On the far side of town, park on the right side of the road, across the street from a small riding stable. This dirt pullout can hold two small trailers. When leaving, unless you want to go to Estes Park, turn around at the Post Office, which is just beyond the riding stable, and return on the road you came on.

Trail #32
Crosier Mountain

Trail rideable	June through September
Best time to ride	June
Maximum elevation	9,250 feet
Difficulty	**Moderate**
Terrain	☙☙ to ☙☙☙ near the summit
Training ability	**+ +**
Length	8.0 or more miles round trip
Elevation gain	2,250
Best features	This route makes a simple spring ride
Obstacles	Dude horses from the stables and from a summer camp
Special notes	Avoid the dude horses in July and August and hunters in the fall; no water for horses on the trail; dogs allowed

This is a reasonable drive and a **Moderate** ride. It makes a good conditioning ride in the springtime because it has a slightly lower elevation than most mountain trails and, although the elevation gain is less than 1,000 feet, it gains it in 4.0 unrelenting miles. It even includes an opportunity to lope through a meadow.

Just west of the riding stable is a dirt road that is someone's driveway. To access the Croiser Mountain Trailhead, lead your horse across the street and follow this dirt road uphill. After a very short

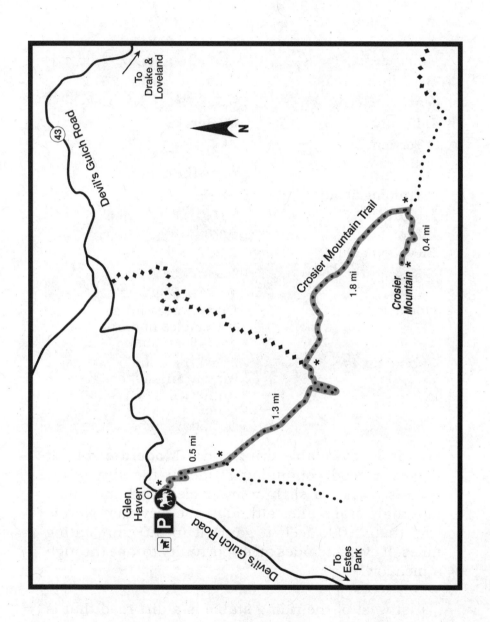

distance, turn right onto a trail that heads up the hill. This trail starts off quite steeply, and is soon followed by a wooden sign indicating it is the trail to Croisier Mountain. This trail is deeply rutted and is frequented by horses from the riding stable and the Cheley girl's summer camp until it reaches Piper Meadow.

This route switchbacks up the hill for 0.5 mile, where a trail to the H Bar G Ranch veers off to the right. Continue straight another 0.5 mile to Piper Meadows, a huge mountain meadow that can be seen from the opposite mountains. A social trail heads off into the meadow at this point. Follow the main trail along the east side of the meadow another 0.2 mile, where an unmarked trail traverses the meadow, destined for the H Bar G Ranch. This route continues up the main trail a little more than 1.0 mile, to a trail junction simply marked "road," which heads down a very steep, rocky and **Dangerous** trail leading to another trailhead on Devil's Gulch Road.

Stay on the main trail traveling through several ecological zones. On the lower part of the mountain, enjoy the ponderosa pine trees as well as Piper Meadow. As the trail climbs, Douglas fir and aspen trees predominate. Then it passes through an area where lodgepole pine trees grow thick and close together, providing shade for the trail. This mature forest has abundant dead and downed trees, ripe for a fire. As the elevation increases the trees are less mature, with little dead wood. After leaving the lodgepole pine trees, the trail crosses some meadows where Douglas fir and aspen trees predominate once again.

At the next junction this route turns right, and continues climbing toward the summit of Croiser Mountain. The other direction leads to a very small trailhead, also on Devil's Gulch Road. Once past the thick trees, enjoy the nice view. The summit is a steep 0.4 mile away, and horses can go to the top. On the way back down, feel free to explore the Piper Meadow area. The two trails mentioned on the way up dead-end on the far side of the meadow, at fences belonging to the ranch. It can be fun to ride on these trails, or even through the meadow, especially if you want to indulge a fantasy of galloping through green meadows.

No description is given for the other trails to Crosier Mountain, due to their steepness, or lack of parking. The Round Mountain Trail from U.S. Highway 34 is not listed in this guidebook for the same reason.

Dunraven Glade Trailhead

Drive to the trailhead	🔑🔑
Parking	🅿️🅿️🅿️
Amenities	Toilet and an emergency call box
Fee Area?	No
Elevation	7,900 feet
Maps	Trails Illustrated 101: Cache La Poudre Big Thompson, and 200 Rocky Mountain National Park; USGS Glen Haven, Estes Park, Pinagree Park

This is a nice roomy trailhead; I have even seen a five-horse trailer being pulled by a Mack truck parked here. This trailhead is named after its access road, but it is often referred to as the Comanche Trailhead since it provides access to the Comanche Peak Wilderness. Sometimes it is referred to as the North Fork Trailhead, since the trail follows the North Fork of the Big Thompson River, and goes by the name North Fork Trail. Some people call it the Lost Lake Trailhead, because that trail ends at Lost Lake. Whatever name you choose, it is a user-friendly trailhead. Those who are coming from Boulder County should come through Loveland, making a long drive.

Directions from Estes Park

Drive to the Dunraven Glade Trailhead by heading north on U.S. Highway 36 from the junction with U.S. Highway 34, passing the Stanley Hotel. Turn right 1.0 mile past that junction onto MacGregor

Avenue. That road makes a ninety-degree turn to the right after 1.0 mile, becoming Devil's Gulch Road, also known as Larimer County Road 43. In 3.0 more miles, the road comes to four very sharp and very steep switchbacks not recommended for large rigs. Continue 4.0 more miles, passing through the tiny town of Glen Haven. Dunraven Glade is marked with a street sign on the left, as well as a wooden sign for the Trails End Ranch for Boys.

Directions from Larimer County or Interstate Highway 25

Drive to the Dunraven Glade Trailhead from Interstate Highway 25, by taking exit 257B. Drive 18 miles west on U.S. Highway 34 through Loveland, following the Big Thompson River. From the Dam Store at the base of the Big Thompson Canyon, it is less than 8.0 miles to the town of Drake. Turn right just past that town, between mileage markers 76 and 75, onto Larimer County Road 43; also know as Devil's Gulch Road. Follow this road along the North Fork of the Big Thompson River for 6.0 miles, and then turn right onto Dunraven Glade. This turnoff is marked with a street sign on the right, as well as a wooden sign for the Trails End Ranch for Boys.

Directions from Larimer County Road 43

Follow the dirt Dunraven Glade road for 2.2 miles, where it dead-ends at a large parking area. If possible, park in the middle of the lot, facing the road, for an uncomplicated departure. Otherwise, park on the right side as you enter the lot. Cars usually park on the west side of the lot, near the trailhead.

Trail #33
North Fork Trail
To Deserted Village and Lost Lake

Trail rideable	June through September
Best time to ride	July
Maximum elevation	10,700 feet
Difficulty	**Moderate** to **Demanding** ·due to the distance and elevation gain
Terrain	♘ to ♘♘
Training ability	✛ ✛
Length	4.2 to 19.4 miles round trip
Elevation gain	200 to 2,800 feet
Best features	This is an interesting and varied trail
Obstacles	Stream crossings
Special notes	Dogs are allowed on a leash until reaching the National Park boundary where Rocky Mountain National Park rules are in force

This fun trail is not too far for those who drive up U.S. Highway 34, and the parking is great. It can be ridden as a very short ride, a very long one, or anything in between.

To access the North Fork Trail, ride to the west side of the parking lot, toward the trailhead and near the restrooms. Ride over the small hill beyond the trail board, and down the other side. Then follow a narrow trail, next to the North Fork of the Big

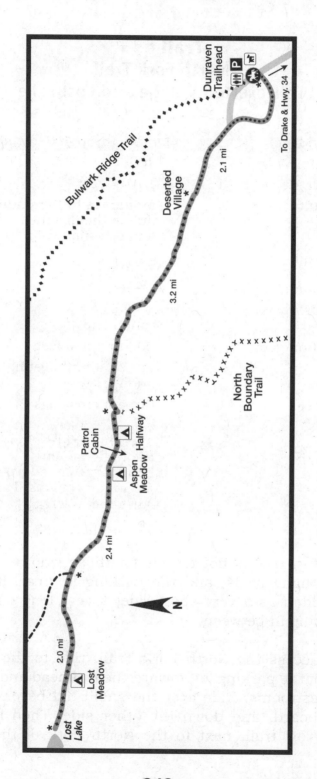

Bulwark Ridge Trail

Dunraven Trailhead

To Drake & Hwy. 34

2.1 mi

Deserted
Village
*

3.2 mi

North
Boundary
Trail

*

Patrol
Cabin

Aspen
Meadow Halfway

2.4 mi

*

2.0 mi

Lost Meadow

*
Lost
Lake

N

Thompson River that is surrounded by blue spruce and Douglas fir trees. Soon the trail fords the river and follows its south side. Before long, it passes the Trails End Ranch boy's camp situated on the north side of the river. Shortly after this leave the main trail, following the trail designated for horses, to ford the river. After crossing the river, the trail climbs up the riverbank and comes to a small dirt road. To the right is a gate for the boys' camp. This route follows the road to the left. The trail seems to enjoy crisscrossing over the river, and does this twice more before arriving at a meadow, 2.1 miles from the parking area. This nice little meadow, called Deserted Village, has the remains of a small cabin on the south side. The trees here are the more common ponderosa pine trees, which flourish with less water than Douglas fir trees.

The Earl of Dunraven came to Estes Park in the 1870's, and attempted to claim it for his personal

hunting grounds. Others opposed this idea, so he built his hunting lodge in Dunraven Glade before leaving the area in 1880. While the site of the lodge, which may have been somewhere along the road leading to the trailhead, has been lost, his name has remained attached to many of the features in this area. This spot was once called Dunraven Meadow, or Dunraven Park. In the early part of the century it was used as hunting resort, but it was apparently abandoned by 1914.

This trail parallels the North Fork of the Big Thompson River the entire 9.7 miles to Lost Lake, which forms part of the headwaters of the river. From the Deserted Village, the trail climbs alongside a lush grassy area for a short distance, and then it curves toward the northwest, climbing steadily uphill through lodgepole pine trees. A sign marks the Rocky Mountain National Park boundary 4.0 miles from the Deserted Village. Before long, this route passes two campsites, one on either side of the trail, and within 0.5 mile of the park boundary it comes to a trail junction for the North Boundary Trail on the left. That trail connects to the Cow Creek Trail after 6.0 miles, but for horses it is a **Dangerous** route that is not described in this guidebook.

The next 1.5 miles ascend fairly gradually. The first campsite after that trail junction is named Halfway, although it is somewhat further than halfway to Lost Lake. A patrol cabin used by park rangers is situated in this area as well. Turning around here makes a 10.5-mile ride round trip.

The next campsite, named Aspen Meadow, allows horses. Pass two more campsites before the trail climbs more steeply and away from the river, coming to the trail junction for the Stormy Peaks Trail on the right. That trail goes over Stormy Peaks Pass and eventually arrives at Pinagree Park. This would be a fun day trip if you decide to camp overnight at one of the nearby stock sites.

At this point, it is only 2.0 more miles to Lost Lake on the main trail. Continue straight and the further the trail continues up the valley, the more it opens out to afford nice views of the mountains. Continue to follow the river past the Sugarloaf campsite, and the Lost Meadow campsite, which allows horses. In less than 1.0 mile, the trail arrives at the lake, which has a hitching post and is a good spot for a well-deserved lunch break.

Sugarloaf Mountain and Mount Dunraven are on either side of the lake, and Rowe Peak, which has several glaciers on its slopes, is to the east. Several larger lakes are above Lost Lake, but no trail leads to them. Unfortunately, in 1911 a dam was built here, turning Lost Lake into a reservoir. Rocky Mountain National Park was able to acquire this area in the 1970's, and removed the dam in 1985. Although the lake is once again its original size, the high water mark will be evident for generations to come by the lack of vegetation on the lakeshore. Return the way you came.

Trail #34
Signal Mountain

Trail rideable	July and August
Best time to ride	August
Maximum elevation	11,262 feet
Difficulty	**Demanding**, due to the terrain and elevation gain
Terrain	U U U U for the steep trail and unstable footing
Training ability	+
Length	10 to 12 miles round trip
Elevation gain	3,362 feet
Best features	The thick forest provides shade
Obstacles	This route ascends a steep hill at the beginning, and the end of the trail is quite rocky
Special notes	Dogs are allowed

This challenging trail is not very aesthetically appealing. The shady trail is covered with snow early and late in the season, but it is cool in the summertime.

To access this trail, ride north out of the parking lot past a sign for the Bulwark Ridge Trail, near the gate on the dirt road that leads to the Trails End Ranch boys camp. This sign indicates that the Indian Trail is 1.0 mile, the Miller Fork Trail is 3.0 miles, Wilderness is 3.0 miles and Signal Mountain is 6.0 miles. After 0.2 mile, the trail veers off to the right. The Trails Illustrated and De Lorme maps call this

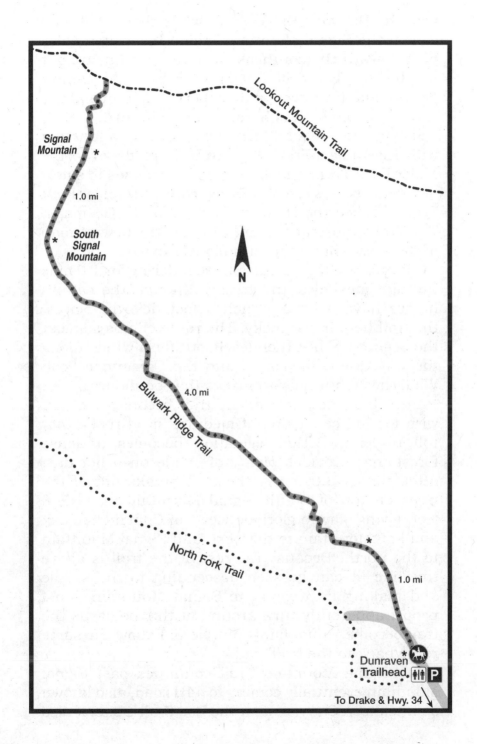

Lookout Mountain Trail

Signal
Mountain *

1.0 mi

South
Signal
Mountain *

N

Bulwark Ridge Trail

4.0 mi

North Fork Trail

1.0 mi *

Dunraven *
Trailhead

To Drake & Hwy. 34

trail the Bulwark Ridge Trail, while the USGS map calls it the Signal Mountain Trail. This route angles back toward the southeast, before heading straight up the hill. The trail is well worn from the camp's horses, and it is steep and slippery. A flat area at the top of this pitch gives horses a place to rest.

Shortly after this hill, the trail arrives at a junction with the Indian Trail. That trail drops down to the Miller Fork Trail, and is too steep for horses to safely negotiate, so it is rated as **Dangerous**. The Miller Fork Trail is called the Donner Hill Trail on USGS maps. The Trails Illustrated map, which is the newest map of the area, shows that it no longer exists.

Continue on the main trail, meandering for 1.0 mile through meadows and trees. Although the camp's horses have worn a trench a foot deep in places, the trail here is not rocky. The route climbs some at the beginning, but then levels out for a while. Along the way, the trail passes into the Comanche Peak Wilderness, but no sign marks that boundary.

After this, the angle of the trail becomes steeper, with footing consisting of medium sized rocks that roll underfoot. The vegetation becomes a dense forest that provides plenty of shade on a hot day. After almost 3.0 miles, the trail breaks out of the trees on top of South Signal Mountain at 11,248 feet, giving way to glorious views of Comanche Peak and Fall Mountain to the west, and Signal Mountain to the north. Because the rest of the trail is above tree line, it can be seen descending to the saddle and making its way up to Signal Mountain. Most people apparently turn around at this point, as the trail becomes quite faint from here. Follow the same route back to the trailhead.

The Signal Mountain Trail continues past Signal Mountain eventually coming to 44H road, also known as Buckhorn Canyon, near the Box Prairie site. It also passes a junction with the Lookout Mountain Trail. That trail goes over Donner Pass, where it crosses the Donner Hill Trail before coming to a spur trail to Lookout Mountain. The main trail continues, following Sheep Creek and passing several trail junctions before coming to Crystal Mountain road, which is the name of the USGS map for this area. Many trails and dirt roads crisscross this area and a horse and rider could wander around there for days. Pinagree Park is west northwest of Signal Mountain, and can be accessed by trail as well.

Trails in the Loveland and Fort Collins area

Bobcat Ridge Natural Area Trailhead

Drive to the trailhead	🔑 🔑 🔑
Parking	🅿 🅿 🅿
Amenities	Restrooms, a drinking fountain, and a frost-free hydrant
Fee Area?	No
Elevation	5,480 feet
Maps	Pick up a brochure with a map at the trailhead, the USGS Loveland map only shows the old roads here

This trailhead is close to Fort Collins and Loveland. It is simple to drive to and has eight pull through parking spots designated for horse trailers.

Directions from Larimer County or Interstate Highway 25

Drive to the Bobcat Ridge Trailhead from Interstate Highway 25, by taking exit 257B onto U.S. Highway 34. Otherwise, from U.S. Highway 287 head west on U.S. Highway 34. Drive through Loveland, continuing 3.8 miles past the last signal in town at Wilson Street. This intersection is 6.0 miles from I-25 and 4.0 miles from U.S. Highway 287. U.S. Highway 34 narrows to a two-lane road 0.4 mile beyond this intersection. 2.2 miles beyond Wilson Street you can spot a gas station at the turnoff for Glade Road. Turn right at the next turnoff 1.6 miles further onto 27 Road. This is between mile markers 86 and 85 and just before Big Thompson Elementary School. Follow 27 Road for 4.7 miles to the turnoff. After 4.0 miles a small brown sign on the right indicates that the Bobcat Ridge Natural area is 0.5 mile further on the left, and soon another one indicates that the turnoff is in 500 feet. Turn left onto West County Road 32C, staying left on the paved entrance road, and avoiding a dirt driveway that heads off to the right.

Directions from northern Larimer County and Interstate Highway 25

Drive to the Bobcat Ridge Trailhead from Interstate Highway 25 Exit 265 or U.S. Highway 287 in Fort Collins, or Taft Hill road, by heading west on Harmony Road. This road becomes Larimer County Road 38E when it continues west past Taft Hill Road. This intersection is noteworthy for the gas station located there, which sells diesel as well as gasoline, and can accommodate a truck pulling a horse trailer. From there, it is almost 10 miles on CR 38E to the Masonville Mercantile. Turn left there onto 27 Road and drive 0.6 mile south. Just past the Masonville Post Office the road curves to the right and a small brown sign announces that the Bobcat Ridge Natural area is 500 feet on the right. This turnoff comes up very fast. Turn right onto West County Road 32C, staying left on the paved entrance road and avoiding a dirt driveway that heads off to the right.

Directions from the turnoff onto West CR 32C from 27 Road.

Before long the route to the trailhead turns to dirt. The entranceway to the Bobcat Ridge Trailhead is on the left 0.5 mile from the intersection with 27 Road. The trailer parking area is located at the far end of the parking lot. This area comfortably holds four trailers and can accommodate eight when necessary. I have seen all eight spaces full, so be prepared to go somewhere else if this is the case when you arrive.

Parking close to the left side of the parking spots gives you room to tie your horses to your trailer. Park near the back of the spot to allow another trailer to pull by you. If they pull up far enough, there is still room to tie your horses to your trailer. To exit the parking area, continue south a short distance to the exit road on the southeast corner of the parking lot.

Trail #35
Valley Loop Trail

Trail rideable	Year round
Best time to ride	Spring and Fall
Maximum elevation	5,800 feet
Difficulty	**Easy,** could be ridden barefoot
Terrain	♘
Training ability	**+ +** for bicycles
Length	4.5 miles
Elevation gain	300 feet
Best features	Year round riding
Obstacles	One small bridge
Special notes	No water and little shade is available on the trail; refrain from riding in this area if it is muddy to avoid damaging the trail

Bobcat Ridge Natural Area, owned by the City of Fort Collins, is very close to Fort Collins and Loveland. The first trail here opened to the public in September of 2006. More trails are planned here. This Natural Area encompasses 2,600 acres and is connected to a network of public lands stretching from the eastern plains to Estes Park. Hopefully someday equestrians will be able to ride the entire network!

Leave your horse at the trailer and walk to the trail board at the start of the trail to pick up a map.

To access the Valley Loop Trail, ride south from the parking lot on a bridle path. This trail turns right

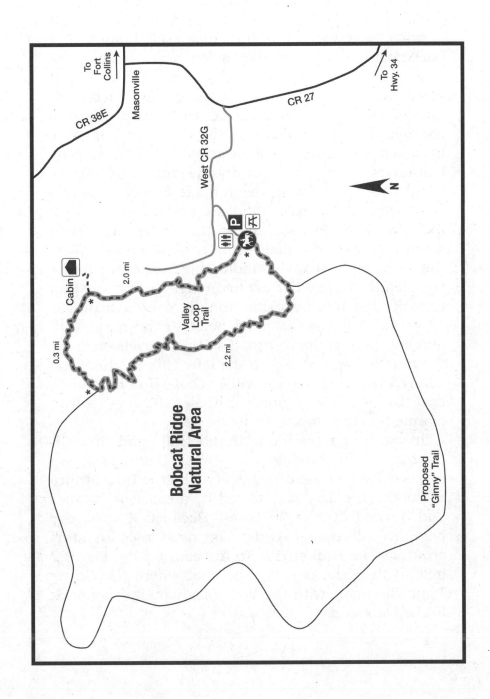

Bobcat Ridge Natural Area

To Fort Collins

CR 38E

Masonville

West CR 32G

CR 27

To Hwy. 34

N

Cabin

2.0 mi

0.3 mi

Valley Loop Trail

2.2 mi

Proposed "Ginny" Trail

after passing the fence that borders the parking area. A cement path lines the main trail making it handicapped accessible but unsafe for horses. The path soon passes a picnic shelter and the first trail junction. It is possible to ride this loop in either direction, but for the sake of description turn right and follow the loop counterclockwise. This trail runs through a beautiful area bordered on the east side by a red sandstone ridge and on the west side by foothills. Cottonwood trees dot the landscape. Notice that the bridle path has been made for horses and a wider, gravel covered, handicapped accessible path is for walkers. Please ride on the bridle path, even when it crosses the pedestrian trail. After 2.0 miles, the path comes to a sign indicating that a trail to the right leads to a cabin. Stay to the right at the junction to visit this nearby cabin that is over a hundred years old. Afterwards head back to the main trail and continue riding north. The trail travels west for 0.3 mile before curving to the left. This is where the Ginny Trail will leave the Valley Loop. Unfortunately, that trail will not be open to horses, however a trail planned further to the west will be.

This route passes along the foothills and through the edge of a ponderosa pine forest. Before long you can see some of the damage done by the Bobcat Fire in 2000. This fire was started by a careless camper and burned over 8000 acres. Because it is so dry here, it will take decades for new trees to start growing. The trail curves to the east for the last 0.2 mile of the ride, passing the spot where the Ginny Trail will merge with the Valley Loop on its way back to the trailhead.

Devil's Backbone Open Space Trailhead

Drive to the trailhead	🔑 🔑 🔑
Parking	**P** **P**
Amenities	Restrooms, a drinking fountain, and a frost-free hydrant
Fee Area?	Not at this time, possible in the future; consider making a contribution in the box provided
Elevation	5,080 feet
Maps	Get a brochure with a map at the trailhead, the USGS Loveland map does not show the trails here

This Open Space area, owned by the Larimer County Open Space Department, is very close to Loveland. While it has been open to the public since 1999, it was not originally open to horses. It received a new parking lot with horse trailer parking in 2003, thanks in part to input from the Larimer County Horseman's Association who helps maintain the trails here. This trailhead is one of several that provide access to a 50-mile long trail network that was completed in 2006.

Directions from Larimer County or Interstate Highway 25

Drive to the Devil's Backbone Trailhead from Interstate Highway 25, by taking exit 257B. Head west on U.S. Highway 34 through Loveland, continuing 2.0 miles past the last signal in town at Wilson Street. U.S. Highway 34 narrows to a two-lane road 1.0 mile beyond this intersection. Drive past a black wooden fence, and a small brown sign for the Devil's Backbone Open Space on the right. A white, water storage tank, which is just past the turnoff, comes into view on the right, just beyond mile marker 88. Hidden Valley Estates uses the same access road from the highway. Turn right and proceed on the paved road a short distance and then turn left onto the gravel road at the large rust colored Devil's Backbone sign. Drive to the far end of the parking lot and back your trailer into one of five trailer parking spaces.

Trail #36
Devil's Backbone trails

Trail rideable	Year round, if snow free
Best time to ride	Summer evenings before sunset, and warm winter days
Maximum elevation	5,400 feet
Difficulty	**Moderate**, with some steep rocky areas and an avoidable **Advanced** stretch
Terrain	♘ ♘ ♘ for short steep rocky areas
Training ability	✚ ✚ for bicycles and dogs
Length	6.1 miles
Elevation gain	320 feet
Best features	This trail is close to town and has great views of Longs Peak at sunset. Riders can turn around at any point, from 1.0 mile to many miles away
Obstacles	Steep and/or rocky areas
Special notes	This trail is hot in the summertime, offering no shade or water along the trail, but the snow melts quickly in the wintertime. Dogs are allowed on a six foot leash. This trail connects to the Blue Sky Trail, and is part of a 50-mile trail system

This geologically interesting area is close enough to Loveland to go for a ride after work in the summertime. Light clouds can create outstanding sunsets here. The trails and parking lot close at dusk so plan evening rides accordingly. The trails here were renamed in 2006. This description uses the new names as shown on the 06/06 Larimer County Parks and Open Lands map, but the trail signposts had not been updated at that time.

To access the Backbone Trail, use the bridle path that starts at the southwest corner of the trailer parking lot. This trail dips through a low, shady area before climbing slightly and joining the main trail. Once on the main trail, continue through a gate and a dry irrigation ditch; horses cannot cross on the bridge. Then the trail parallels the Devil's Backbone for 2.0 miles. These "hogbacks", which can be seen from north of Fort Collins to south of Colorado Springs, are the result of an ancient sea bed that has been exposed and eroded by the forces of nature that are continually reshaping our environment. On the east side of the valley a new subdivision is being built, and closer to the trail are the remnants of an old Gypsum mine which, although somewhat unsightly, has not been reclaimed for historical reasons.

After passing a bench on the left, the trail arrives at the Wild Loop trail. The western half of the Wild Loop is parallel to the eastern half of the Wild Loop. The western half is closer to the rock formation however, and is not open to horses to help limit erosion in that area. This loop is the first of three loops on this trail, each one connected to the next one by the main trail, which is ridden on the outbound ride and again on the return ride.

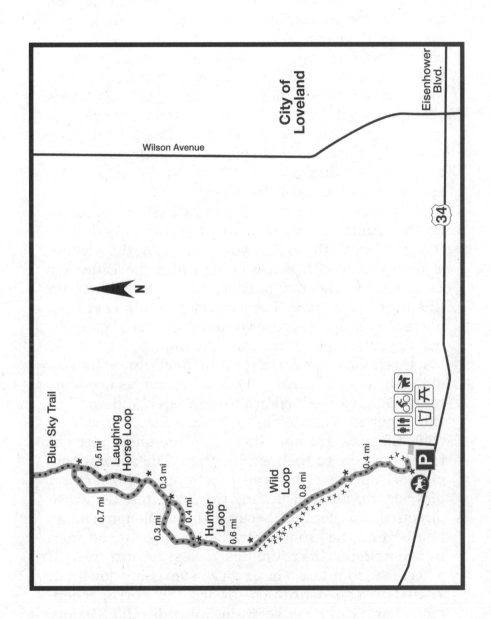

City of Loveland

Wilson Avenue

Eisenhower Blvd.

34

Blue Sky Trail

Laughing Horse Loop

0.5 mi

0.7 mi

0.3 mi

0.3 mi

0.4 mi

Hunter Loop

0.3 mi

0.6 mi

Wild Loop

0.8 mi

0.4 mi

P

N

Continue on the Wild Trail, passing the junction where the western part of this loop joins the main trail. Next, this route crosses the valley, and passes the only tree along this route before climbing up a steep and narrow segment to a trail junction. To reduce your interactions with other trail users on this part of the trail, look for people coming down, and wait for them to descend before heading up this section of trail. The quality of this steep area of trail varies, due to its heavy usage and difficult footing, so judge for yourself if it is safe to ride your horse over it. If not, then dismount and lead your horse past the spot with questionable footing.

At the next junction, you can ride either direction on the Hunter Loop trail, but this route heads left, toward the north, where you can enjoy the view of a large valley with a few houses and the Blue Sky Trail running through it. Bicycles are not allowed on this part of the loop. Then the loop heads east on a narrow trail that dips down and then rises up again before reaching another trail junction.

At this junction, turn left and keep riding northward, along the top of the ridge. Follow the trail as it swings to the east, where it comes to a flat area and another trail junction. Turn left onto the Laughing Horse Loop trail. Bicycles are not allowed on the short piece of trail from here to the next junction. The second part of the loop, past the trail junction, is shorter and bicycles are allowed. Riding this trail in a clockwise direction is preferable, because the challenging areas just beyond the junction are better approached from this direction. This route heads west toward the cliff where it encounters a large rocky step going downhill. Then the trail continues toward the north, where more homes can be seen dotting the ridge. Before long, it travels down the hill toward the east, where the trail junction for the Blue Sky Trail is situated.

That trail continues a short distance further north on the ridge, before it descends into the valley to the west. The Parks and Open Lands trail crews have done a marvelous job of making this steep drop-off into a user-friendly trail. To extend your ride to a total of 9.0 miles round trip, turn left onto the Blue Sky Trail, and ride down the hill into the valley you saw from the Hunter Loop. Then continue south on this trail until you reach two cottonwood trees that offer welcome shade on summer days and a bench to eat your lunch. For an even longer ride, continue on this trail as far as you want to, passing two junctions for the Indian Summer Trail along the way. Return the way you came, or turn right at the Indian Summer Trail and right again onto the Blue Sky Trail. For a further description of the Blue Sky and Indian Summer Trails, see trail #41. Turn around wherever you want to stop and ride back to the Laughing Horse Loop.

This route, however, continues east on the Laughing Horse Loop, which has been rated **Advanced**. If you do not want to ride this piece of the loop, return the way you came. Just past the Blue Sky Trail junction the trail makes an abrupt turn to the south. Horses must make a large step up, onto a rock, at the same time as the turn. Let your mount look it over, and go up where he or she is comfortable, usually close to where you first approach it. After going up this one large step, carefully traverse a slabby spot that is somewhat slippery. Before long, this part of the loop rejoins the main trail where the loop began.

When the Laughing Horse Loop returns to the junction with the main trail, this route stays left and heads south, back down the main trail it came on. At the following trail junction stay left, and follow the other half of the Hunter Loop. This part of the loop soon comes around a hill and heads west, descending to the junction with the Wild Loop. Turn left there and head down the steep and narrow trail you came on, looking for other trail users before descending. At the bottom of the hill, the trail angles west toward Devil's Backbone, passing the lone tree again. Follow this trail back to the trailhead.

Coyote Ridge Natural Area Trailhead

Drive to the trailhead	🔑 🔑 🔑
Parking	🅿 🅿 🅿
Amenities	None
Fee Area?	No
Elevation	5,032 feet
Maps	Get a brochure with a map at the trailhead; the USGS Loveland map does not show the trails here

This trailhead is simple to drive to and to turn around in. It received a new parking lot in 2005 with five pull-through horse trailer parking spaces. While this area is owned by the City of Fort Collins, a trail that provides access to Larimer County's trail network was added in 2006.

Directions from southern Larimer County or Interstate Highway 25

Drive to the Coyote Ridge Trailhead by traveling west on Colorado State Highway 402 from Exit 255, or on U.S. Highway 34 from Exit 257B. Turn right onto Wilson Avenue, at the furthest west traffic signal in Loveland. Coyote Ridge is 5.0 miles north of U.S. Highway 34. The parking area is 1.0 mile north of 57th Street, on the left and at the bottom of a slight hill, and just past a sign for Coyote Ridge Ranch.

Directions from Northern Larimer County

Drive to the Coyote Ridge Trailhead by traveling west to Taft Hill Road in Fort Collins and turning south.

The trailhead is on the right and at the bottom of a slight hill, 3.5 miles south of the junction with Harmony Road, and 1.0 mile south of Trilby Road.

Directions from the turnoff

After pulling off the paved road, turn right and drive to the designated trailer parking area, at the north end of the parking lot.

Trail #37
Coyote Ridge Natural Area

Trail rideable	Year round
Best time to ride	Spring and Fall
Maximum elevation	5,600 feet
Difficulty	**Moderate** with one unavoidable, **Demanding** stairway after 2.0 miles
Terrain	♘ to ♘♘♘♘ for one Demanding area with large steep steps
Training ability	**+ +** for bicycles
Length	4.0 to 7.1 miles round trip, or more if desired
Elevation gain	578 feet
Best features	Year round riding, great views of Loveland, Fort Collins, and the Front Range; riders can turn around at any point, from 1.0 mile to many miles away
Obstacles	This trail has one very steep hill with large steps, and occasional bicycles
Special notes	Very little shade and no water are available on the trail, except from a hydrant 1.0 mile from the trailhead

This area is owned by the city of Fort Collins, and is a designated wildlife preserve. The route is interesting as it crosses various habitats. Since the trail is a part of a 50-mile trail network, a ride can be extended as far as desired. It could also be used as a 2.0 to 4.0 mile round trip training ride, turning around after enjoying the great views, and before descending the difficult stairway.

The actual trailhead for this area is at the southwest corner of the automobile parking area. Since that area is cement, an alternate entrance has been constructed on the west side of the trailer parking area where horses can access the trail. The first 1.0 mile of this trail is a fairly level, gravel road that is not open to vehicles. A hitching post, a frost-free water hydrant, and a visitor center with restrooms are located at that point. Beyond the visitor center, the trail travels up a continuous 1.0 mile hill. A north facing area, at the first turn in the trail, can be icy in the wintertime. The ice can be avoided by riding a large loop out to the right in the grass. The views at the top of the ridge are engaging to the east, as well as the west. A sighting tool has been installed there to identify distinctive features. The first 2.0 miles of this trail could be a good first time trail ride for a novice rider or horse.

Continue along the ridge to a steep stairway dropping into the valley. Riders may want to dismount to negotiate this challenging feature. From here the trail is called the Rimrock Trail, and this area is part of the Devil's Backbone Open Space. Cross the valley, watching for prairie dog holes. Ride up the next ridge and around the small loop in either direction, passing a junction with the Blue Sky Trail.

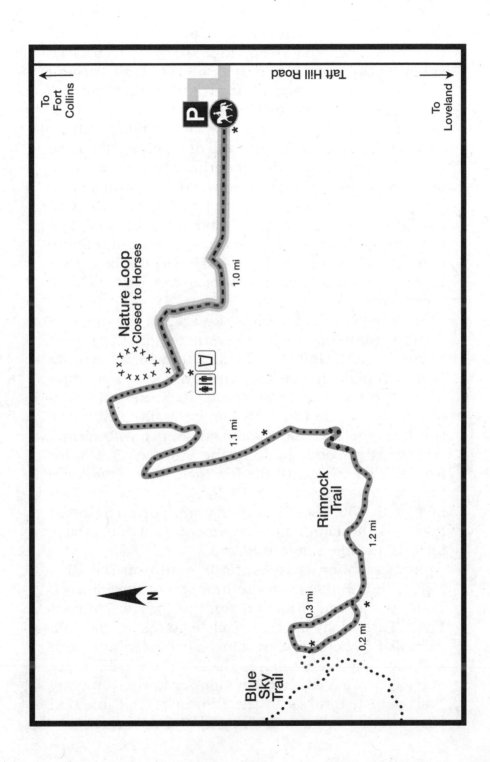

To
Fort
Collins

Taft Hill Road

To
Loveland

P

Nature Loop
Closed to Horses

1.0 mi

1.1 mi

Rimrock
Trail

1.2 mi

0.3 mi

0.2 mi

Blue
Sky
Trail

N

Return the way you came, or to continue on that trail ride down the steep ridge 0.1 mile to a large valley. At the junction with the Blue Sky Trail, turning right leads to a narrow, rolling trail. That trail follows the valley northward for 3.0 miles, before reaching a road underpass. The trail crew has installed rubber mats, improving the footing and dampening the noise just for horses. After the underpass, the trail comes to a flat area with large cottonwood trees and a large slab of rock that makes a nice bench. This is a good place for a lunch break. Beyond this nice spot, the trail enters a busy campground, so turn around here and return the way you came. This would be a 13.3 mile ride round trip, but horses can turn around anywhere along the trail.

Turning left onto the Blue Sky Trail at the junction with the Rimrock Trail has several options. That trail heads down the hill for 0.2 mile after which the route swings out to the west to give an eagle that nests along the cliff plenty of space. It passes two trail junctions for the Indian Summer Trail. Continuing south on the Blue Sky Trail leads to two cottonwood trees that provide shade in the summer, 1.4 miles from the junction with the Rimrock Trail. From here the trail reaches the Devil's Backbone trails in 1.0 mile, with 150 feet of elevation gain. Turning around there, at the Laughing Horse Loop junction, would make a 12-mile ride round trip.

Another option is to continue south on the Blue Sky Trail 0.3 mile from the junction of the Rimrock Trail to the trail junction for the Indian Summer Trail. Turn right on that trail heading up the hill, gaining 350 feet of elevation before heading south and then east, returning to the Blue Sky Trail in 2.1 miles. Turn left at that junction, onto the Blue Sky Trail, which returns to the Rimrock Trail junction after another 1.0 mile making a 10.6-mile ride.

Whichever option you choose, on the return trip ride up the hill at the junction with the Rimrock Trail, and turn either way at the junction of the Rimrock loop to return to the Coyote Natural Area Trailhead the way you came.

Horsetooth Mountain Park, Main Trailhead

Drive to the trailhead	🔑 🔑 🔑
Parking	🅿 🅿 🅿
Amenities	Restroom, picnic tables, hitching posts
Fee Area?	Yes
Elevation	5,900 feet
Maps	A brochure and a map are available at the trailhead for these trails; the USGS map is Horsetooth Reservoir, but these trails are not shown on that map

This trailhead near Ft. Collins offers designated horse trailer parking for two trailers. These trails and the parking lot close at dusk.

Directions from Larimer County and Interstate Highway 25

Drive to the Horsetooth Mountain Park Trailhead by traveling west on Harmony Road from Interstate Highway 25 Exit 265 or U.S. Highway 287 in Fort Collins. This road becomes Larimer County Road 38E when it continues west past Taft Hill Road. This intersection is noteworthy for the gas station located on its northwest corner which sells diesel as well as gasoline, and can accommodate a truck pulling a large horse trailer. From there, it is 6.4 miles on CR 38E to the trailhead, which is on the right side of the road and is marked by a sign. The horse trailer parking is on the west side of the parking lot, and is accessed by making a left turn near the far end of the parking lot before parking on the right. A park ranger is often available near the self-service fee station to collect the required fee. Otherwise, unless you have an annual park pass displayed, the $6.00 fee (as of 2008) should be put in the lock box and the stub left on the windshield.

This fee grants you access to 28 miles of trails covering 2,772 acres in Horsetooth Mountain Park as well as the trails in Lory State Park. Those trails are accessible from the Horsetooth Park trailheads and encompass another 2400 acres. Horsetooth Mountain Park is also part of the Larimer County Lands and Open Spaces trail system. With so many trails, one could ride here a dozen times without repeating the same ride twice. If you think you will ride, hike, or boat here more than ten times in one calendar year, it is a better value to purchase a yearly pass than to pay the daily fee. Pick up a map when you pay your fee. The trail system here is convoluted and extensive, and can be quite confusing.

Larimer County Parks and Open Lands is working to preserve the integrity of the ponderosa pine forest here. Due to the drought and a pine beetle infestation, which may be a result of the drought, some of the trees have died creating a fire hazard. You may see tree thinning activity, or the resulting tree stumps, as you ride through the park. Hopefully, this tree thinning will create a sustainable forest that is not a fire hazard to nearby homes.

Trail #38
Wathen Trail

Trail rideable	Year round, if snow free
Best time to ride	Early spring and late fall
Maximum elevation	6,900 feet
Difficulty	**Moderate**
Terrain	♘ ♘ for steep trail
Training ability	**+ +**
Length	6.5 miles round trip
Elevation gain	1,000 feet
Best features	A short loop to get oriented
Obstacles	Mountain bikes, challenging trail segments
Special notes	Water available seasonally, dogs are allowed on a leash

This trail is a nice introduction to the type of trails encountered at Horsetooth Park and demonstrates how to get in and out of the park from this trailhead. The one disadvantage to riding in Horsetooth Park from this trailhead is that it takes 45 minutes to ride to the area where most of the trails come together, and another 45 minutes to get back, making all the routes here fairly long.

Access this trail from the parking lot by riding west from the trailer parking onto the South Ridge Trail. This trail heads west and is fairly flat for a short distance, then it switchbacks to the right and traverses the hill as it climbs. At the top of this climb it veers left, near a bench and the junction with the Soderburg Trail. That trail leads back to the parking lot, but it

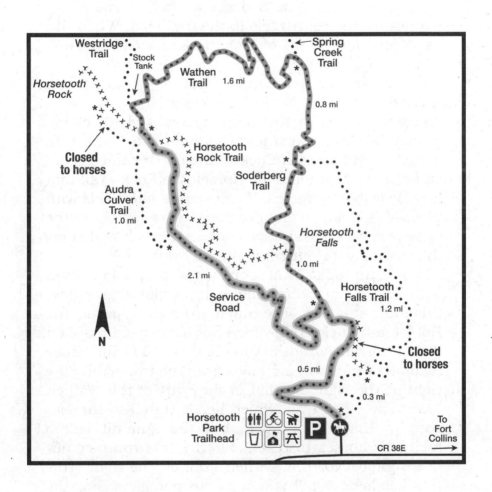

Westridge
Trail

Spring
Creek
Trail

Stock
Tank

Wathen
Trail   1.6 mi

Horsetooth
Rock

0.8 mi

**Closed
to horses**

Horsetooth
Rock Trail

Soderberg
Trail

Audra
Culver
Trail
1.0 mi

Horsetooth
Falls

1.0 mi

2.1 mi

Service
Road

Horsetooth
Falls Trail
1.2 mi

**Closed
to horses**

0.5 mi

0.3 mi

Horsetooth
Park
Trailhead

P

To
Fort
Collins

CR 38E

N

has a trail marker indicating that it is for hikers only. The trail climbs less slowly after this, coming to a trail junction in a short distance. Stay on the South Ridge Trail as it curves to the left. The sign indicates this is the Audra Culver Trail; the map, however, shows this as a continuation of the South Ridge Trail. The road on the right, the Soderberg Trail, is one of the options for the return trip to the trailhead. When you see a junction on the left for the Audra Culver Trail, continue on the road.

The Audra Culver Trail starts as a nice walk through the trees with little elevation gain. As it reaches the top of the ridge, glorious views of the mountains to the west and Glade Road to the south, as well as Horsetooth Rock to the north can be seen. Unfortunately, it joins the Horsetooth Rock Trail that is impassable to horses. If you want a short ride with nice views this is a great option. Grassy areas on the ridge make a pleasant spot to take a break and enjoy the views before returning the way you came.

The South Ridge Trail soon comes to a trail junction with no trail markers, only a memorial sign, where this route stays left. The trail to the right is part of the Horsetooth Rock Trail, which has a steep staircase on it that horses cannot negotiate. Soon the trail comes to another junction 2.6 miles from the trailhead. Stay right at the signpost that is the start of the Wathen Trail. The other trail, which heads uphill to the left, goes to Horsetooth Rock, but the summit is too rocky for horses to reach. Shortly this route comes to a signpost for the Wathen Trail on the right. This trail heads downhill at a fairly steep angle, losing the elevation that was gained on the first part of the ride.

Near the top of the Wathen Trail, a signpost shows a turnoff to a waterhole. This is one of several springs in the park that has been tapped to send water to stock tanks, when they are flowing. After 1.6, miles the Wathen Trail arrives at the valley floor. It then crosses the end of a meadow and Spring Creek, where horses may be able to get a drink, before intersecting with the Spring Creek Trail. This route turns right here, and before long the trail drops steeply into a busy area where three trails come together. A bench and the stream encourage hikers to linger here. The trail approaching this trail junction is challenging for horses, so riders may want to dismount. Once down the steep part, the trail is again at Spring Creek, the same stream this route crossed earlier. Where the creek drops down the hill, as the trail does, it is called Culver Falls.

At this point, riders can take either trail option, so both descriptions follow. Turning to the right is the more direct and easier option. This route crosses the creek on a small dirt covered bridge, and traverses

up the short hill ahead until reaching a meadow. It continues to climb up the side of the meadow and then the trail widens to a road. After 1.0 mile the trail joins the South Ridge Trail. Turn left and ride down the hill the way you came.

Turning left at the three-way junction leads to the Horsetooth Falls Trail to the south. This trail should only be ridden in this direction and never when any snow is on the ground, due to an unsafe bridge. Before long, the short spur trail to Horsetooth Falls intersects the main trail on the right. During a wet spring, the falls can be quite attractive; in the autumn they usually have no water in them at all. From there, the parking lot is only 1.0 mile away, and the trail is popular with hikers and families for this reason. The next part of the trail is the challenging part, with stair steps going up and down, and then crossing a bridge with no railings. After the bridge, the trail veers to the left heading steeply up stair steps on the far side. While this combination is not difficult from this direction, it could be disastrous if the horse slipped on the stairs when approaching the bridge from the south. The Soderburg Trail and the Horsetooth Falls Trail merge into one trail for the last 0.2 miles before arriving back at the parking lot.

Trail #39
Westridge Trail

Trail rideable	Year round, if snow free
Best time to ride	Early spring and late fall
Maximum elevation	7,000 feet
Difficulty	**Moderate**
Terrain	♘ ♘ for short steep steps
Training ability	**+ +**
Length	8.9 miles round trip
Elevation gain	1,100 feet
Best features	A real mountain experience close to town
Obstacles	Mountain bikes are common on the lower portions of this trail, and some challenging trail segments are encountered
Special notes	Water available seasonally, dogs are allowed on a leash

It is surprising how much this area feels like it is in the mountains. It even smells like the mountains! So when you want a trip to the mountains, and it is too cold or too far to go there, come to Horsetooth Mountain Park instead.

Access this trail from the parking lot by riding west from the trailer parking onto the South Ridge Trail. This trail heads west and is fairly flat for a short distance, then it switchbacks to the right and traverses the hill as it climbs. At the top of this climb, it veers left near a bench and the junction

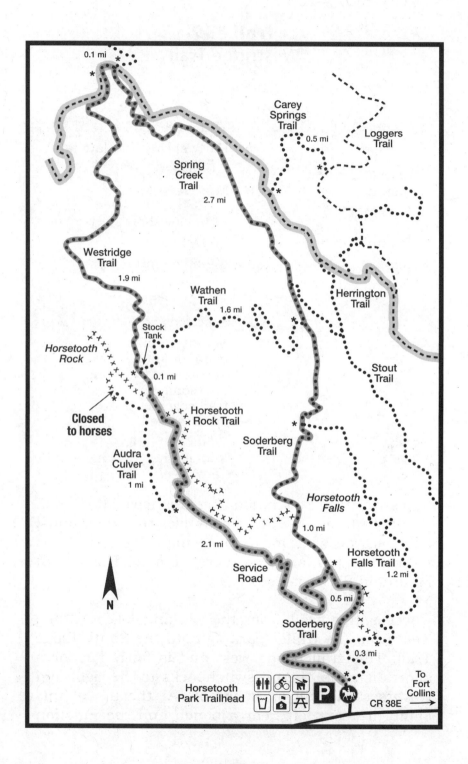

0.1 mi

Carey
Springs
Trail

Loggers
Trail

0.5 mi

Spring
Creek
Trail

2.7 mi

Westridge
Trail

1.9 mi

Wathen
Trail

1.6 mi

Herrington
Trail

Stock
Tank

*Horsetooth
Rock*

Stout
Trail

0.1 mi

**Closed
to horses**

Horsetooth
Rock Trail

Soderberg
Trail

Audra
Culver
Trail

1 mi

*Horsetooth
Falls*

1.0 mi

Horsetooth
Falls Trail

1.2 mi

2.1 mi

Service
Road

0.5 mi

Soderberg
Trail

N

0.3 mi

Horsetooth
Park Trailhead

P

To
Fort
Collins

CR 38E →

286

with the Soderburg Trail. That trail leads to the parking lot, but it has a trail marker indicating that it is for hikers only.

The trail climbs less slowly after this, coming to a trail junction in a short distance. Stay on the road as it curves to the left. The sign indicates this is the Audra Culver Trail; the map, however, shows this as a continuation of the South Ridge Trail. The road on the right, the Soderberg Trail, is one of the options for the return to the trailhead. When you see a junction on the left for the Audra Culver Trail stay on the road. The South Ridge Trail comes to a trail junction with no trail markers, only a memorial sign, where this route stays left. The trail to the right is part of the Horsetooth Rock Trail, which has a steep staircase on it that horses cannot negotiate. Soon the trail comes to another junction. Stay right at the signpost, which is the start of the Wathen Trail. The other trail, which heads uphill to the left, goes to Horsetooth Rock, but the summit is too rocky for horses to reach. Continue straight past a signpost for the Wathen Trail on the right. This is the beginning of the Westridge Trail. Soon another signpost shows a turnoff to a waterhole. This is one of several springs in the park that has been tapped to send water to stock tanks when water is available.

This route heads north for 1.9 miles along the side of the mountain below Horsetooth Rock on the Westridge Trail, and is a real mountain experience. As the trail reaches the ridge on the north sporting a plethora of antennae, it curves to the east and follows the ridge until the trail ends.

At the dirt service road, turn right. The Mill Creek and Spring Creek trails intersect the road after 0.1 mile. The trailhead can be reached via the Spring Creek Trail or the Towers Trail. The first option follows Spring Creek Trail south 2.7 miles. Horses may be able to drink out of Spring Creek, on the right, near the junction with the Wathen Trail, when there is water in the stream. The second option continues south on the Towers Trail, until reaching the junction for the Herrington Trail, which angles off to the right. Stay right and follow that trail 0.5 mile over the ridge and back down. When the Herrington Trail intersects the Spring Creek Trail, this route turns left.

Both options continue south on the Spring Creek Trail. Soon the trail drops steeply into a busy area where three trails come together. A bench and a stream encourage hikers to linger here. The descent approaching this junction is challenging for horses, so riders may want to dismount.

At this point, riders can take either trail option, so both descriptions follow. Turning to the right is the more direct and easier option. This route crosses the creek on a small dirt covered bridge, and traverses up the short hill ahead until it reaches a meadow. It

continues to climb up the side of the meadow, and then the trail widens to a road. After 1.0 mile the trail joins the South Ridge Trail. Turn left and ride down the hill the way you came.

Turning left at the three-way junction leads to the Horsetooth Falls Trail, to the south. This trail should only be ridden in this direction, and never when any snow is on the ground. Before long, the short spur trail to Horsetooth Falls intersects the main trail on the right. During a wet spring the Falls can be quite attractive; in the autumn they probably have no water in them at all. From here, it is 1.0 mile to the parking lot, and the trail is popular with hikers and families for this reason. The next part of the trail is the challenging part, with stair steps going up and down, and then crossing a bridge with no railings. After the bridge, the trail veers to the left, heading steeply up the steps on the far side. While this combination is not difficult from this direction, it could be disastrous if the horse slipped when approaching the bridge from the south. The Soderburg Trail and the Horsetooth Falls Trail merge into one trail for the last 0.2 mile before arriving back at the parking lot.

Other Options

The possibilities for combining various trails here, and with the trails in Lory State Park, are many. I often come with an idea of where I want to ride, and end up doing something totally different, because I make a wrong turn or decide to explore a trail that I may not have been on before. Relax and enjoy the ride, and eventually you will be able to find your way to the large meadow with Spring Creek Trail running through it. From that point, if you head south on Spring Creek Trail, all trails lead to the parking lot.

Horsetooth Mountain Park, Soderburg Trailhead

Drive to the trailhead	𝄞 𝄞 𝄞
Parking	P P P
Amenities	Restrooms, a drinking fountain, a frost free hydrant, and picnic tables
Fee Area?	Yes
Elevation	5,450 feet
Maps	A brochure and a map of these trails is available at the trailhead; the USGS map is Horsetooth Reservoir, but these trails are not shown on this map

This trailhead is quite close to Ft. Collins, and it is simple to drive to it. The parking lot provides uncomplicated access to Horsetooth Mountain as well as the Blue Sky Trail that opened in June 2006. These trails and the parking lot close at dusk.

Directions from Larimer County or Interstate Highway 25

Drive to the Soderburg Trailhead by traveling west on Harmony Road from Interstate Highway 25 Exit 265, or U.S. Highway 287 in Fort Collins. This road becomes Larimer County Road 38E west of Taft Hill Road. That intersection is noteworthy for the gas station located on its northwest corner which sells diesel as well as gasoline, and can accommodate a truck pulling a large horse trailer. From here, drive 5.7 miles on CR 38E, to the turnoff for the Soderberg Trailhead and Inlet Bay on the right side of the road, marked by a sign. Turn right and follow the paved road 1.3 miles, to the paved parking lot on the left with an entrance gate. Past the parking lot, the access road becomes a private road. When leaving, use the designated exit at the south end of the parking lot. This lot has spaces long enough for a trailer or two automobiles, although at this time, none of them have been designated specifically for horse trailers.

A parking lot designated for the Blue Sky Trail is planned for the future. Until then, if this lot is full, horse trailers can park in the Marina parking lot. Access that parking area by driving through the fee station as described below. After the fee station, stay to the right to drive to the marina parking area. Ride on the Inlet Bay Trail, located between the parking area and the road, to access the trailhead to the north or the Blue Sky Trail to the south.

If you do not have a Larimer County Park Pass displayed, the $6.00 (as of 2008) fee should be put in the lock box and the stub left on the windshield. If you would like to purchase a yearly pass, the marina has a fee station that is open during boating season. To approach this fee station from the access road, stay right at the sign that reads "entrance". After the pull-through fee station drive forward slowly, staying left until the stop sign, and then turning right to continue on to the Soderberg parking lot.

The fee grants you access to Horsetooth Mountain Park, as well as being able to ride, but not drive, into Lory State Park to the north. This is also the trailhead for the Blue Sky Trail, which travels southward. With 50 miles of trails, one could ride here a dozen times without repeating the same ride twice. If you think you will ride, hike, or boat here more than ten times in one calendar year, it is a better value to purchase a yearly pass than to pay the daily fee.

Pick up a map for Horsetooth Park or the Blue Sky Trail at the trailhead. The trail system in Horsetooth Park, while extensive, is convoluted and can be confusing. When in doubt, follow the trail signs. When the ground is wet, the trails in the valley are very muddy. Entering and leaving Horsetooth Park by the service road, which has been renamed the Towers Trail, might be an option, but refrain from riding the Nomad Trail if it is muddy, to avoid damaging the trail.

Larimer County Parks and Open Lands is working to preserve the integrity of the ponderosa pine forest here. Due to the drought and a pine beetle infestation, which may be a result of the drought, some of the trees have died, creating a fire hazard. You may see tree thinning activity, or the resulting tree stumps as you ride through the park. Hopefully, this tree thinning will create a sustainable forest that is not a fire hazard to nearby homes.

Trail #40
Nomad Trail

Trail rideable	Year round, as long as the ground is dry
Best time to ride	Fall and winter
Maximum elevation	5,550 feet
Difficulty	**Easy,** could be ridden barefoot
Terrain	♘
Training ability	**+**
Length	7.2 miles round trip
Elevation gain	100 feet
Best features	**Easy** trails, good footing, no horseshoes needed
Obstacles	Bicycles allowed. Plenty of horses being ridden, small bridges
Special notes	No shade or water, avoid this trail if it is muddy, dogs are allowed on a leash

This is a great little ride. It does not get any easier than this.

Access the trail on the north side of the parking area, near the sign for the trailhead. Ride on the Swan Johnson Trail for .75 miles, where it ends at a service road called Towers Trail. Although only the Nomad Trail is shown on the map going north up the valley, there are in fact two trails. This route follows the one to the west; so turn left onto the service road and ride for a short distance. Turn right onto the Nomad Trail at the next junction near a

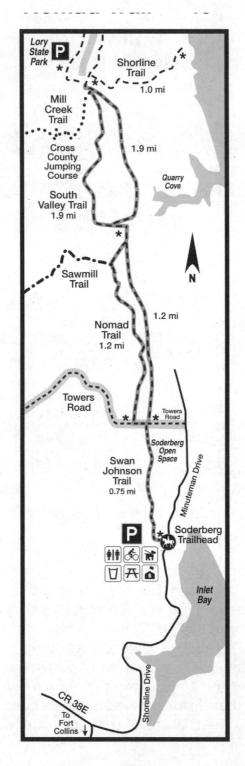

small pond. After 1.2 miles, the two trails merge. Continue riding north and soon this route leaves Horsetooth Mountain Park and enters Lory State Park. The trail is now called the Valley Trail, which ends at a parking lot in less than 2.0 miles. The trail on the northern end of the valley splits into two trails as well. This route stays left at the split. This trail passes an old cross-country jumping course along the last 1.0 mile to the parking lot. Turn right just before the parking lot.

Before long another junction comes into view. Turning left there will take you to the optional 2.5 mile trail extension. Soon that trail comes to a junction for the Shoreline Trail. Turn right there and ride 1.0 mile to the shore of Horsetooth Reservoir. On the way back, stay left at both junctions.

Turn right at the second junction near the parking lot to return to the trailhead. This option, although not on the map, is closer to Horsetooth Reservoir and at one point comes quite close to Quarry Cove. When the trail crosses back into Horsetooth Mountain Park, the two trails merge and become the Nomad Trail. When the trail forks again, this route stays left for the sake of diversity. When that trail ends at the gravel road, turn right. To return to the trailhead, turn left onto the Swan Johnson Trail at the next junction.

Trail #41
Stout Trail loop

Trail rideable	Year round, as long as the ground is dry
Best time to ride	Early spring and late fall
Maximum elevation	6,400 feet
Difficulty	**Moderate**
Terrain	♘ ♘
Training ability	+
Length	6.5 miles round trip
Elevation gain	950 feet
Best features	Low elevation, interesting views, and a more open feel than the rest of Horsetooth
Obstacles	Mountain bikes are common here
Special notes	This trail has very little shade and no water; dogs are allowed on a leash

This is a great winter trail with impressive views of Horsetooth Reservoir as well as all of Fort Collins and beyond. It can be hot in the summer as it has little shade.

To access this route, ride north past the trail board on the north side of the parking lot. Follow the Swan Johnson Trail .75 miles, where it ends. Turn left there onto a service road called the Towers Trail. Ride up the hill, passing a junction for the Nomad Trail. Before long, the trail comes to a signpost for the Stout Trail where this route turns left, headed south. After 0.5 mile, the trail passes near the edge

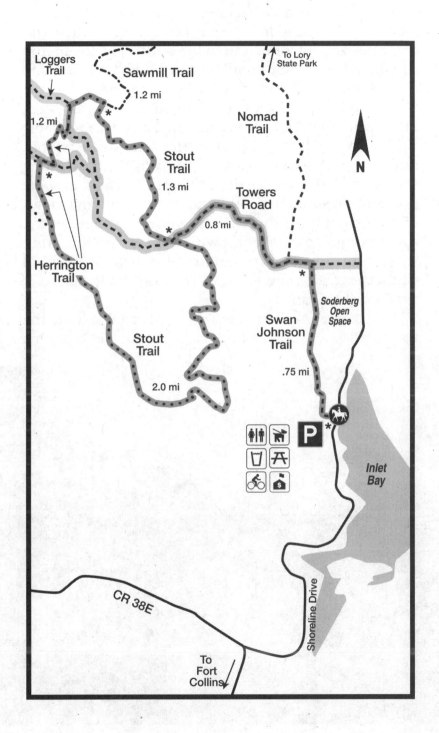

Loggers
Trail

Sawmill Trail

1.2 mi

To Lory
State Park

1.2 mi

*

Nomad
Trail

Stout
Trail

1.3 mi

N

Towers
Road

0.8 mi

*

Herrington
Trail

*

Soderberg
Open
Space

Swan
Johnson
Trail

Stout
Trail

.75 mi

2.0 mi

P *

Inlet
Bay

Shoreline Drive

CR 38E

To
Fort
Collins

of the park at its southernmost spot. Social trails can make it difficult to follow the trail there. A fence and dirt road are downhill and to the south. A **Closed** and unlabeled trail that should be avoided, as it is quite dangerous, heads off to the west from the fence.

This route continues straight ahead, to the west and uphill, before heading north. Great views of Fort Collins, the southern part of Horsetooth Reservoir, and two of the dams can be enjoyed from all along the loop. 1.0 mile further, the trail reaches some ponderosa pine trees on a ridge, with terrific views of Longs Peak through the trees. After 0.5 mile, the route comes to a junction with the Herrington Trail, where this route turns right and heads downhill until the trail reaches the Towers Trail, where it turns right again.

From there, taking the Towers Trail back to the trailhead is a shorter and more direct option. This

route however, turns left again after a short distance, onto a continuation of the Herrington Trail. When the trail reaches an old road called the Loggers Trail, this route turns to the left and heads north, until it arrives at a signpost for the Sawmill Trail. Then it turns right onto the Sawmill Trail and heads downhill, passing a small cabin along the way. At the next junction, turn right onto the Stout Trail to finish the Stout Trail loop. Along the way, the trail crosses two bridges that are covered with dirt, which makes them quieter for the horses, but the lack of railings makes them somewhat less safe. When the trail arrives at the Towers Trail, this route turns left and returns to the trailhead the way it came. This loop, as described, totals 6.5 miles.

Rather than finishing the Stout Trail loop, another option is to continue on the more challenging Sawmill Trail until it reaches the valley floor. Then turn right onto the Nomad Trail, and follow it to the Towers Trail. To return to the trailhead, make a left turn onto the road, shortly followed by a right turn at the junction for the Swan Johnson Trail.

Trail #42
Blue Sky Trail

Trail rideable	Year round, as long as the ground is dry
Best time to ride	Springtime
Maximum elevation	5,500 feet
Difficulty	**Moderate**, could be ridden barefoot
Terrain	♘
Training ability	**+ +**
Length	13.4 miles round trip or more
Elevation gain	300 feet
Best features	This trail has little elevation gain; riders can turn around at any point, or access this trail from Coyote Ridge or Devil's Backbone trailheads
Obstacles	Bicycles are common here; the first part of the trail goes through a very busy campground and a road underpass
Special notes	This trail has no water and very little shade, dogs are allowed on a leash; the Indian Summer Trail option adds 1.4 miles and a 350 feet of elevation gain to the ride increasing the rating to **Moderate**

This was the final jewel of Larimer County's trail network to be put in place, opening in June 2006. It connects all the other trails, as well as being a nice trail on its own. A description of the entire trail is given here. Most likely, trail users will use parts of this trail in conjunction with other open space trails that are described in this guidebook. This description can be used when accessing this trail from these other open space areas.

Access this trail by leading your horse to the south end of the parking lot, and continue across the road on which you drove. If your mount is very dependable, ride him along the Inlet Bay Trail between the road and the campground. Soon this trail ends, and this route continues on the road through the campground. This is a very busy campground, complete with children and barking dogs where you may be more comfortable leading your horse than riding. After the campground, this route accesses the Blue Sky Trail that continues to the south. Before long, this trail passes through a road underpass. Thankfully, the underpass has rubber mats on the floor to make it safer and quieter for horses to walk through. After that challenge, you are in the Devil's Backbone open space, and the only obstacles are other trail users.

The entire length of the Blue Sky Trail runs south, along the west side of a ridge with beautiful red sandstone outcroppings, except at the very end of the trail, where it traverses up to the top of the ridge. Along the first part of the trail, on the right side, is a private dirt road that provides access to a ranch and the houses dotting the hillside. The trail is rolling, with good footing and some blind turns. Before long the houses are left behind, and Rimrock Ranch can be seen in the valley on the right. This ranch has beautiful pastures with mature cottonwood trees,

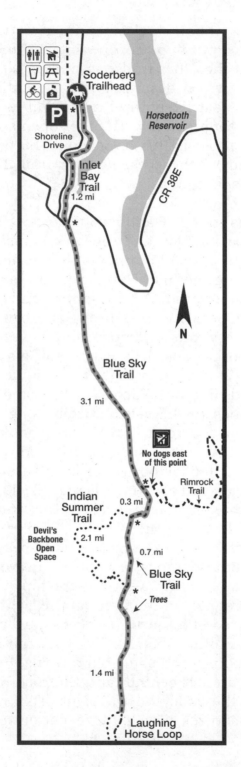

Soderberg
Trailhead

Horsetooth
Reservoir

Shoreline
Drive

Inlet
Bay
Trail
1.2 mi

CR 38E

N

Blue Sky
Trail

3.1 mi

No dogs east
of this point

Rimrock
Trail

Indian
Summer
Trail

0.3 mi

Devil's
Backbone
Open
Space

2.1 mi

0.7 mi

Blue Sky
Trail

Trees

1.4 mi

Laughing
Horse Loop

and horses are often seen grazing there. The strip of land the trail follows through this area used to be part of Rimrock Ranch.

Continue following the trail, which leaves the ranch behind and enters an area that was previously platted as the Indian Creek subdivision. Larimer County Parks and Opens Lands was able to purchase this area when the developer was unable to sell the individual lots quickly enough to meet his financial obligations.

Soon the trail comes to a junction with the Rimrock Trail, 3.0 miles from the underpass. That trail leads to the Coyote Ridge Natural Area, trail #36, via a steep 0.1 mile trail. This route continues down the hill. Most of Blue Sky Trail stays near the ridge on the east side of the valley. For the next 1.5 miles, however, the trail curves westward to limit its impact on a golden eagle that has nested on the cliff there for many years.

After 0.3 mile the route comes to a junction with the Indian Summer Trail. That loop is 1.4 miles long with 350 feet of elevation gain. It returns to the Blue Sky Trail 0.7 mile further south and can be ridden in either direction. In the springtime, the Indian Summer Trail is one of the most fabulous trails in this guidebook. Due to the elevation gain and distance from the trailheads very few trail users are seen here. The lack of trees encourages an abundance of spring wildflowers. As the trail reaches is highest point the views to the east are fabulous. To ride this trail turn right at that junction and head up the hill. When this trail rejoins the Blue Sky Trail, turn left to return the way you came for a 12-mile ride round trip or turn right to continue south on the Blue Sky Trail to the trees described below, which are only 0.4 mile away.

This route continues south, down the valley on the Blue Sky Trail. The trail returns to the east side of the valley after 1.1 miles, where there is an area seasonally shaded by two cottonwood trees. Two benches have been placed there which make this a nice place for lunch. This spot is an obvious turnaround spot, and would make an 11.4-mile ride round trip. Past this spot the trail begins climbing up the side of the ridge on the west side of the valley in its final 1.0 mile. The trail crew has done an amazing job of designing and installing this trail. This was a daunting task that they handled with aplomb, creating a user-friendly trail that horses handle with ease. The Blue Sky Trail and this description end on the top of the ridge, where the trail intersects the Laughing Horse Loop trail, which is part of the trails described under the Devil's Backbone Trail #35. That 1.2 mile long loop trail connects to the other trails there. The west side of this loop has a **Moderate** rating and the east side of the loop is rated **Advanced**.

Other Options

By this time, you realize the endless possibilities for combining various trails in Horsetooth Mountain Park, and in Lory State Park, not to mention the trails accessible from the Blue Sky Trail. I often come with an idea of where I want to ride and end up doing something totally different, because I make a wrong turn or decide to explore a trail that do not remember. In this situation a map makes it simple to choose a new route.

Lory State Park

Drive to the trailhead	🔑🔑
Parking	🅿️🅿️🅿️
Amenities	Restroom, picnic table, hitching post
Fee Area?	Colorado State Park fees apply
Elevation	5,500 feet
Maps	A brochure and a map of these trails is available at the trailhead; the USGS map is Horsetooth Reservoir, but these trails are not shown on this map

While it can be somewhat confusing to drive to Lory State Park, once there, it is a great trailhead with lots of pull through parking. You can even access the fee station from your rig. This park is by far the most trailer friendly area I have seen.

Lory State Park has plenty of trails, but many of the shorter ones are not open to horses. All the trails that are open to horses are described here, as well as how to access the trails in Horsetooth Mountain Park, which are also covered by the entrance fee. When the ground is wet, the trails here are a very muddy, and riding on them causes extensive trail damage. Please do not create additional work for Larimer County Horseman's Association and others who maintain the trails in this state park.

Directions from Interstate Highway 25 to North Fort Collins

Drive to Lory State Park by heading west on U.S. Highway 14 from exit 269, staying right when it merges with U.S. Highway 287.

Directions from Southern Larimer County or Boulder County to North Fort Collins

Drive to Lory State Park by heading north on U.S. Highway 287 through Fort Collins. As the highway approaches the north edge of town, it curves to the left and continues to the west.

Alternate directions from Loveland

Drive west to the last signal in Loveland at Wilson Street. Turn right on Wilson and continue to the first signal in Fort Collins at Harmony Ave. Turn left at that intersection onto Larimer County Road 38E. At the top of the hill turn right onto Larimer County Road 23. Drive the length of Horsetooth Reservoir, crossing two dams. This route has been blocked off in the past due to Homeland Security but it has been open since 2006. When you arrive at Larimer County Road 25G, turn left and continue 1.6 miles on this road, until the pavement ends at Lory State Park, then turn left onto a well-maintained gravel road. Continue by following the directions at the end of this section.

Directions from U.S. Highway 287 north of Fort Collins

Continue driving west on U.S. Highway 287 until the highway angles off to the northwest. Stay in the left lane and continue straight, toward the west, on Old Highway 287, also known as Larimer County Road 54G. A brown sign there indicates that Lory State

Park is straight ahead. Follow this road past Taft Hill Road and through the town of LaPorte. Take the Rist Canyon Road, also known as Larimer County Road 52E, which angles off to the left just past and across the street from Vern's restaurant. A sign for the park with an arrow is situated almost a full block before the actual turn, which is not marked. This turnoff is 3.0 miles from the start of CR 54G, and 1.7 miles from the intersection of Taft Hill and CR 54G.

Continue on CR 52E until reaching a green sign identifying the tiny town of Bellvue. Turn left onto Larimer County Road 23N at the three-way intersection in front of the building with Bellvue painted on it. Drive south on this road 1.3 miles until reaching the intersection with Larimer County Road 25G on the right, marked with a sign indicating that is the way to Lory State Park. After turning right, continue 1.6 miles on this road, until the pavement ends at Lory State Park, then turn left onto a well-maintained gravel road. The fee station is on the right, after 0.3 mile on the gravel road. Park users who do not have a State Park Pass can drive through and pay the daily or yearly fee at the window on the north side of the building. Trail maps are also available here.

Continue driving south on the gravel road from the fee station. A riding stable that is open in the summertime is on the left, 0.3 mile from the fee station. The first of the four parking lots on the left side of the road is located there as well. These trail descriptions are from the second parking lot, located 0.6 mile further along the road with a sign identifying it as the Eltuck Picnic Area. It has the same amenities as the third lot, but it is less busy. That lot is 1.0 mile further up the road, adjacent to the parking lot used by cars, and is also nice with plenty of pull through parking. Parking at that lot reduces the round trip mileage listed for these trails by 2.0 miles.

Trail #43
Valley Trails

Trail rideable	Year round, as long as the ground is dry
Best time to ride	Fall and winter
Maximum elevation	5,600 feet
Difficulty	**Easy**, could be ridden barefoot
Terrain	⊌
Training ability	✛
Length	8.0 miles round trip
Elevation gain	100 feet
Best features	**Easy** trails, good footing, no horseshoes needed
Obstacles	Bicycles are common, plenty of horses are ridden here, and the trail crosses some small bridges
Special notes	Dogs are allowed on a leash, no shade and no water are available on this trail

This trail is a nice winter or training ride. Bridle paths start at the riding stables and the Timber Picnic area, just past the entrance station, and they parallel the road on both the east and the west sides. These trails are appropriately named the East Valley and West Valley Trails respectively. They are each 2.2 miles long, and can be accessed at various points along the road. For the sake of the description, the trail narrative and mileage start from the Eltuck Parking area.

To access this route from the area near the hitching post and restrooms at the Eltuck Parking area, ride east on the trail leaving the parking lot. That trail soon intersects the East Valley Trail where this route turns right. Enjoy the nice views of Orchard Cove before coming to a junction with the Shoreline Trail. That trail leads to the edge of Horsetooth Reservoir in 1.0 mile and is open to horses. This route continues straight toward the south. Just past that junction is the end of the gravel road, where the third and fourth parking lots are located.

Although only one trail, named the South Valley Trail, is shown on the map going south, the trail splits into two trails. For some diversity, this route follows the one to the left that is closer to Horsetooth Reservoir, at one point coming quite close to Quarry Cove. Where the two trails merge, less than 2.0 miles from the third parking lot, this route leaves Lory State Park and enters Horsetooth Mountain Park.

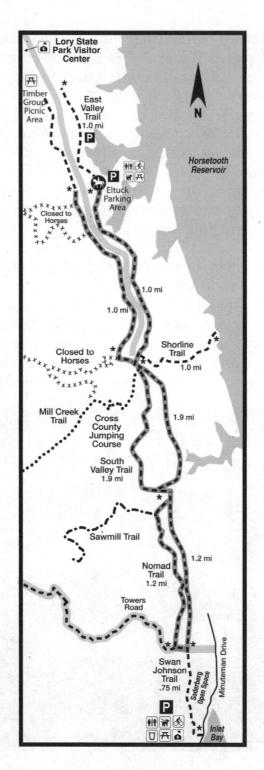

Lory State Park Visitor Center

Timber Group Picnic Area

East Valley Trail 1.0 mi

P

Horsetooth Reservoir

N

Closed to Horses

Eltuck Parking Area

1.0 mi

1.0 mi

Closed to Horses

Shorline Trail 1.0 mi

1.9 mi

Mill Creek Trail

Cross County Jumping Course

South Valley Trail 1.9 mi

Sawmill Trail

Nomad Trail 1.2 mi

1.2 mi

Towers Road

Swan Johnson Trail .75 mi

Soderberg Open Space

Minuteman Drive

P

Inlet Bay

This route is now on the 1.2-mile long Nomad Trail. The southern part of the Nomad Trail also splits into two trails. For the sake of description, stay left at the fork, and then turn right when the trail ends at a dirt service road named Towers Trail. Ride on this road for a short distance; passing a trail junction for the Swan Johnson Trail on the left that accesses the Soderberg Trailhead in 0.7 mile. Stay on Towers Trail, turning right at the signpost for the Nomad Trail near some trees and a small pond. When the trail crosses back into Lory State Park, this route stays left at the fork in the trail. The trail passes an old cross-country jumping course along the last 1.0 mile to the car parking lot.

This route stays to the left at the parking lot, and returns on the West Valley Trail. None of the trails heading west from the West Valley Trail are open to horses. The Eltuck parking area is on the right and a trail connects the West Valley Trail to the main road near there. Following these directions results in a ride that resembles two large loops, with a short piece of trail that is ridden twice connecting the two loops.

Trail #44
Mill Creek Trail

Trail rideable	Year round, as long as the ground is dry
Best time to ride	Fall and winter
Maximum elevation	6,600 feet
Difficulty	**Moderate** due to total distance and elevation gain
Terrain	♘ ♘
Training ability	✦
Length	9.5 miles round trip
Elevation gain	1,400 feet
Best features	The uncomplicated access to mountain trails
Obstacles	Bicycles are allowed and plenty of horses are ridden here
Special notes	Dogs are allowed on a leash, the trail described has no water

Most of this ride is actually in Horsetooth Mountain Park. The State Park fee allows you to ride, but not drive, into that 2,410-acre park as well as parking and riding in Lory State Park. While endless trail options exist there, this route describes one, with an alternate route. Once you and your horse are familiar with the trails described, make up your own routes. Get a map of the park at the Horsetooth Mountain Park's Main Trailhead or its Soderburg Trailhead and keep it with your tack, as a map is indispensable here and this area is not shown on either the Lory State Park maps or on commercial maps.

Access this route from the Eltuck parking area by crossing the main road, and turning left onto the West Valley Trail. None of the trails heading west from the West Valley Trail are open to horses. Ride south 1.0 mile, continuing past the main trailhead auto parking area, to a junction for Mill Creek Trail. Stay right there and the trail soon heads up the hill. Within 0.5 mile the trail crosses into Horsetooth Park. After another 1.0 mile of climbing, this route arrives at another trail junction.

The signpost there indicates that Loggers Trail is to the left. Stay right to continue on Mill Creek Trail. This route follows Mill Creek Trail until it ends at a dirt service road named Towers Trail, 3.5 miles from where it started. Turn left on the road and follow it to the first junction on the left. Turn left onto Carey Springs Trail at that junction. This 0.5-mile trail does not get as much traffic as the other trails, and a small meadow alongside the trail makes a nice place to take a break. A seasonal spring has been tapped to provide water for horses in a stock tank here. This route continues downhill and turns left when this short trail ends at the Loggers Trail. Ride north on the Loggers Trail until it ends at the junction that was passed on the ride up. Turn to the right onto the previously ridden Mill Creek Trail, which returns to the parking area.

A longer option would be to ride all the way down the hill on the Towers Trail from the end of the Mill Creek Trail, making an optional side trip to Carey Springs. After 2.5 miles, the Towers Trail comes to a signpost for the Nomad Trail near some trees and a small pond. Turn left, and after traveling north 1.2 miles through the meadow, the trail crosses back into Lory State Park. Stay left when the trail forks. Continue riding on this trail, named the South Valley

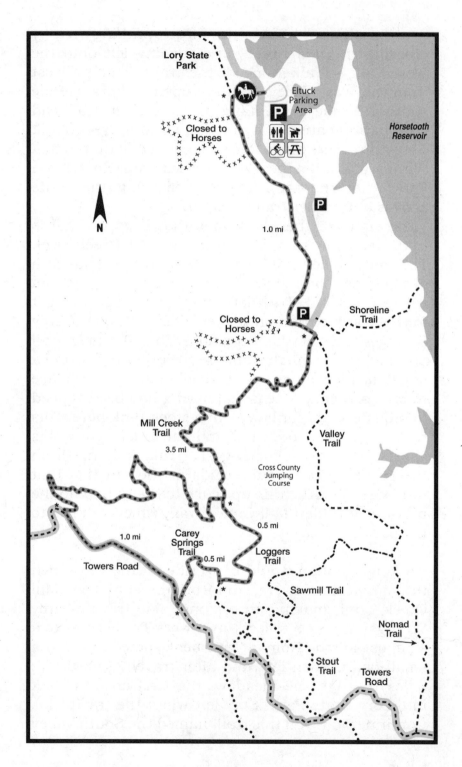

Trail, for 2.0 miles. The trail passes an old cross-country jumping course along the last 1.0 mile to the main trailhead. Stay to the left at this parking area to return the way you came, on the West Valley Trail to parking area two. Look for the trail to Eltuck Picnic area on your right 1.0 mile past the trailhead. This route totals 11.5 miles round trip.

Trail #45
Spring Creek Trail

Trail rideable	Year round, as long as the ground is dry
Best time to ride	Fall and winter
Maximum elevation	6,900 feet
Difficulty	**Advanced** due to short steep areas and total distance
Terrain	♘ ♘
Training ability	✚
Length	12 miles round trip
Elevation gain	1,400 feet
Best features	The uncomplicated access to mountain trails
Obstacles	Bicycles are allowed and plenty of horses are ridden here
Special notes	Dogs are allowed on a leash

This ride crosses over the ridge and continues into the drainage to the west. From there, you can see Horsetooth Rock and much of Horsetooth Mountain Park.

Access this route from the Eltuck parking area, by crossing the main road and turning left onto the West Valley Trail. None of the trails heading west from the West Valley Trail are open to horses. Ride south 1.0 mile, continuing past the main trailhead parking, to a signpost for the Mill Creek Trail. Turn right onto the Mill Creek Trail, which soon heads up the hill.

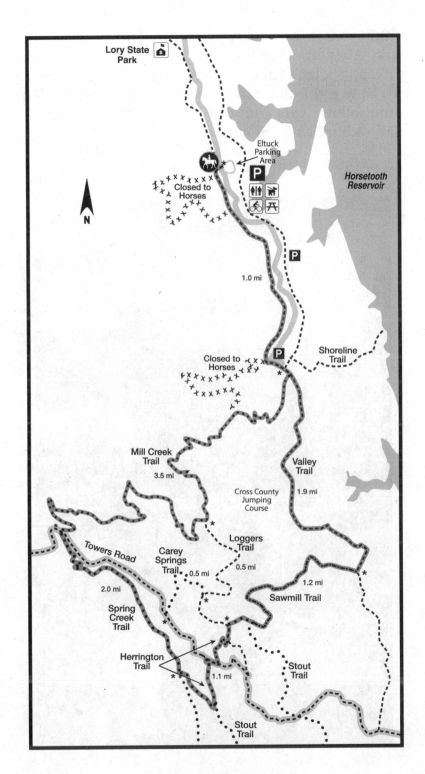

Lory State Park

Eltuck Parking Area

Horsetooth Reservoir

Closed to Horses

N

1.0 mi

Closed to Horses

Shoreline Trail

Mill Creek Trail

3.5 mi

Valley Trail

1.9 mi

Cross County Jumping Course

Loggers Trail

0.5 mi

Towers Road

Carey Springs Trail

0.5 mi

2.0 mi

Sawmill Trail

1.2 mi

Spring Creek Trail

Herrington Trail

1.1 mi

Stout Trail

Stout Trail

Within 0.5 mile the trail crosses into Horsetooth Park. After another 1.0 mile of climbing, this route arrives at a trail junction. The Loggers Trail is to the left. Stay right and continue on Mill Creek Trail. The route follows this trail until it ends at a dirt service road. 3.5 miles from where it started.

At the end of the Mill Creek Trail, cross the dirt road to access the Spring Creek Trail. This is a nice trail that makes a steady descent for 2.0 miles to a large meadow. The Wathen Trail, on the right, crosses Spring Creek where your horse may be able to get a drink, and then heads up the hill toward Horsetooth Rock. Ride that trail another day using the Horsetooth Mountain Park Trailhead. Continue riding south on the Spring Creek Trail and turn left at the next junction, onto the Herrington Trail.

Climb up the ridge and down the other side, ignoring the junction for the Stout Trail, and then turn right onto the dirt Towers Trail. Follow the road a short distance to the south until you reach another signpost for the Herrington Trail on the left. Turn left there, onto a continuation of the Herrington Trail. When it reaches the old road named Loggers Trail this route turns left, headed north to the Sawmill Trail. Then it turns right and heads downhill on the Sawmill Trail, passing a small cabin. This trail has been improved recently, but it is still rather steep and includes a section with a sign for riders to dismount. After 1.3 miles this trail ends.

Turn left there, onto the Nomad Trail and head north 0.2 mile to the Lory State Park boundary. Stay left when the trail divides and continue on the South Valley Trail another 2.0 miles, passing the old cross-country jumping course. Stay left, on the West Valley Trail at the parking lot, and ride the last 1.0 mile to the Eltuck parking area, where a trail leaves the West Valley Trail and crosses the road to the parking lot.

PART III

REFERENCES

Reference

- *About Saddle Fit* video, David Gedadek, www.aboutthehorse.com
- *How to Shit in the Woods*—A great little book with helpful advice for those who are new to spending the day in the mountains. I especially like the chapter for women titled "How not to pee in your boots."
- *NATRC Rider's Manual* —A guide to Competitive Trail Riding Rules as well as helpful trail riding information can be purchased from NATRC. See appendix B.

Maps

De Lorme Mapping publishes the Colorado Atlas and Gazetteer that includes topographic maps of the entire state in road atlas form. This paperback map book is an indispensable and reasonably priced reference source for locating trailheads. I keep one in my tow vehicle and one in my house to make it simple to look up trails and trailheads to get the big picture. These are available at outdoor recreation outlets, as well as other map sellers and bookstores.

National Geographic Trails Illustrated Maps publish user-friendly maps that are waterproof and tear resistant. They do not cover all areas of the state; rather they are for specific areas such as Rocky Mountain National Park. They are numbered as well as named. While the larger scale of these maps allows one map to show an area covered by 10 USGS maps, some of the detail is lost. On the other hand, they have added some really nice information to some of their maps. The Rocky Mountain National Park map shows mileages and campsites. It also shows trails that are not open to horses by using a different line than the trails that are open to horses. They have the only map available for the Lion Gulch and Homestead

Meadows trails. That map, numbered 101, shows each of the homesteads and labels them with the name of the homesteaders.

USGS maps are the original topographic maps developed by the U.S. government in the mid 1900s. These are quite detailed; however, a daylong ride can entail two or three maps. This amount of detail is probably more important for hiking than for riding. For areas not covered by Trails Illustrated maps, these are the only option. Newly created trails, such as those in Open Space areas and Lyon Gulch are not shown on these maps yet. USGS maps are available at REI. See below for their address.

Map reading is an indispensable skill. Maps are designed to be user friendly and it is not difficult to learn to read them. They are interesting enough that I frame some of them and hang them on my walls, so they are simple to access whenever I want to look up some bit of information.

If you do not know how to read a map, ask a friend who is a skilled map reader to show you how to find your way around on a map, or call a hiking store like REI or EMS, and ask about map reading classes. When you read a trail description in this guidebook that interests you, make a note of the maps needed and check whether you have them, or if you need to purchase them.

Catalogs

- *Books on Horses* by Breakthrough Publications Inc. www.booksonhorses.com, 1-800-276-8419. This is a catalog of horse publications, from children's books to training videos.
- National Bridle Shop Catalog www.nationalbridleshop. com 1-800-251-3474. This retail outlet offers clothing and more for horse and rider.
- Schneiders offers an all-inclusive catalog that offers both English and Western tack and riding wear, and everything from blankets and sponges, to grooming products and supplements.
- Sportack www.sportack.com 1-800-248-8225. This small catalog offers clothing and gear for horse and

rider designed specifically for endurance riding, but that can also be great for use on long trail rides.
- State Line Tack Catalog www.statelinetack.com 1-800-228-9208. This subsidiary of Petsmart sells gear for horse and rider.
- Two Horse Enterprises has a guide to trail riding and horse camping information and items. Contact them to obtain their free catalog at P.O. Box 15517, Fremont, CA 94539.

Stores
- EMS (Eastern Mountain Sports) 2550 Arapahoe Avenue in Boulder. This is an outdoor recreation store with all the basics.
- REI (Recreational Equipment Inc.) 4025 S. College St. in Fort Collins, or 1789 28th St. in Boulder. Visit them for maps and map reading classes, search and rescue cards, rain ponchos, water containers, socks, and other useful things like granola bars and lip balm on a string to wear around your neck.

USEFUL CONTACT INFORMATION
Agencies

- Colorado Department of Agriculture State Board of Stock Inspection
  (303) 294-0895 Contact them for the telephone number of your local brand inspector.
- Department of Wildlife
  Hunting information (970) 472-4300, or
  (303) 291-7227.
- National Forest Service
  Visitor Information Fort Collins office (970) 498-2770, then 0 for the information desk. Contact them for gate closure and camping information, and to check for current fire restrictions.
- National Forest Service
  Visitor Information, Boulder Office (303) 541-2500, then 0 for the information desk.
  Contact them for gate closure and camping information and to check for current fire restrictions. This office also issues permits for backcountry camping in the Indian Peaks Wilderness.
- Rocky Mountain National Park
  Contact them for information regarding the current snow line, road closure information, general information, and volunteer opportunities at (970) 586–1206, from 8:00 A.M.–4:30 P.M. daily. For information about backcountry campsites and reservations call (970) 586-1242.

Horseman's Associations

- Back Country Horsemen, Northern Colorado Branch
  Vicky Buchanan, 17257 W CR 84, Ault, CO 80610
  Contact them for membership information.
- Back Country Horsemen, Front Range Branch
  Julie Chaney P.O. Box 1524, Elizabeth, CO 80107.

Contact them for membership information.
- Boulder County Horseman's Association
  P.O. Box 19601, Boulder CO 80308-2601 Contact them for membership information or to purchase their compilation of trail descriptions from past newsletters, Happy Trails.
- Estes Park Equestrian Club
  C/o Cindy Brandjord 437 Whispering Pines Drive, Estes Park, CO 80517, or phone her at (970) 577-1331 or cell (970) 215-4886. Contact them for membership information and possibly short-term horse boarding.
- Larimer County Horseman's Association
  P.O. Box 270375, Fort Collins, CO 80527-0375. Contact them for membership information.
- North American Trail Ride Conference
  P.O. Box 224, Sedalia, CO 80135. www.NATRC.org, E-mail: narc@natrc.org. Contact them for information about competitive trail riding, or to purchase their informative Rider's Manual.
- Roundup Riders of the Rockies Heritage and Trails Foundation, Inc.
  9902 N. Heather Dr., Castle Rock, CO 80108-9133 (303) 858-0465.

This group is a 501(c) 3 tax exempt organization that raises funds that they give to many organizations who build trails in Colorado, including the National Forest Service, the Continental Divide National Scenic Trail, the Department of Colorado State Parks, etc.

If you would like to make a tax-exempt contribution that will be used to improve the trails in Colorado, this organization is a great place to make donations.

ABOUT THE AUTHOR

I love mountains and have spent most of my free time there. As a teenager, I backpacked and skied in the area around Lake Tahoe, Nevada, and I joined the ski patrol when I was sixteen. I yearned to go to the Alps from the time I was a child, and was able to spend a year in Europe while in college. My vacations have taken me trekking in the Himalayas, and I came to Colorado when I was twenty-eight years old to live near the Rocky Mountains. Since then I have hiked, ski-patrolled, gone on backcountry ski trips, and introduced other people to the joys of skiing and backpacking, both individually, and by leading trips for the Sierra Club.

I have always loved horses, and talked my parents into purchasing one for me when I was twelve years old. I started a three year old gelding a few years later. As an adult, I always thought I would have another horse someday, but the years passed without one. Then I met my husband, David. Although he had grown up on a farm in Kansas, he had never owned a horse. He thought living in the mountains, and having a horse would be the best life he could imagine, with me by his side of course.

This is how two people in their forties decided to embark on a life that revolves around horses. I no longer have the physical ability to carry a pack, ski, or sleep on the ground, but I can still spend the day in the mountains on my Tennessee Walking Horse. I have applied the knowledge I gained from years of exploring the mountains to trail riding. Having the advantage of living near Rocky Mountain National Park, I could investigate parking options at trailheads without being encumbered by a trailer.

I am surprised that I see so few other horses on the trails in Rocky Mountain National Park. I hope that by showing horse owners how to take their mounts to the mountains, more of them will begin to enjoy the magic that I find there.

Quick Order Form

To order a copy of **Get out of the Ring** please use the following information.

- **Telephone orders:** Call (970) 203-9995
- **E-mail orders to:** Kimstarling@mesanetworks.net
- **U. S. Postal service:**   Kim Starling
  P. O. Box 1022
  Loveland, CO 80539
- **Fax orders:** Fax this form to (303) 225-5460

Name:_____

Address:_____

City:_____ State_____

Zip_____

Telephone: (_____)_____

E-mail address:_____

Please send _____ copies of **Get Out of the Ring** to the address above, at a cost of $24.95 per book. Tax and shipping is $6.00 for the first book and $1.50 for each additional book shipped to the same address.

Payment: Credit Card: __   Check __

Amount: $_____

 Visa____ Master Card____

Card Number:_____

Name on card:_____

Expiration Date: _____